CW01649379

Francis Frith's
Canals & Waterways

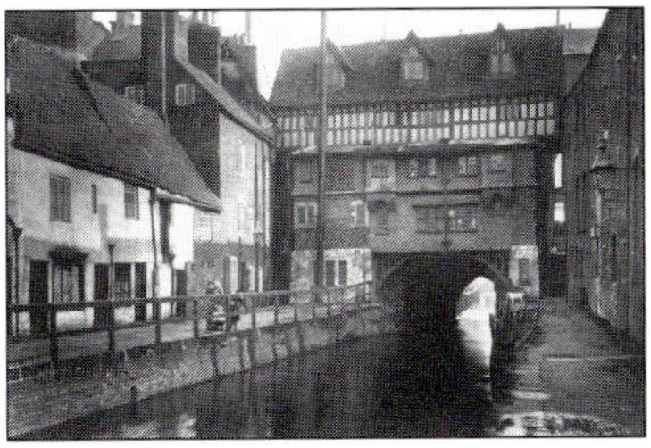

PHOTOGRAPHIC MEMORIES

Francis Frith's
CANALS & WATERWAYS

Dennis Needham

THE FRANCIS FRITH COLLECTION
FRITH BOOK Co

First published in the United Kingdom in 2000 by
Frith Book Company Ltd

British Library Cataloguing in Publication Data

Canals & Waterways
Dennis Needham
ISBN 1-85937-129-9

Frith Book Company Ltd
Frith's Barn, Teffont,
Salisbury, Wiltshire SP3 5QP
Tel: +44 (0) 1722 716 376
Email: info@frithbook.co.uk
www.frithbook.co.uk

Printed and bound in Great Britain

Front Cover: Market Drayton, Tyrley Locks 1911 63346

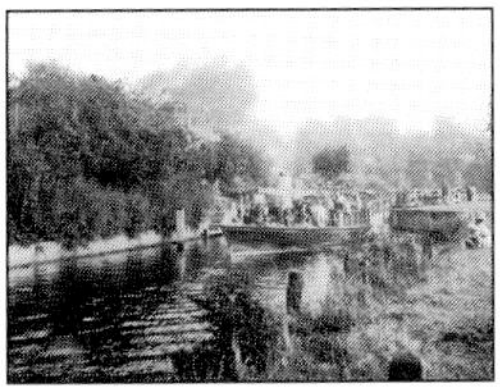

Contents

FRANCIS FRITH: *Victorian Pioneer*

FRANCIS FRITH, Victorian founder of the world-famous photographic archive, was a complex and multitudinous man. A devout Quaker and a highly successful Victorian businessman, he was both philosophic by nature and pioneering in outlook.

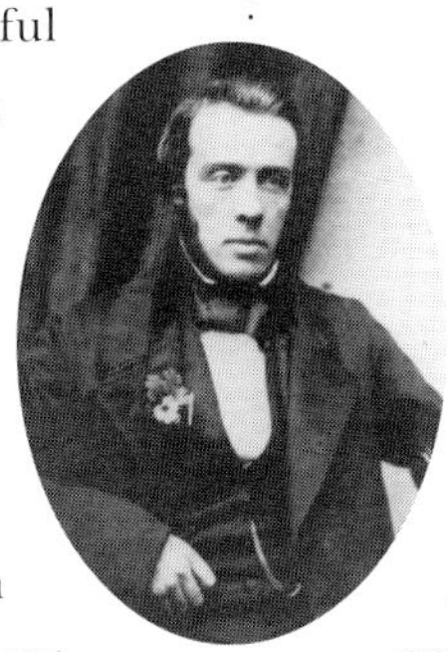

By 1855 Francis Frith had already established a wholesale grocery business in Liverpool, and sold it for the astonishing sum of £200,000, which is the equivalent today of over £15,000,000. Now a multi-millionaire, he was able to indulge his passion for travel. As a child he had pored over travel books written by early explorers, and his fancy and imagination had been stirred by family holidays to the sublime mountain regions of Wales and Scotland. 'What a land of spirit-stirring and enriching scenes and places!' he had written. He was to return to these scenes of grandeur in later years to 'recapture the thousands of vivid and tender memories', but with a different purpose. Now in his thirties, and captivated by the new science of photography, Frith set out on a series of pioneering journeys to the Nile regions that occupied him from 1856 until 1860.

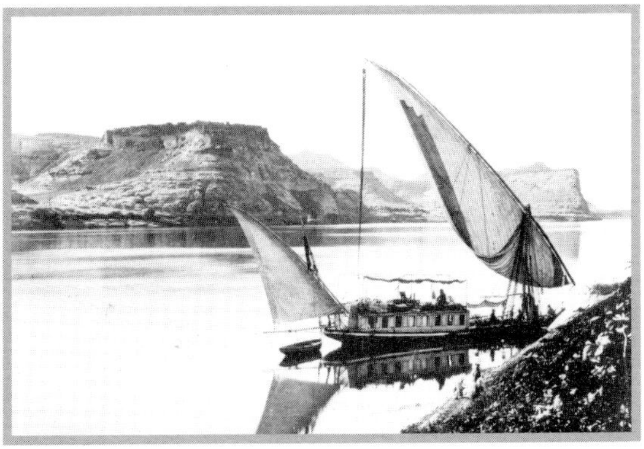

INTRIGUE AND ADVENTURE

He took with him on his travels a specially-designed wicker carriage that acted as both dark-room and sleeping chamber. These far-flung journeys were packed with intrigue and adventure. In his life story, written when he was sixty-three, Frith tells of being held captive by bandits, and of fighting 'an awful midnight battle to the very point of surrender with a deadly pack of hungry, wild dogs'. Sporting flowing Arab costume, Frith arrived at Akaba by camel seventy years before Lawrence, where he encountered 'desert princes and rival sheikhs, blazing with jewel-hilted swords'.

During these extraordinary adventures he was assiduously exploring the desert regions bordering the Nile and patiently recording the antiquities and peoples with his camera. He was the first photographer to venture beyond the sixth cataract. Africa was still the mysterious 'Dark Continent', and Stanley and Livingstone's historic meeting was a decade into the future. The conditions for picture taking confound belief. He laboured for hours in his wicker dark-room in the sweltering heat of the desert, while the volatile chemicals fizzed dangerously in their trays. Often he was forced to work in remote tombs and caves where conditions were cooler. Back in London he exhibited his photographs and was 'rapturously cheered' by members of the Royal Society. His reputation as a photographer was made overnight. An eminent modern historian has likened their impact on the population of the time to that on our own generation of the first photographs taken on the surface of the moon.

Venture of a Life-Time

Characteristically, Frith quickly spotted the opportunity to create a new business as a specialist publisher of photographs. He lived in an era of immense and sometimes violent change. For the poor in the early part of Victoria's reign work was a drudge and the hours long, and people had precious little free time to enjoy themselves.

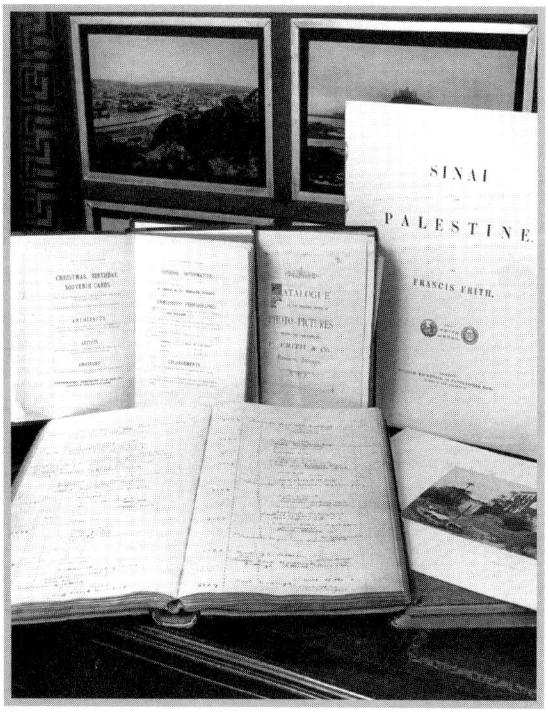

Most had no transport other than a cart or gig at their disposal, and had not travelled far beyond the boundaries of their own town or village. However, by the 1870s, the railways had threaded their way across the country, and Bank Holidays and half-day Saturdays had been made obligatory by Act of Parliament. All of a sudden the ordinary working man and his family were able to enjoy days out and see a little more of the world.

With characteristic business acumen, Francis Frith foresaw that these new tourists would enjoy having souvenirs to commemorate their days out. In 1860 he married Mary Ann Rosling and set out with the intention of photographing every city, town and village in Britain. For the next thirty years he travelled the country by train and by pony and trap, producing fine photographs of seaside resorts and beauty spots that were keenly bought by millions of Victorians. These prints were painstakingly pasted into family albums and pored over during the dark nights of winter, rekindling precious memories of summer excursions.

The Rise of Frith & Co

Frith's studio was soon supplying retail shops all over the country. To meet the demand he gathered about him a small team of photographers, and published the work of independent artist-photographers of the calibre of Roger Fenton and Francis Bedford. In order to gain some understanding of the scale of Frith's business one only has to look at the catalogue issued by Frith & Co in 1886: it runs to some 670

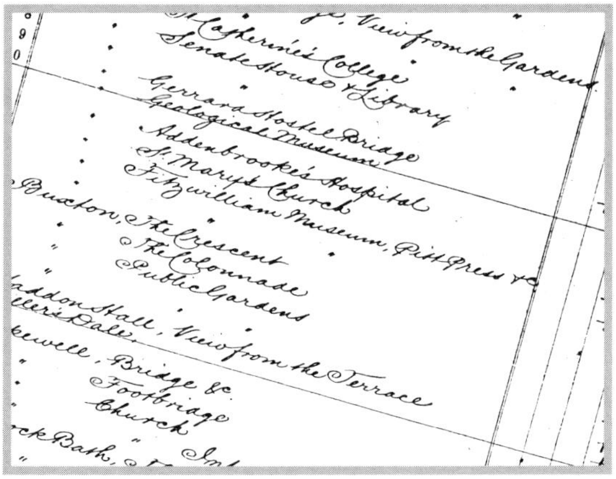
St Catherine's College, View from the Gardens
Senate House & Library
Gerrard Hostel Bridge
Geological Museum
Addenbrooke's Hospital
St Mary's Church
Fitzwilliam Museum, Pitt Press &c
Buxton, The Crescent
The Colonnade
Public Gardens
addon Hall, View from the Terrace
llers Dale
kewell, Bridge &c
Footbridge
Church
ck Bath

pages, listing not only many thousands of views of the British Isles but also many photographs of most European countries, and China, Japan, the USA and Canada – note the sample page shown above from the hand-written *Frith & Co* ledgers detailing pictures taken. By 1890 Frith had created the greatest specialist photographic publishing company in the world, with over 2,000 outlets – more than the combined number that Boots and WH Smith have today! The picture on the right shows the *Frith & Co* display board at Ingleton in the Yorkshire Dales. Beautifully constructed with mahogany frame and gilt inserts, it could display up to a dozen local scenes.

Postcard Bonanza

The ever-popular holiday postcard we know today took many years to develop. In 1870 the Post Office issued the first plain cards, with a pre-printed stamp on one face. In 1894 they allowed other publishers' cards to be sent through the mail with an attached adhesive halfpenny stamp. Demand grew rapidly, and in 1895 a new size of postcard was permitted called the court card, but there was little room for illustration. In 1899, a year after Frith's death, a new card measuring 5.5 x 3.5 inches became the standard format, but it was not until 1902 that the divided back came into being, with address and message on one face and a full-size illustration on the other. *Frith & Co* were in the vanguard of postcard development, and Frith's sons Eustace and Cyril continued their father's monumental task, expanding the number of views offered to the public and recording more and more places in Britain, as the coasts and countryside were opened up to mass travel.

Francis Frith died in 1898 at his villa in Cannes, his great project still growing. The archive he created continued in business for another seventy years. By 1970 it contained over a third of a million pictures of 7,000 cities, towns and villages. The massive photographic record Frith has left to us stands as a living monument to a special and very remarkable man.

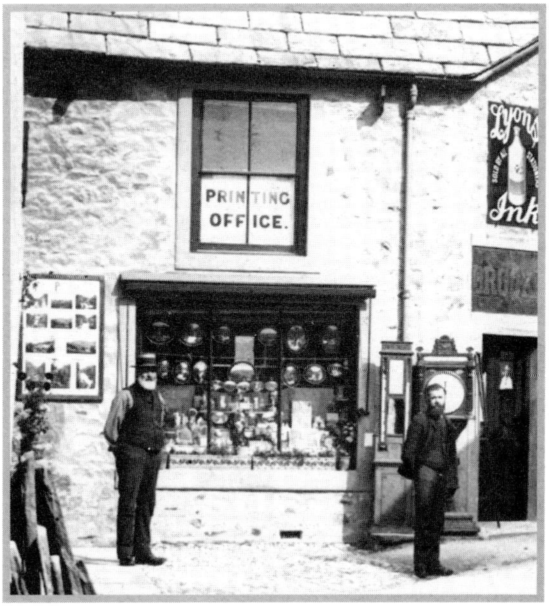

Frith's Archive: *A Unique Legacy*

Francis Frith's legacy to us today is of immense significance and value, for the magnificent archive of evocative photographs he created provides a unique record of change in 7,000 cities, towns and villages throughout Britain over a century and more. Frith and his fellow studio photographers revisited locations many times down the years to update their views, compiling for us an enthralling and colourful pageant of British life and character.

We tend to think of Frith's sepia views of Britain as nostalgic, for most of us use them to conjure up memories of places in our own lives with which we have family associations. It often makes us forget that to Francis Frith they were records of daily life as it was actually being lived in the cities, towns and villages of his day. The Victorian age was one of great and often bewildering change for ordinary people, and though the pictures evoke an impression of slower times, life was as busy and hectic as it is today.

We are fortunate that Frith was a photographer of the people, dedicated to recording the minutiae of everyday life. For it is this sheer wealth of visual data, the painstaking chronicle of changes in dress, transport, street layouts, buildings, housing, engineering and landscape that captivates us so much today. His remarkable images offer us a powerful link with the past and with the lives of our ancestors.

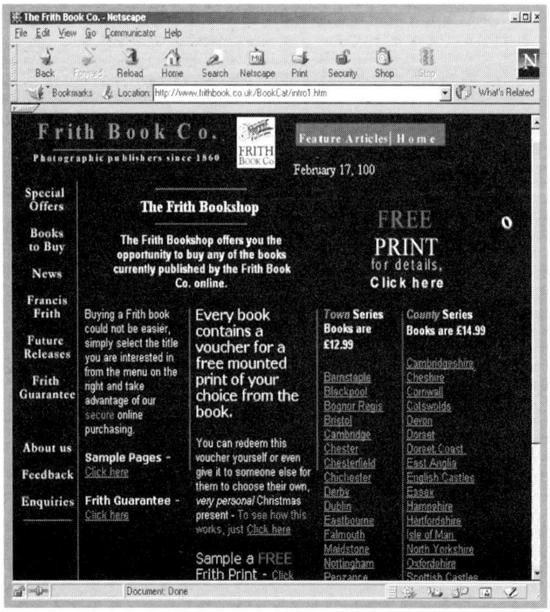

See Frith at www. frithbook.co.uk

Today's Technology

Computers have now made it possible for Frith's many thousands of images to be accessed almost instantly. In the Frith archive today, each photograph is carefully 'digitised' then stored on a CD Rom. Frith archivists can locate a single photograph amongst thousands within seconds. Views can be catalogued and sorted under a variety of categories of place and content to the immediate benefit of researchers. Inexpensive reference prints can be created for them at the touch of a mouse button, and a wide range of books and other printed materials assembled and published for a wider, more general readership - in the next twelve months over a hundred Frith local history titles will be published! The day-to-day workings of the archive are very different from how they were in Francis Frith's time: imagine the herculean task of sorting through eleven tons of glass negatives as Frith had to do to locate a particular sequence of pictures! Yet the archive still prides itself on maintaining the same high standards of excellence laid down by Francis Frith, including the painstaking cataloguing and indexing of every view.

It is curious to reflect on how the internet now allows researchers in America and elsewhere greater instant access to the archive than Frith himself ever enjoyed. Many thousands of individual views can be called up on screen within seconds on one of the Frith internet sites, enabling people living continents away to revisit the streets of their ancestral home town, or view places in Britain where they have enjoyed holidays. Many overseas researchers welcome the chance to view special theme selections, such as transport, sports, costume and ancient monuments.

We are certain that Francis Frith would have heartily approved of these modern developments, for he himself was always working at the very limits of Victorian photographic technology.

The Value of the Archive Today

Because of the benefits brought by the computer, Frith's images are increasingly studied by social historians, by researchers into genealogy and ancestory, by architects, town planners, and by teachers and schoolchildren involved in local history projects. In addition, the archive offers every one of us a unique opportunity to examine the places where we and our families have lived and worked down the years. Immensely successful in Frith's own era, the archive is now, a century and more on, entering a new phase of popularity.

The Past in Tune with the Future

Historians consider the Francis Frith Collection to be of prime national importance. It is the only archive of its kind remaining in private ownership and has been valued at a million pounds. However, this figure is now rapidly increasing as digital technology enables more and more people around the world to enjoy its benefits.

Francis Frith's archive is now housed in an historic timber barn in the beautiful village of Teffont in Wiltshire. Its founder would not recognize the archive office as it is today. In place of the many thousands of dusty boxes containing glass plate negatives and an all-pervading odour of photographic chemicals, there are now ranks of computer screens. He would be amazed to watch his images travelling round the world at unimaginable speeds through network and internet lines.

The archive's future is both bright and exciting. Francis Frith, with his unshakeable belief in making photographs available to the greatest number of people, would undoubtedly approve of what is being done today with his lifetime's work. His photographs, depicting our shared past, are now bringing pleasure and enlightenment to millions around the world a century and more after his death.

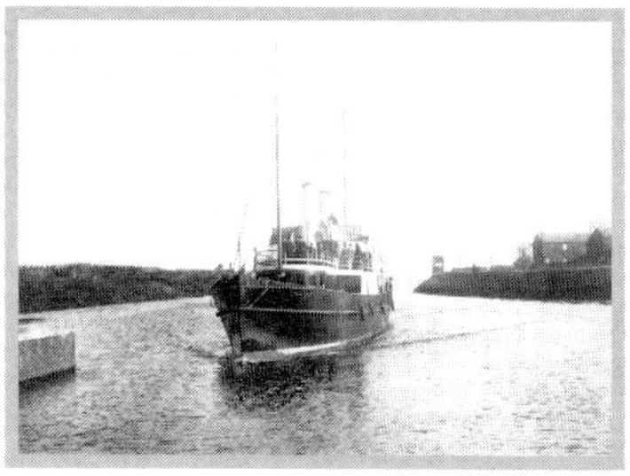

CANALS & RIVERS – *An Introduction*

SINCE THE EARLIEST days of man, our rivers and waterways have provided a basic form of transport and travel. For those who braved the sometimes turbulent waters in the earliest recorded boats, the search for food was probably the main motive for travelling in this way - and adventure was often what they found.

The Romans arrived on these shores two thousand years ago and gave us the first canals. They dug artificial channels to link existing rivers, but they did not seem to know of locks, even though these had been in use in China for centuries.

For a thousand years after the Romans left, we navigated on rivers as best we could; little was done to improve their natural courses. But by the 16th century, things were stirring in the west country: a canal was built to link Exeter with the sea after an artificial barrier had been built across the river by a local noblewoman.

But it was the imperatives of the industrial revolution that propelled the development of canals. The sources of the raw materials for industry were being exploited, and new ways to use them were being developed. Manufactories were being built, and moving finished products to markets was proving a huge problem. Thus was the canal age born.

At this remove, it is difficult to comprehend the quantum leap forward in transport that canals became. Previously, horse and cart was the only method, usually on diabolical roads. In the 18th century, it could take ten days or more to move a couple of tons of products from the new pottery works in the Stoke-on-Trent area to Liverpool docks - and a large percentage would be broken in transit. Then a canal was built. Suddenly, twenty tons or more could be transferred in three days with virtually no breakage. Since then, the railways and better roads have improved load capacity and transit times. But to create a similar step forward today, it would be necessary to invent a system that could move 600 tons over the same journey in about thirty minutes.

Costs dropped dramatically too. Before London was linked to the coalfields of the Midlands by canal, fuel delivered to the capital by pack-horse would cost over £12 a ton just for the transport. After canals were built, this dropped to 13p per ton.

The first area to start to exploit artificial

waterways as a form of bulk transport was the north-west. St Helens and Manchester were among the first towns to construct canals. The late 18th century was the peak time for construction. Every town wanted to be in on the act, and many fortunes were lost on crackpot schemes. However, many fortunes were made, as entrepreneurs and investors climbed aboard the bandwagon: this enthusiasm for new technology is a mirror image of today's obsession with IT.

One of the pioneer canal engineers was James Brindley. A millwright from Leek in Staffordshire, he planned to link our main rivers by canal, forming a St Andrew's cross of water across central England. He was instrumental in getting this plan well under way before his death in 1772. The Severn was linked with the Trent, the Mersey with the Thames. Prior to this, canals had tended to be locally-promoted and small-scale, with no overall plan.

At the centre of this spider's web of water is Birmingham. There are actually more miles of water here than there are in Venice - and the water is a great deal cleaner as well. Today, boaters actually holiday in the city. Unquestionably, the arrival of canals saw the city develop from little more than a village to a vast industrial centre. It became the engineering heartland of the country; canals delivered raw materials to its factories, and took away the finished products for distribution around both this country and the world.

Even before the idea of constructing canals had fired the imagination of investors and industrialists alike, several of our rivers were being improved to allow easier passage of boats, including the Thames, the Wey and the Great Ouse. Other rivers were soon improved as well, and smaller canal sections were built to avoid the more treacherous lengths of the rivers.

Early in the canal age, a standard size for locks - and thus boats - was set. What was to become the narrowboat was 70ft long with a beam of 7ft. These vessels had long holds to carry the cargo, with a small cabin at the stern where the boatman and his family lived. These boats were family concerns. The husband would often work off the boat, setting locks or moving swing bridges. The children

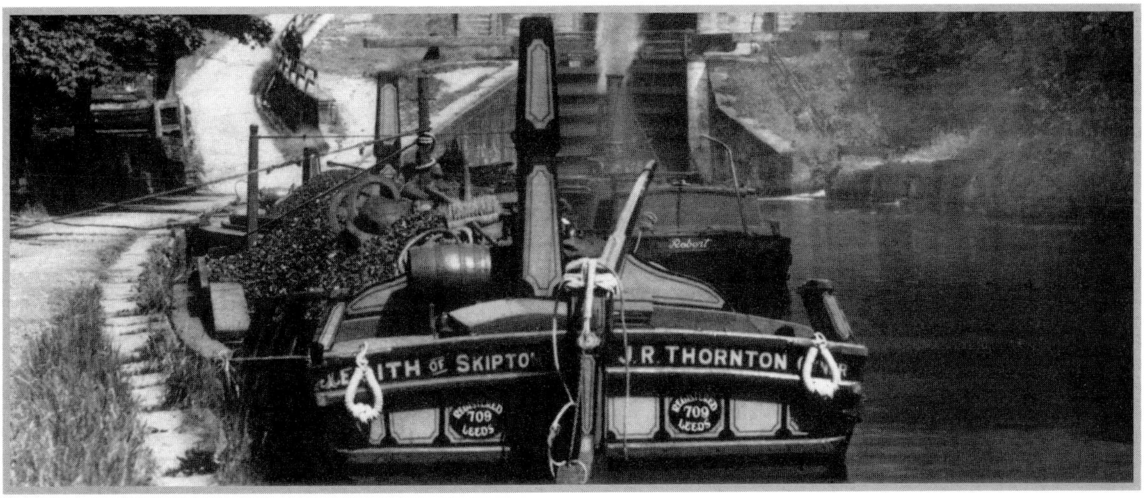

Bingley, Five Lock Rise c1900 B98501

would be responsible for driving the horse, and the wife would steer, preparing food at the same time. This was cooked on a single coal-fired stove just inside the rear cabin doors. As these boats became home, families tended to decorate them. Brassware was always popular, and the distinctive paintings of roses and castles were adopted to brighten their surroundings.

In fact, it was this standard size (which was decided by Brindley, who foresaw a shortage of water if he built larger chambers) that would eventually lead to the demise of water-borne freight. A payload of between 20 and 35 tons (depending on bulk) was all that could be loaded on a narrowboat. This could be doubled on a barge, and many later canals were built to what is known today as wide beam size: 70ft x 14ft.

The Canal Age - as it became known - lasted from the 1770s for around fifty years. By the mid 1800s, railways were making increasing inroads into canal freight business; many of the privately owned canal companies made approaches to the newcomers, offering their businesses for sale. The Great Western Railway and the London and North Western Railway were both owners of extensive canal systems by the end of that century.

It was during the years of canal construction that many new and innovative civil engineering techniques were tried for the first time by an increasingly ambitious set of canal builders. Many of their greatest achievements are recorded within the covers of this book. Brindley, as the pioneer, chose routes that followed the contours of the land through which he built. Transit times were nothing then; limitations of engineering knowledge decided everything.

Yet Brindley was not afraid to try something different. He built an aqueduct on the Bridgewater Canal in Lancashire to take his new navigation across the river Irwell. This endured until the growing use of the Manchester Ship Canal meant that an alternative crossing was needed. Thus was the Barton Swing Aqueduct built. Brindley also took to tunnelling. His Trent & Mersey Canal needed to cross a watershed on the

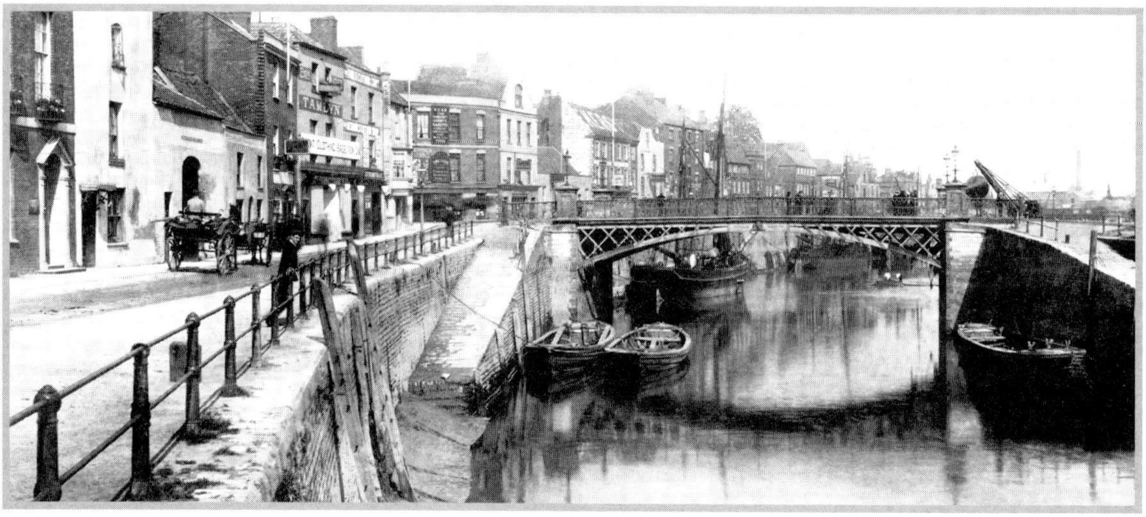

Bridgwater, The Bridge 1903 50451

Staffordshire/Cheshire border. Harecastle Tunnel took eleven long years to build; at 2897 yards, it was a stupendous undertaking for its day.

Half a century later, as canal construction neared its end, engineering geniuses like Thomas Telford were throwing cast iron troughs across valleys, marching boldly through hillsides and over dales.

These were stirring days, and ones that added to our vocabulary. Construction workers were known as navigators. Abbreviated to 'navvies,' the word has become today's term for labourers. The changes wrought on village communities as the canals were dug must have been quite horrific. Isolated areas that hardly ever saw a stranger were suddenly invaded by hard-working, hard-drinking and hard-living men. Their wages often went on drink, and affrays were common.

The canal engineers were responding to ever-increasing demands for transport. They set out on horseback, with minimal equipment and poor maps, to seek out the easiest route between A and B. Did they succeed? We only have to look at the topography today to see that where those pioneers dug their canals, the railway builders followed; and a century later, the motorway construction gangs were to be found at work in the same places. Those early canal surveyors were indeed astonishingly accurate and astute as they wove their watery threads across our landscape.

Several of the canals featured in this book are now part of history. They served their purpose and were successively run down and abandoned, and only survive today in a severely truncated form. The Bude and the Grand Western are two examples.

It is also clear, from examining these photographs, that the concept of canals as seedy areas in the wrong part of town is not altogether justified. Of course, the centres of industry were not sparklingly clean, but to get between those places, canals had to pass through some of the most delightful parts of our fair land; a situation that obtains to this day. The towing paths that once echoed to the ring of horses' hooves are now padded by walkers. Enjoyable for a short stroll or a long distance walk, these footpaths are available to all.

One aspect of canal construction that is clear from these wonderful historic records is that much of the infrastructure given to us by the waterways remains. Venerable buildings that we can see and admire today were built because the canal or river passed that way. Later, towns would grow up alongside the railways, to be followed by places convenient to the motorway network.

Since those first canals were built, efficient transport has become the vital need of any civilised society. The navigable waterways of England became the catalyst for growth in this country; they are a worthy forerunner of today's complex and sophisticated transport system. And yet we still fail to learn from our mistakes. After the last war, a group of men formed the Inland Waterways Association to campaign for the retention of the canals which, at that time, were being abandoned as fast as possible. Half a century later, the parts that were sold off are now complicated barriers to restoration. Similarly, for the last thirty years we have been selling off redundant railway land. That these short-sighted decisions will return to haunt the next generation is as sure as the tide.

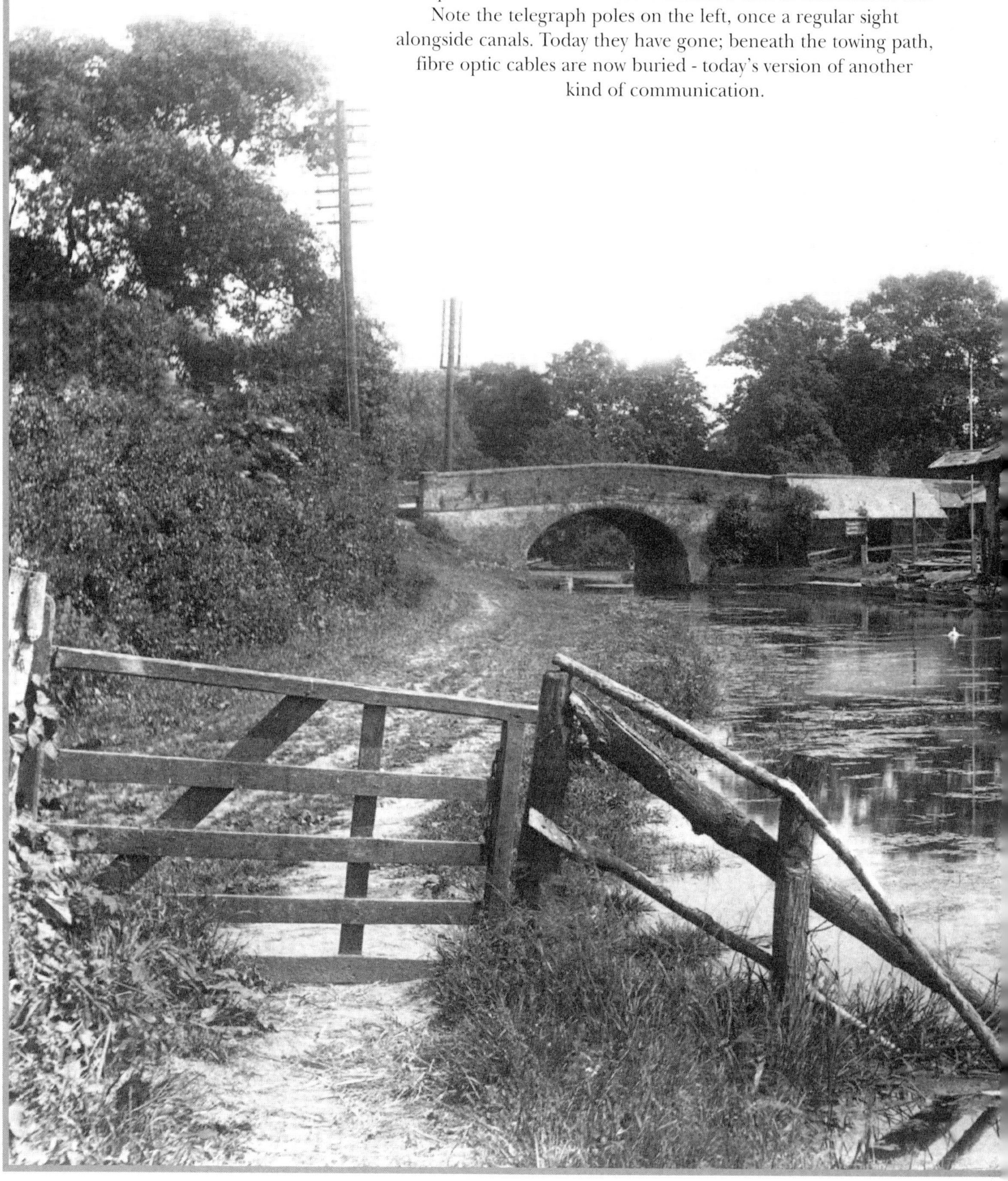

ODIHAM

The Canal Wharf 1906 55854

Here we see the upper reaches of the Basingstoke Canal in Hampshire. The surface weed indicates a lack of commercial use. Note the telegraph poles on the left, once a regular sight alongside canals. Today they have gone; beneath the towing path, fibre optic cables are now buried - today's version of another kind of communication.

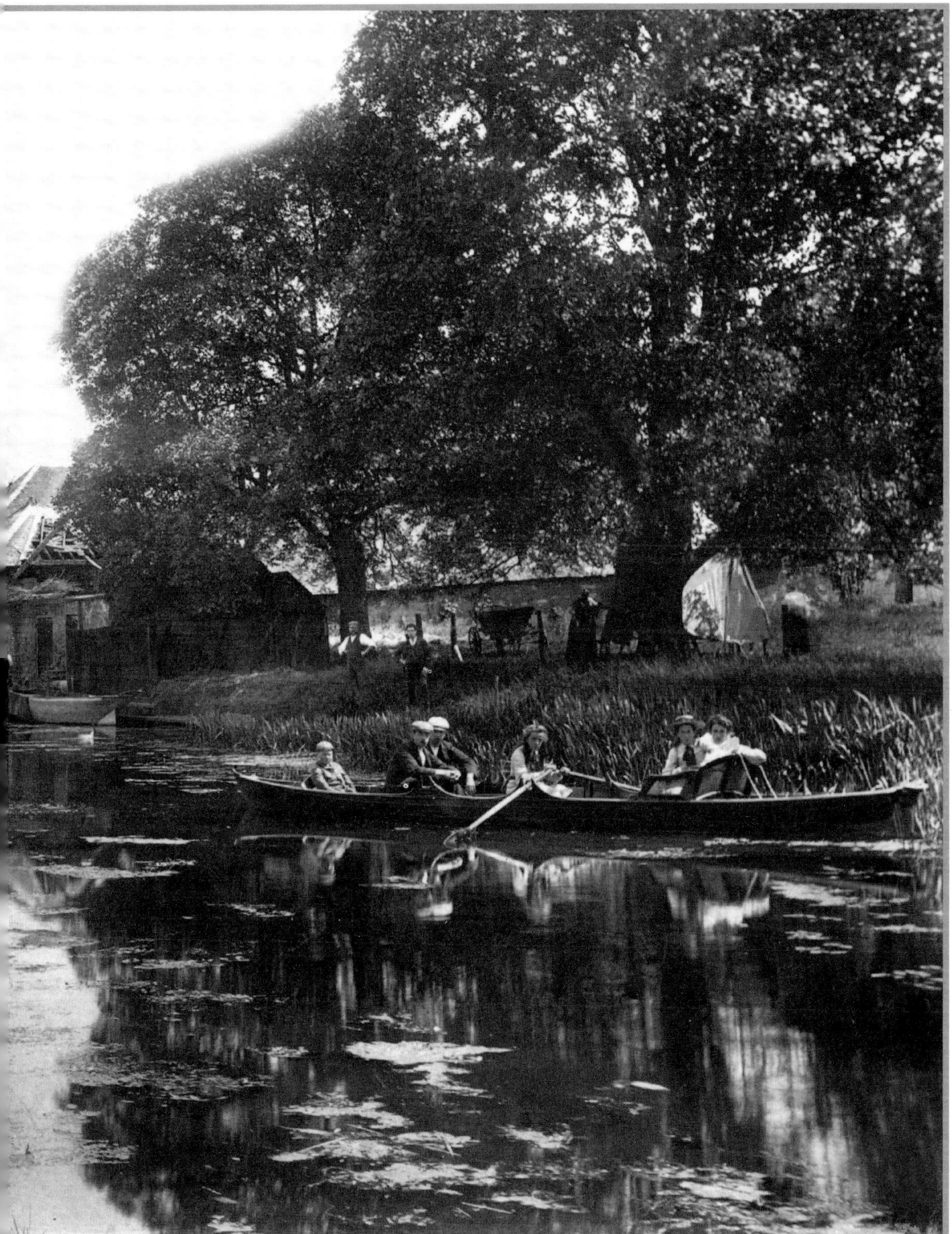

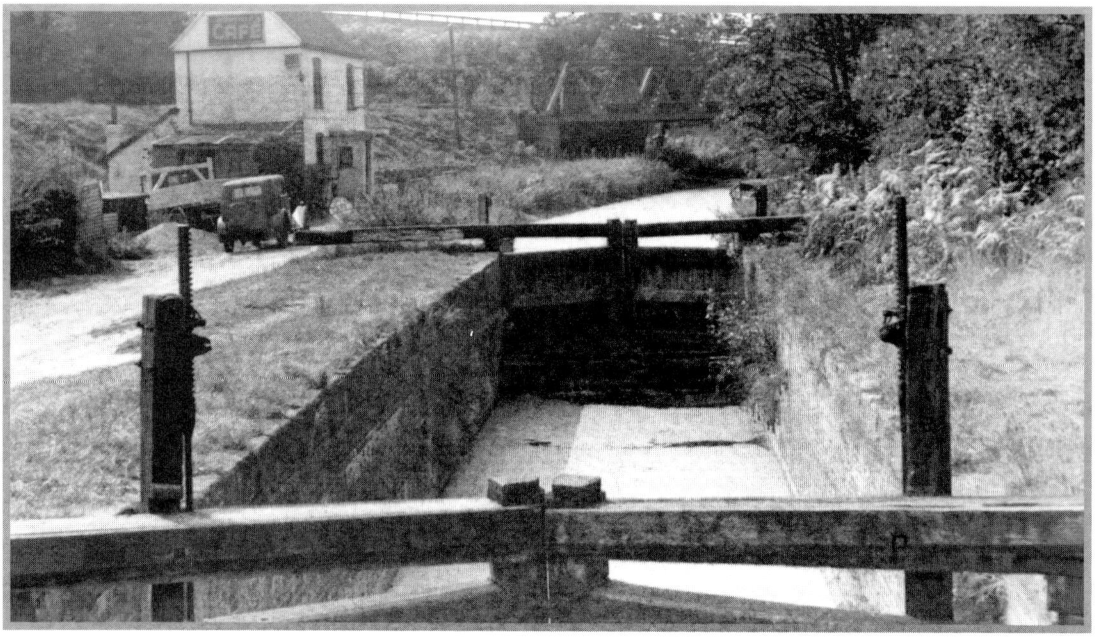

BROOKWOOD, THE BASINGSTOKE CANAL c1955 B232014
This is the bottom chamber of the Deepcut flight of 14 locks. The bridge immediately beyond the lock used to take a railway into Pirbright army camp, just behind the trees to the right. Note the chain around the bottom gates; these were not completely necessary, as the canal was impassable by this time. It was restored and re-opened in 1991.

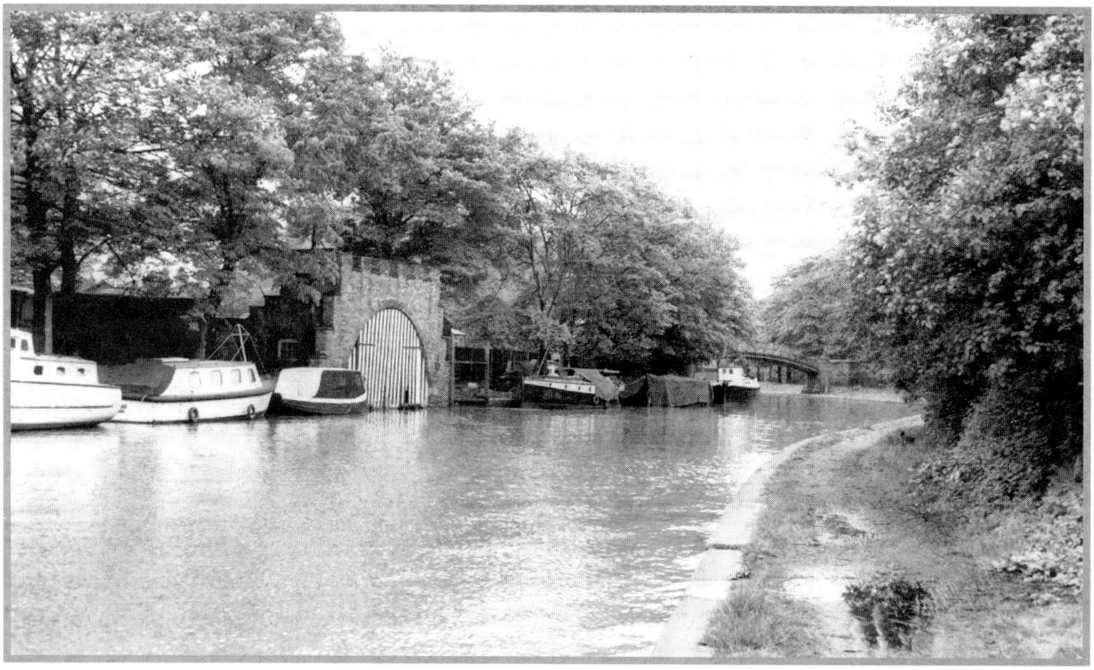

WORSLEY, THE BOATHOUSE c1960 W145053
This scene on the Bridgewater Canal in Greater Manchester is essentially unchanged to this day. This was the first really commercial canal, carrying coal from mines - just to the left of our cameraman - into Manchester.

Runcorn
The Locks c1955
This is an historic view, as these locks, linking the Manchester Ship and the Bridgewater canals, were infilled in 1966. There were 10 chambers, each one duplicated to speed the flow of traffic.

Runcorn
The Locks c1955
A pair of boats prepare to enter a lock. The left hand one - the 'Stafford' - sports its Fellows, Morton & Clayton livery, a company that stopped trading when the canals were nationalised in 1948. The right hand boat is the 'Shad', an ex-FMC motor in the colours of its new owners.

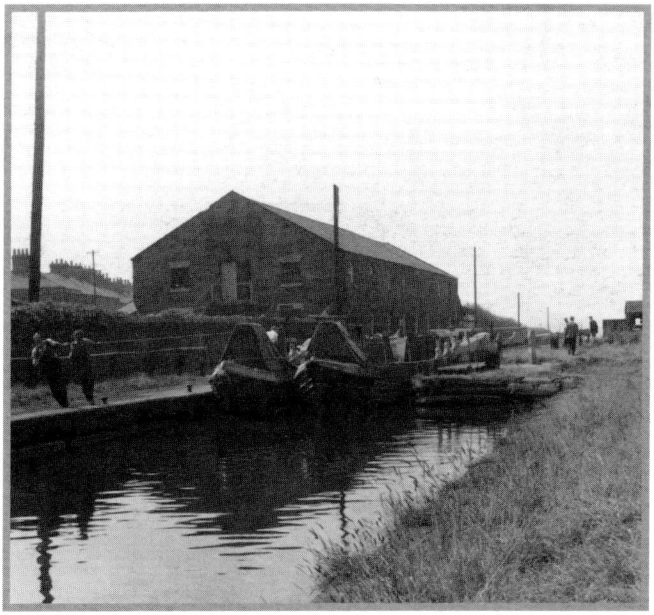

Runcorn, The Locks c1955 R67003

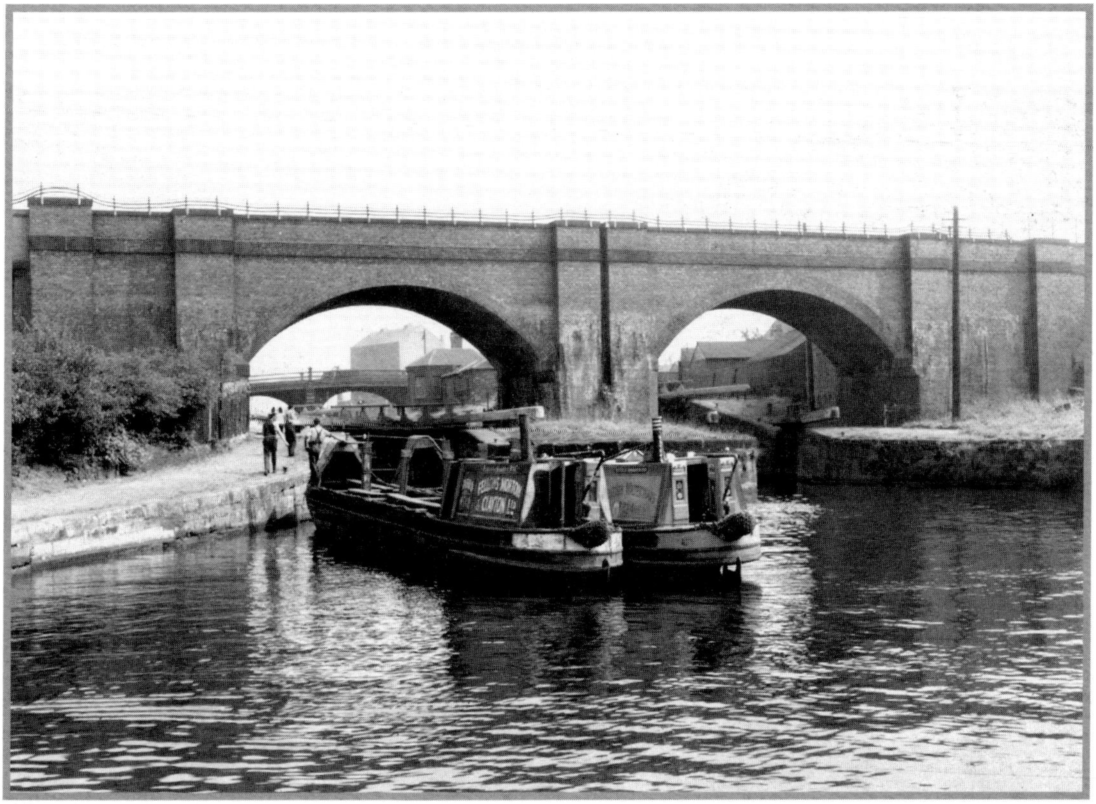

Runcorn, The Locks c1955 R67002

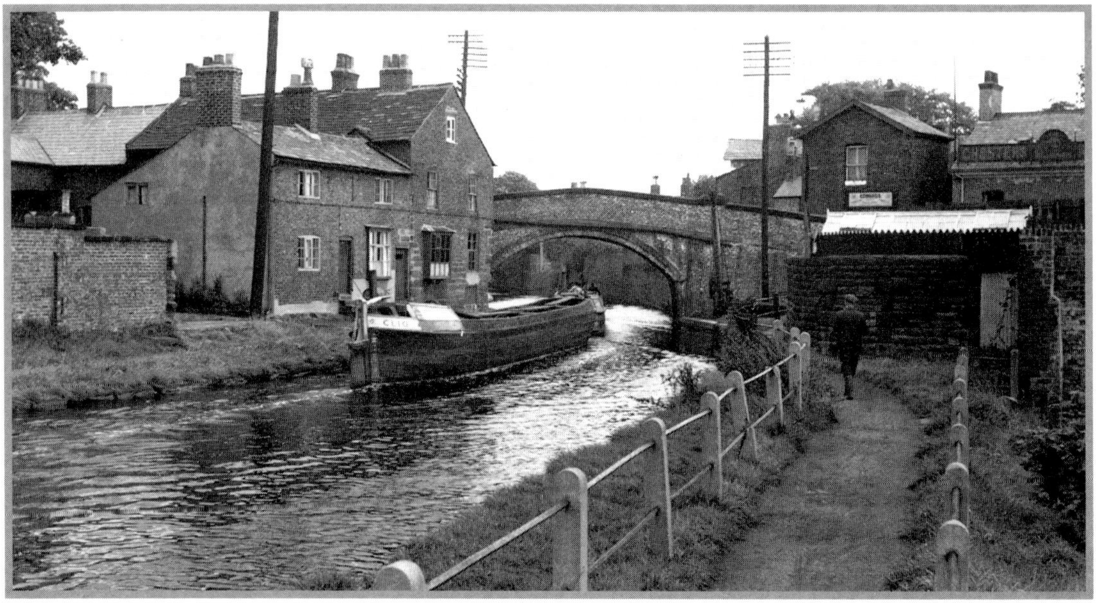

LYMM, THE CANAL c1960 L122026
The Bridgewater Canal flows through the pretty town of Lymm in Cheshire. An empty pair of boats head towards Manchester, probably to collect coal. Unusually, the butty has no steerer, although the tiller is in place. Perhaps he/she had just popped below to put the kettle on. Heating and cooking was performed on a coal-fired range, the chimney for which can be seen behind the tiller.

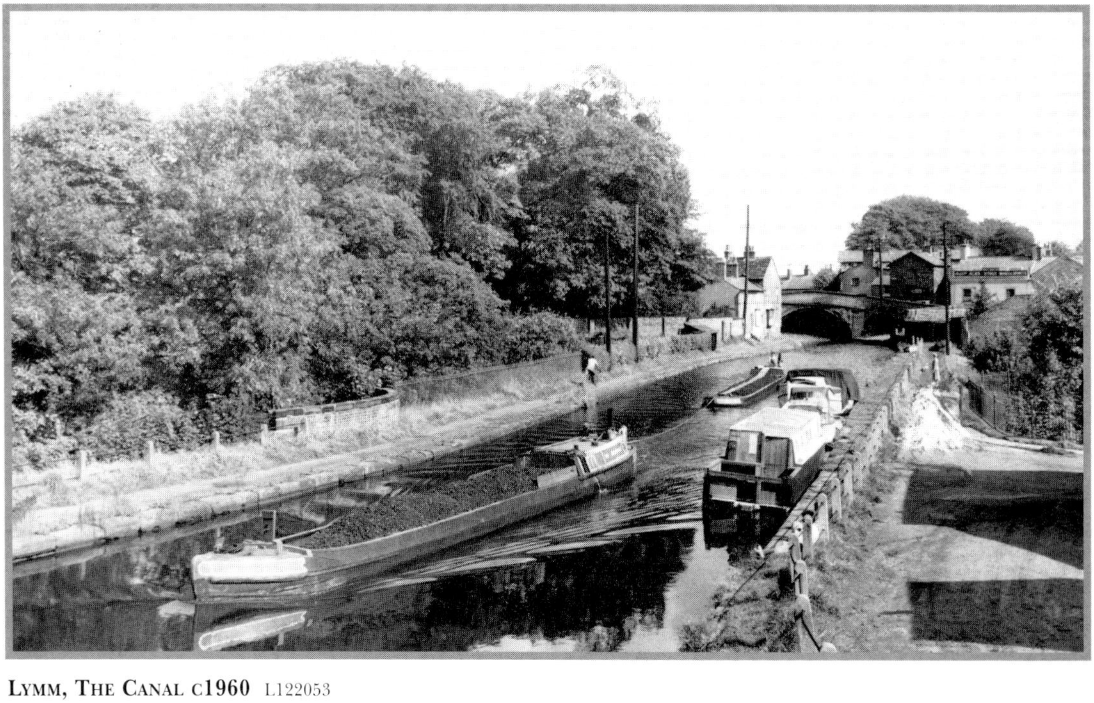

LYMM, THE CANAL c1960 L122053
A few yards from the site of photograph No L122026, a pair of loaded boats head south towards the Trent & Mersey Canal. They were owned by Horsefield Ltd. Early versions of holiday cruising boats can be seen tied up on the right.

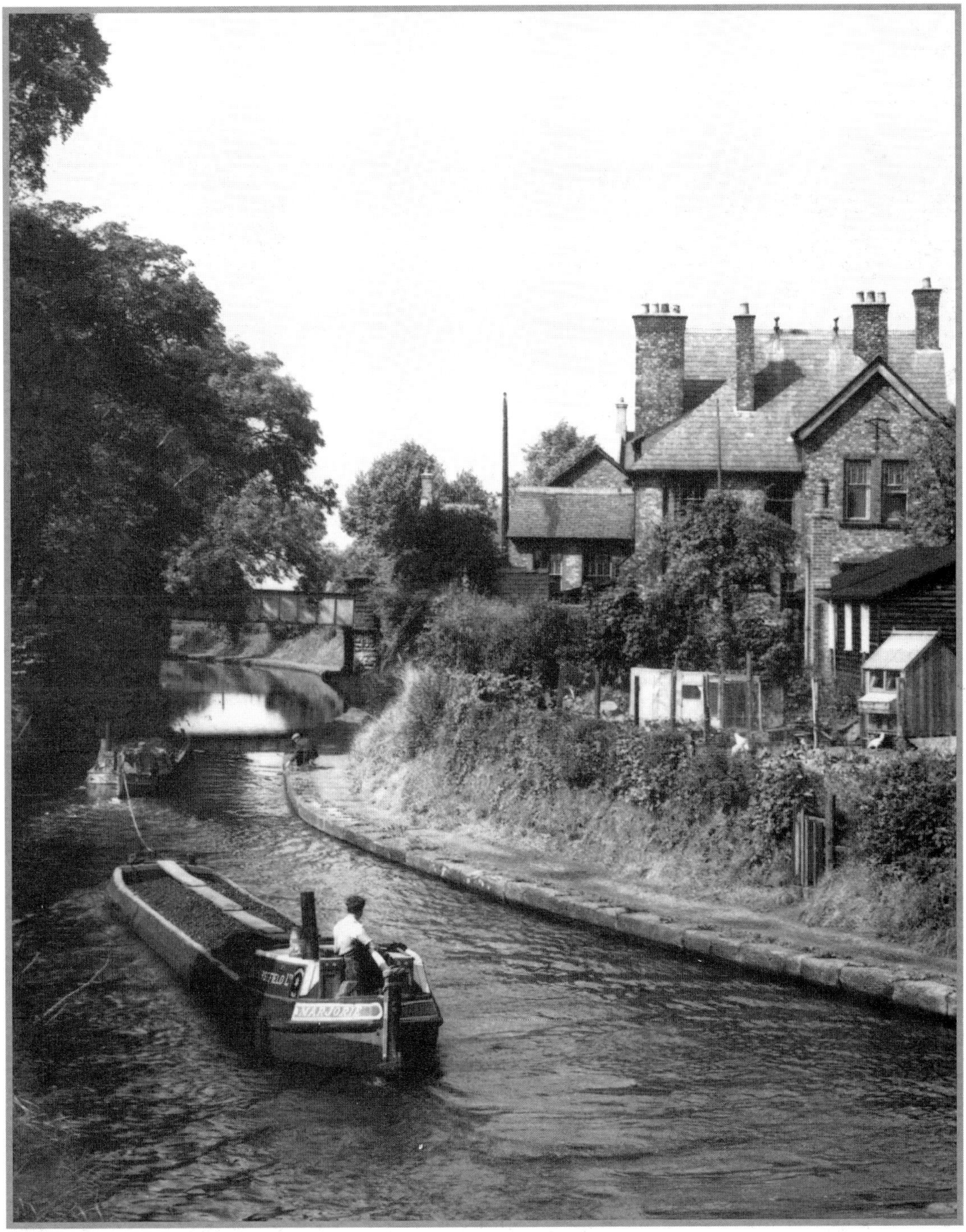

Lymm, The Canal c1960 L122054

Here we have a second view of the loaded boats we saw in photograph No L122053. Now, the name of the butty can be distinguished: 'Marjorie'. By the time this photograph was taken, commercial carrying in narrowboats was almost at an end; it was kept going in many cases by early canal enthusiasts, for whom working long anti-social hours in all weathers was actually a pleasure.

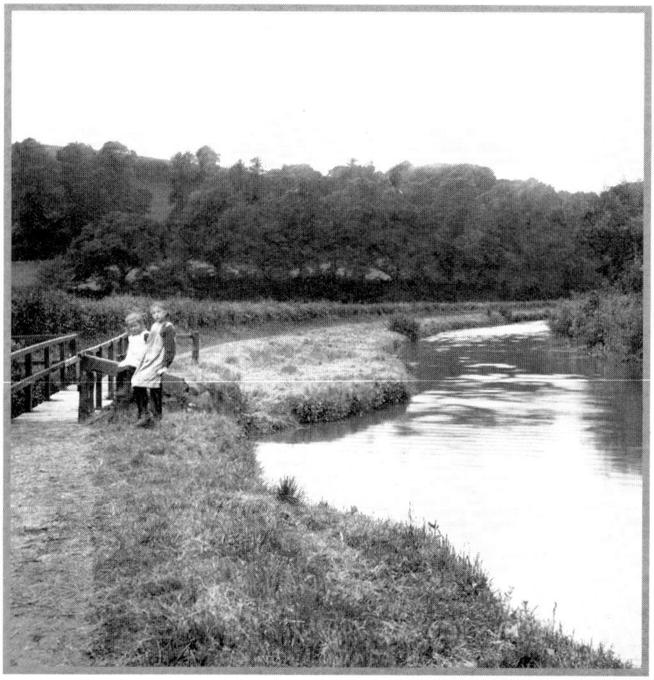

BUDE, ON THE CANAL 1920 69567

BUDE

On the Canal 1920

The Bude Canal was something of an oddity. For its first 2 miles, it was a barge canal - as seen here. Then, freight was trans-shipped into small tubs with wheels. These were horse-drawn and, instead of locks, used slopes called inclined planes. Power was provided at these points, and the tubs were hauled up (or down) to change water levels.

BUDE

The Canal from the Bridge 1890

The harbour, with the sea lock in the far distance, still exists today, albeit completely altered. The quay to the right belonging to Hockin & Co is now a car park. In the right distance, the building that used to be a blacksmith's shop is now a museum. Houses line the left hand bank. In the foreground are examples of the tub boats mentioned earlier.

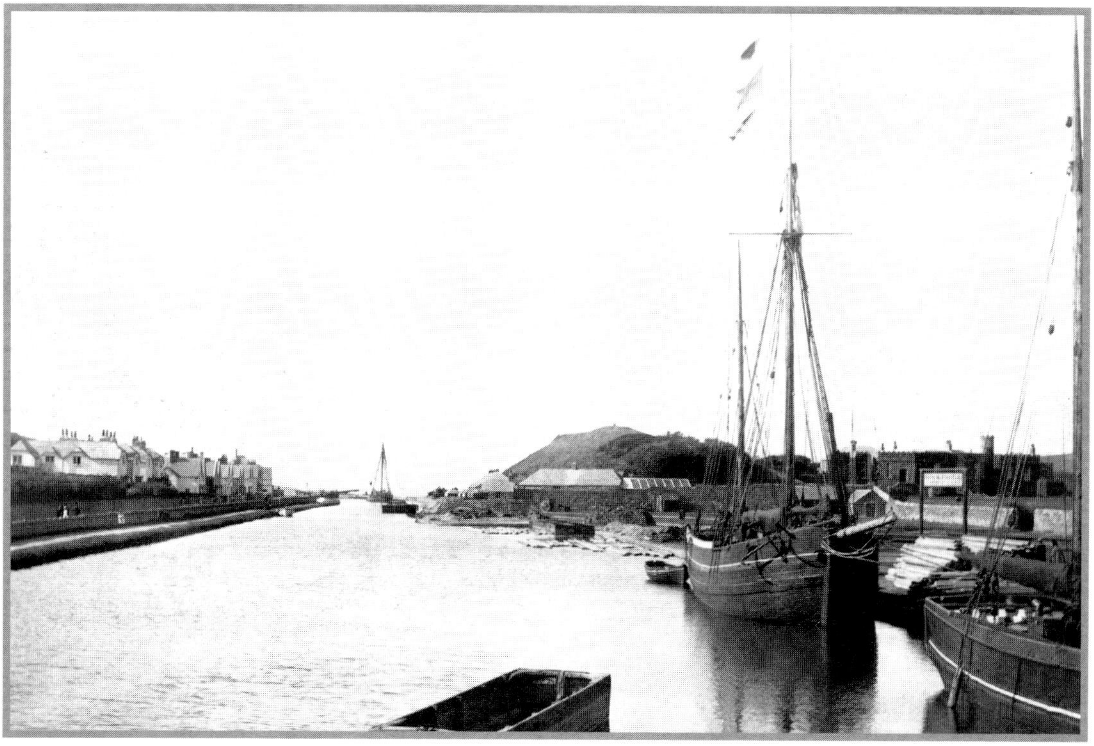

BUDE, THE CANAL FROM THE BRIDGE 1890 23780

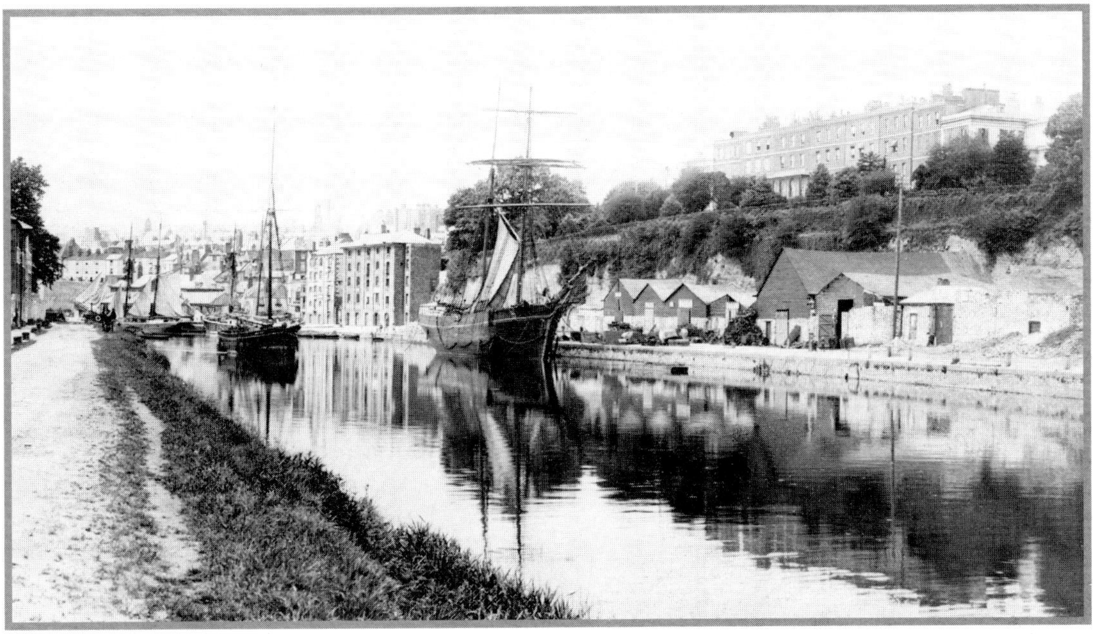

EXETER, THE PORT 1896 38034
A little-known fact is that Exeter's was the first artificial canal in England with locks. The Romans built several channels in the north, but this, constructed in 1566, pre-dated the northern canals where many people think the canal age started.

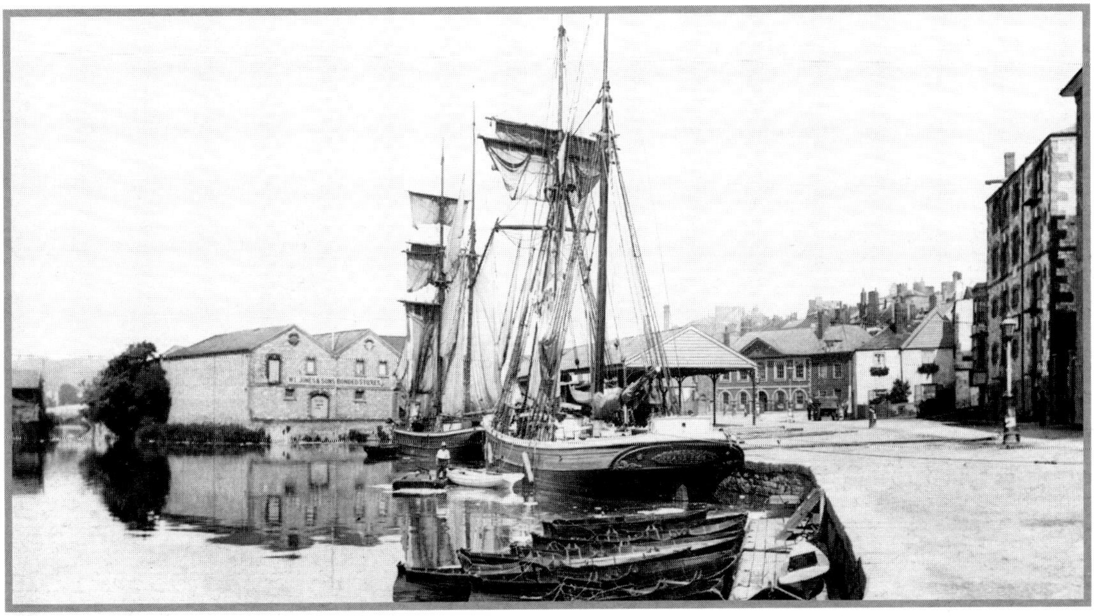

EXETER, IN THE PORT 1896 38036
Final improvements on the Exeter Canal, completed in 1832, allowed larger vessels, such as the 'Hans Emil' pictured here, to reach the Port. Note the bonded warehouse to the left of centre. An indication of the kind of cargoes passing through the Port is gained from noting the wharf-side businesses. W L Jones' bonded store (seen in photograph No 38035) is now centre shot.

EXETER

In the Port 1896 38035

The Exeter Canal was just over 5 miles long, and trade along it to these quays continued until 1972. Subsequently, a maritime museum was established; this has now dispersed, a victim of council indifference. As the canal's owners, they seem curiously at a loss to know how best to exploit this wonderful asset.

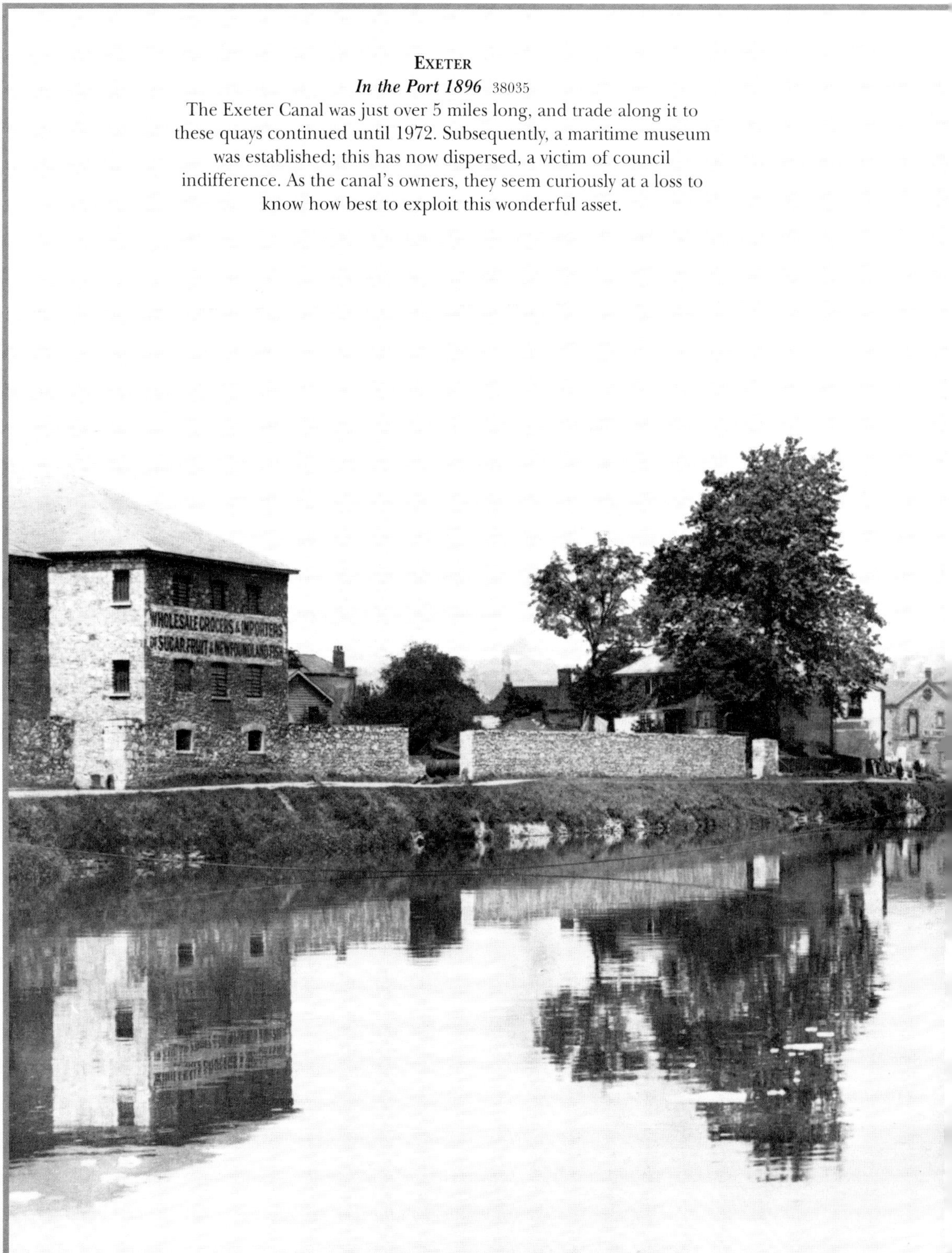

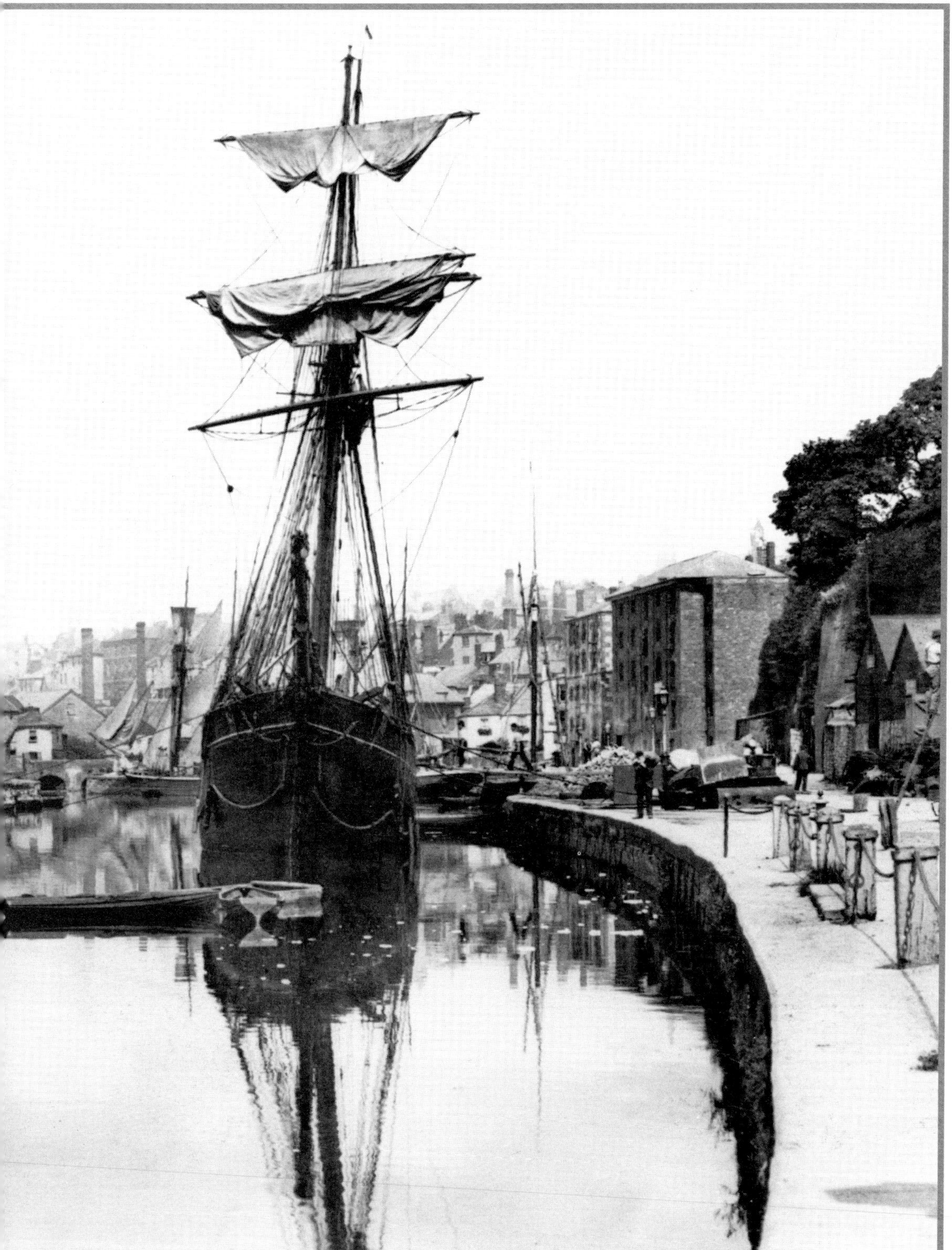

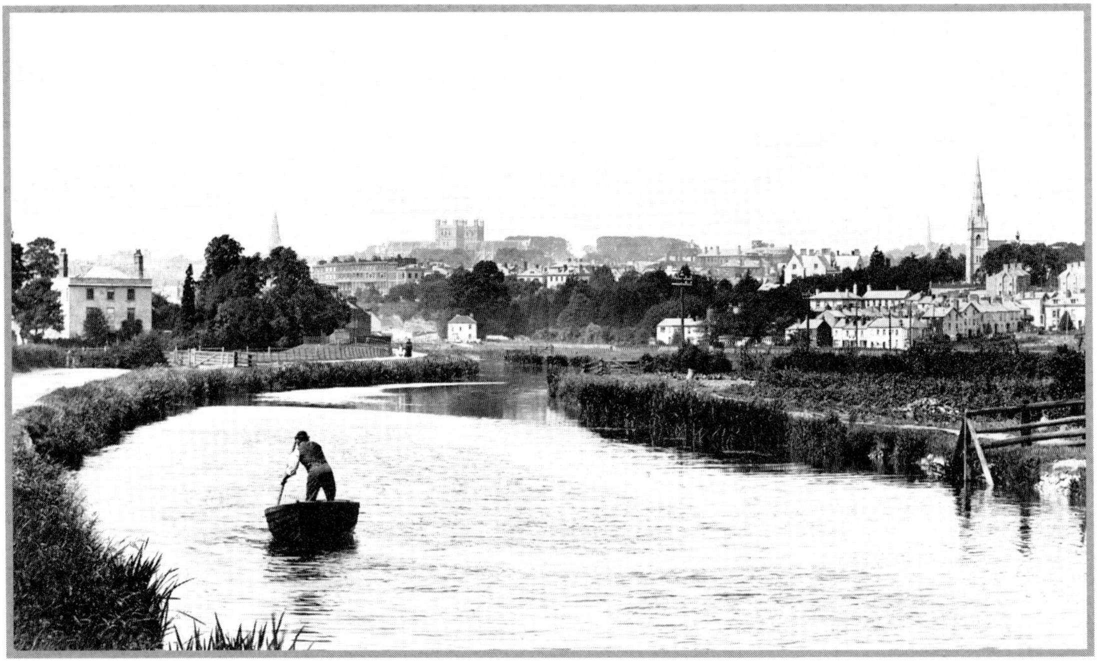

EXETER, FROM THE CANAL 1896 38033
Exactly what the lone oarsman is doing is open to speculation. Note the towing path to the left, with a lady and child out for a stroll. Then, as now, this is a popular walk. The path extends for the full length of the canal.

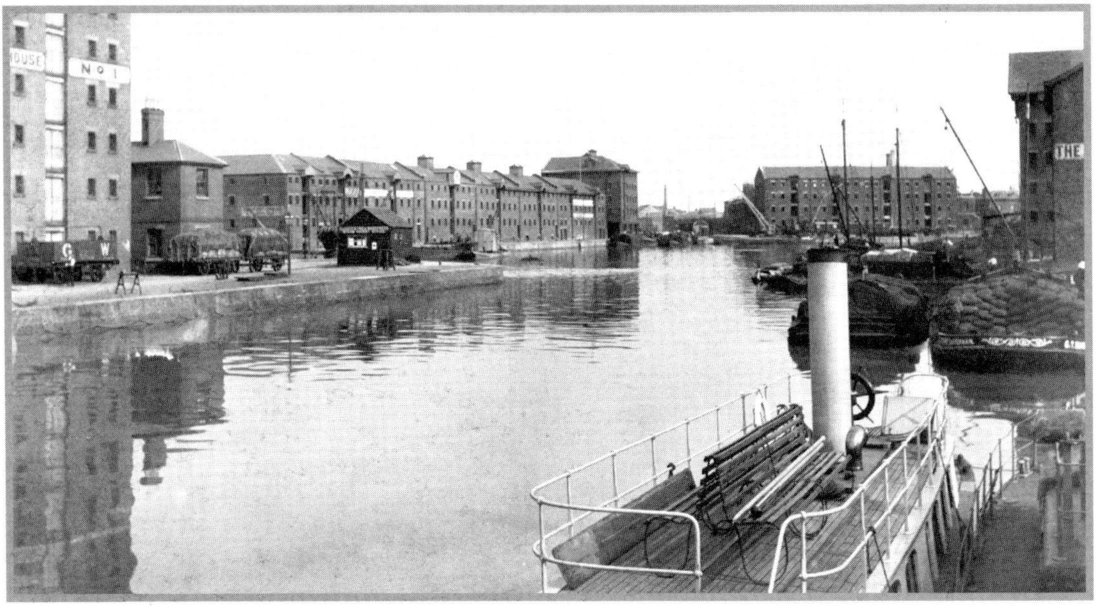

GLOUCESTER, THE DOCKS 1912 65114
Gloucester was linked to the sea by the Gloucester & Sharpness Canal, opened in 1827 and built to avoid the river Severn, which is treacherous hereabouts. Many of these wonderful old buildings exist to this day. The pleasure steamer indicates that canal cruising was clearly popular in the early 19th century. The docks are now extensively developed, and there is a fascinating waterways museum on the site.

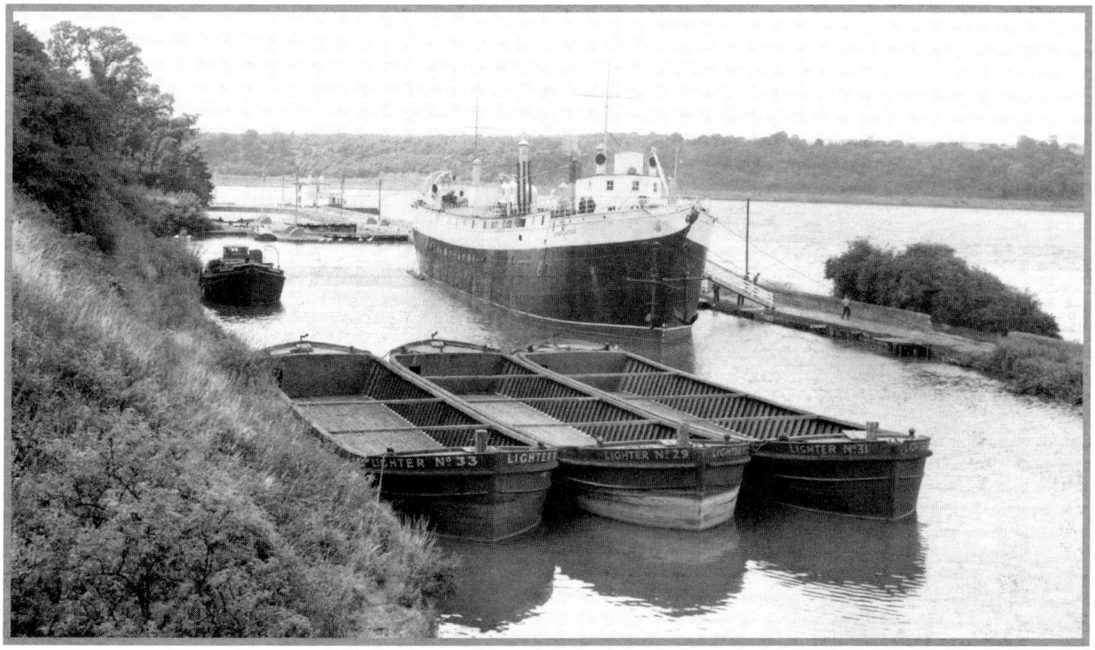

SHARPNESS, THE TRAINING SHIP 'VINDICATRIX' c1955 S502018

SHARPNESS

The Training Ship 'Vindicatrix' c1955

Having just taken refuge from the turbulent river Severn, this venerable craft now offers shore leave to her crew. Note the size of the twin anchors hanging from the bow. The lighters in the foreground were used to carry freight from Sharpness port to Gloucester,

HAREFIELD

The Canal c1965

A pair of empty working narrowboats on the Grand Union Canal near Harefield. When this picture was taken, there was still some commercial traffic around: within five years, almost two centuries of carrying on the GU would come to an end.

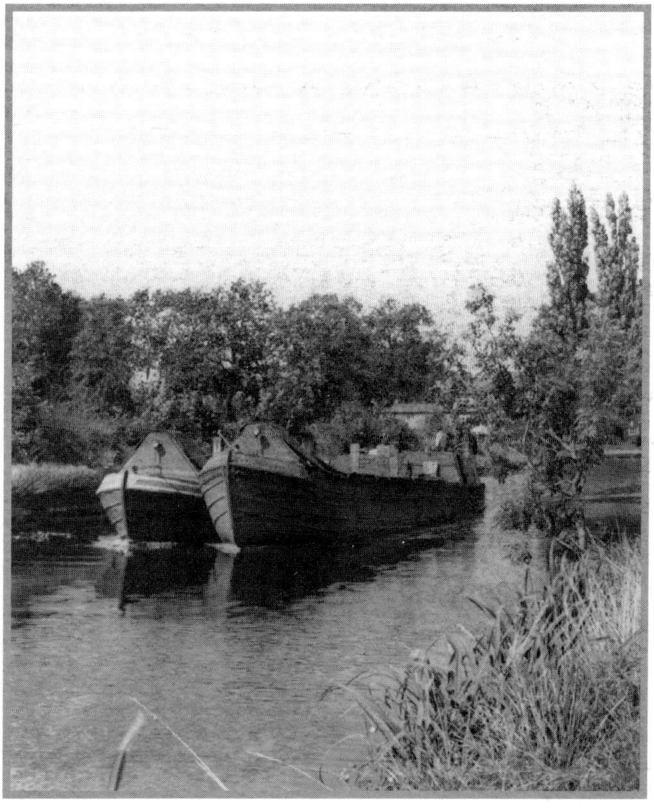

HAREFIELD, THE CANAL c1965 H428034

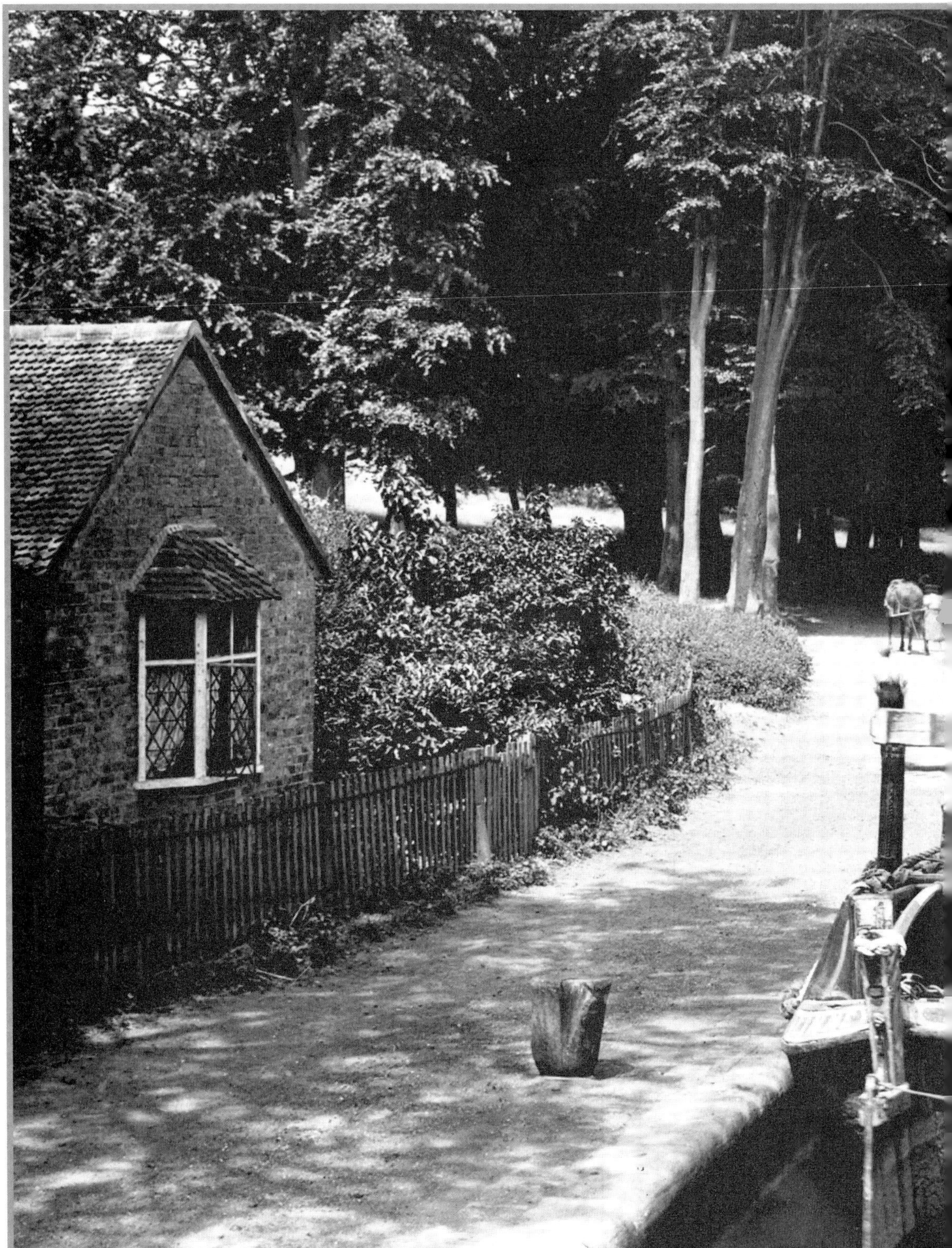

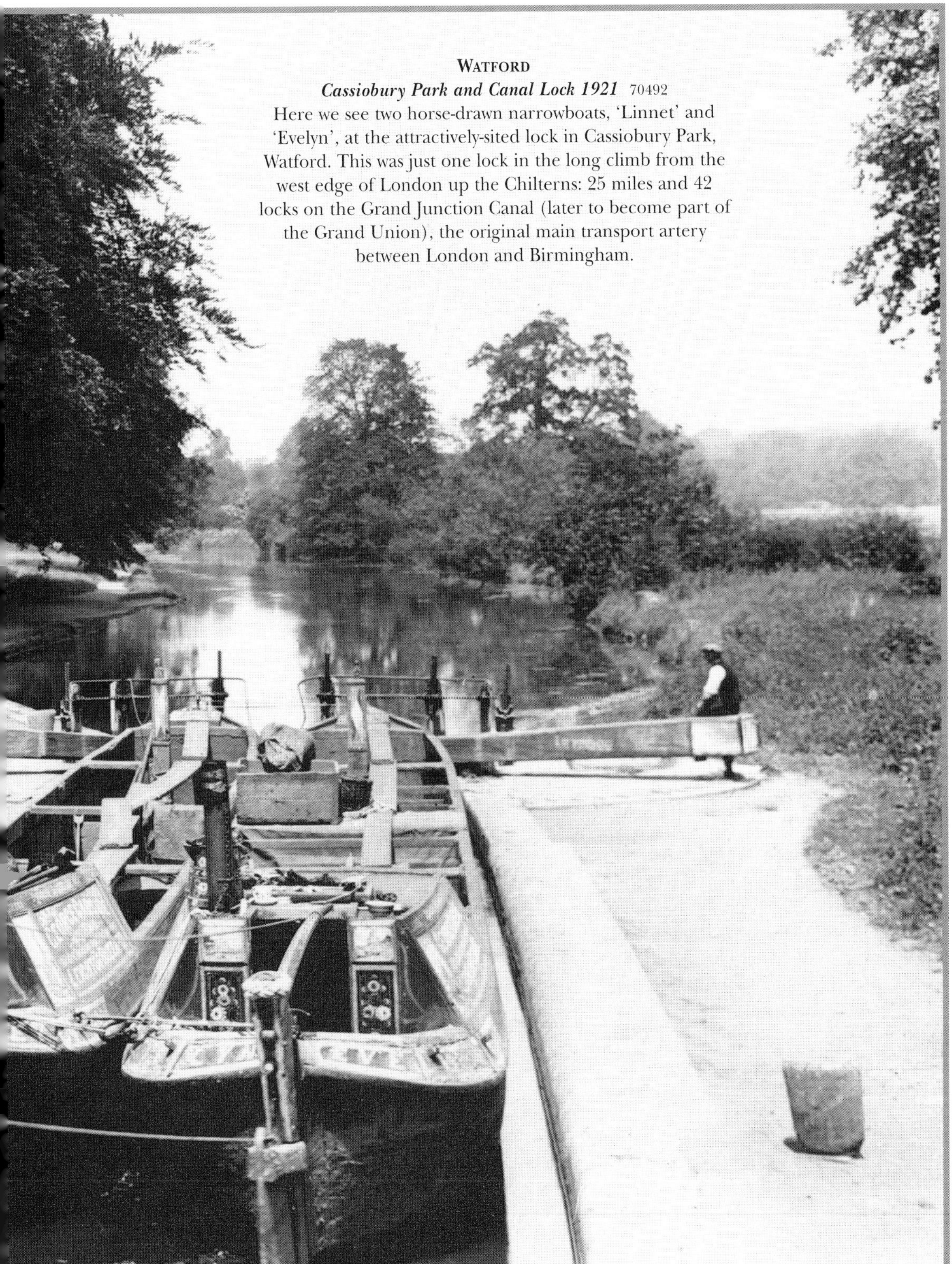

WATFORD

Cassiobury Park and Canal Lock 1921 70492

Here we see two horse-drawn narrowboats, 'Linnet' and 'Evelyn', at the attractively-sited lock in Cassiobury Park, Watford. This was just one lock in the long climb from the west edge of London up the Chilterns: 25 miles and 42 locks on the Grand Junction Canal (later to become part of the Grand Union), the original main transport artery between London and Birmingham.

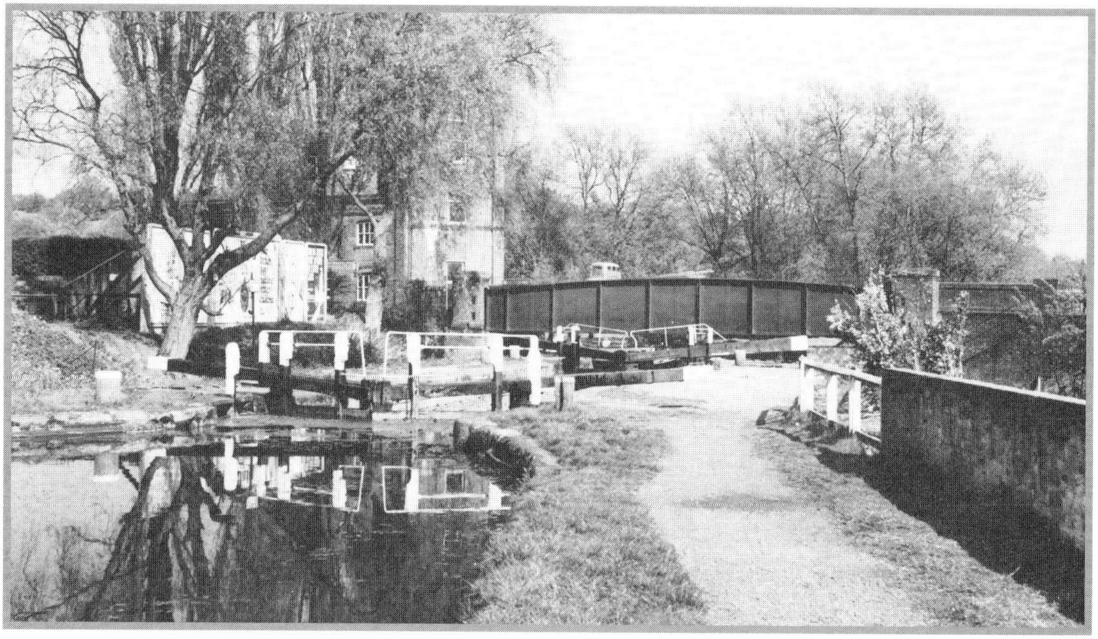

BERKHAMSTED, THE CANAL AND LOCKS c1965 B407108

This is the Grand Union Canal. The line was built by the Grand Junction company between London and Braunston (Northants). Following an amalgamation with several other connected waterways, the Grand Union was formed in 1929. A Thames Trader lorry is crossing the iron bridge.

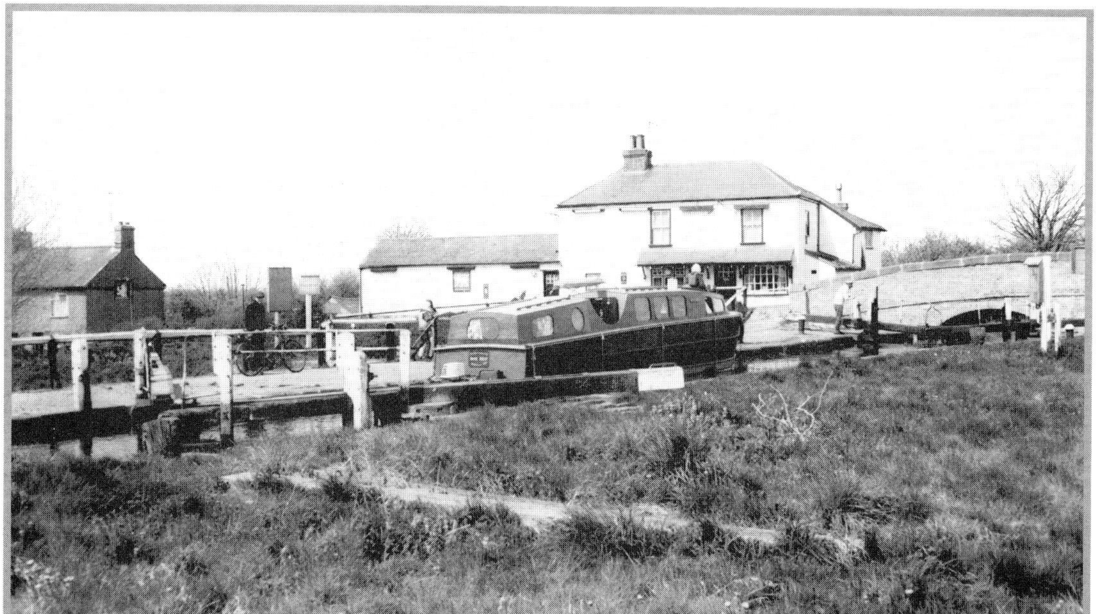

TRING, MARSWORTH LOCKS c1960 T81054

The bottom Marsworth Lock at Startops End is being used by an early pleasure cruiser. The white building is the White Lion pub, still dispensing excellent food and drink to boaters and landlubbers alike.

AYLESBURY
The Canal 1897
Children are trying their luck at fishing in the Aylesbury Arm of the Grand Junction Canal. Just beyond the bridge is the delightfully named Hills and Partridges Lock.

AYLESBURY
The Canal 1921
A pair of loaded working boats on the Aylesbury Arm near Broughton on the edge of town. The wooden stumps (bottom left) are known as strapping posts, and were used to tie up boats. Their state in this view appears to be somewhat poor. Two ladies, dressed in the fashions of the day, take their ease.

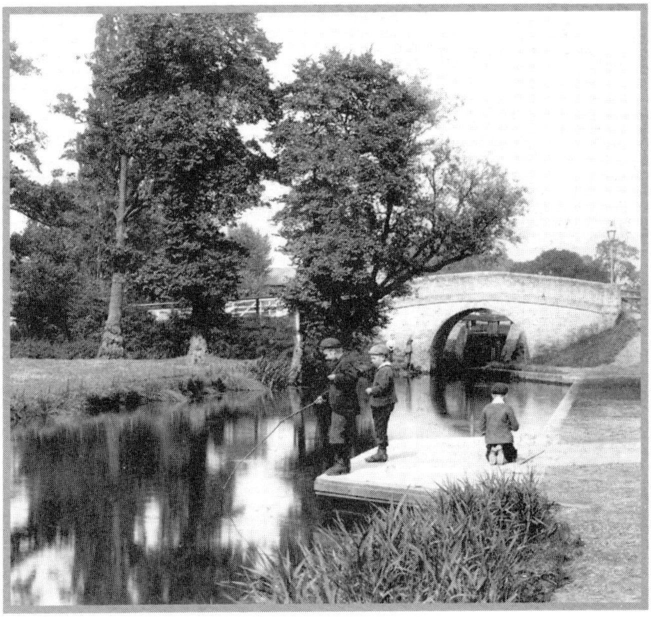

AYLESBURY, THE CANAL 1897 39642

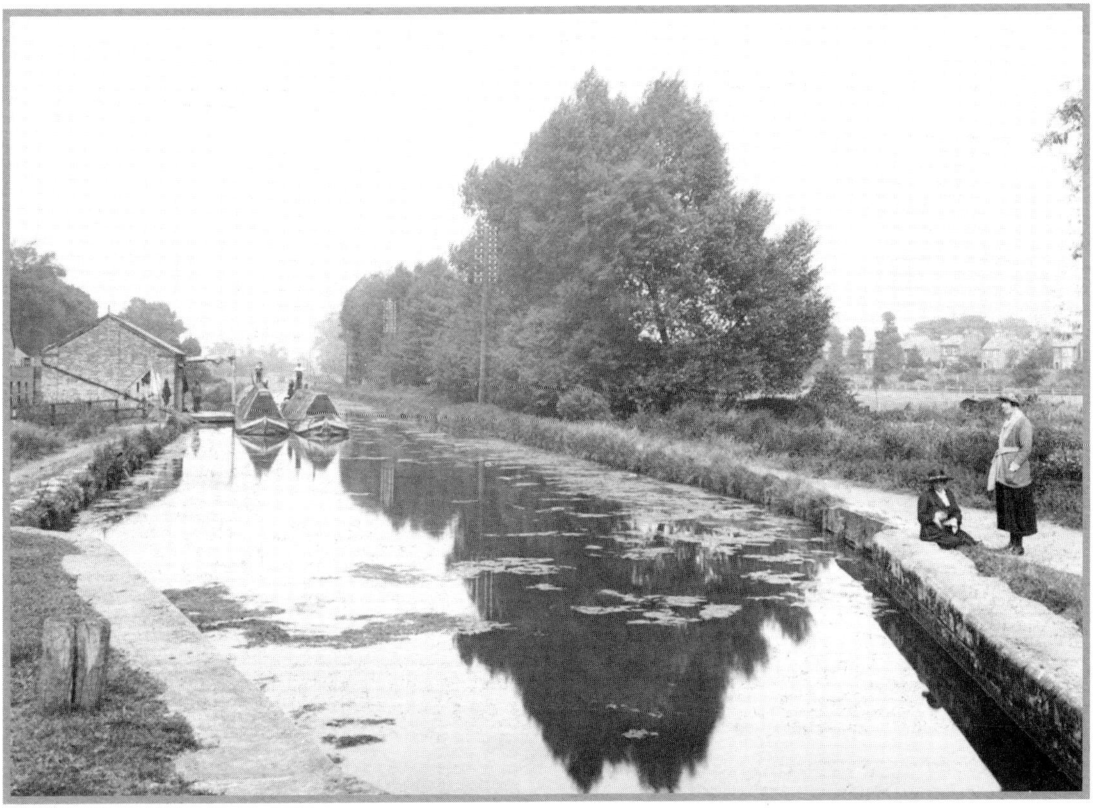

AYLESBURY, THE CANAL 1921 70564

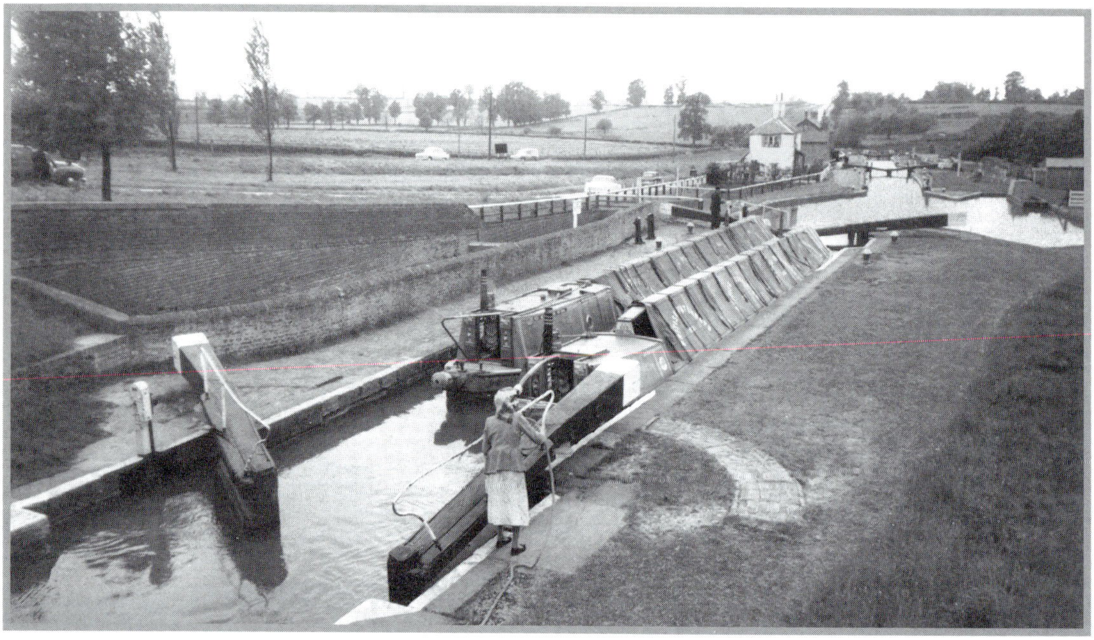

LEIGHTON BUZZARD, THE THREE LOCKS c1955 L211054
These are Soulbury Three Locks on the Grand Union Canal north of Leighton Buzzard. The lady is using the rope over the gate to take the last forward movement off the butty boat. Note that the top gate on the second chamber is already open, ready for them. The white building is the Three Locks pub, built to serve canal boatmen.

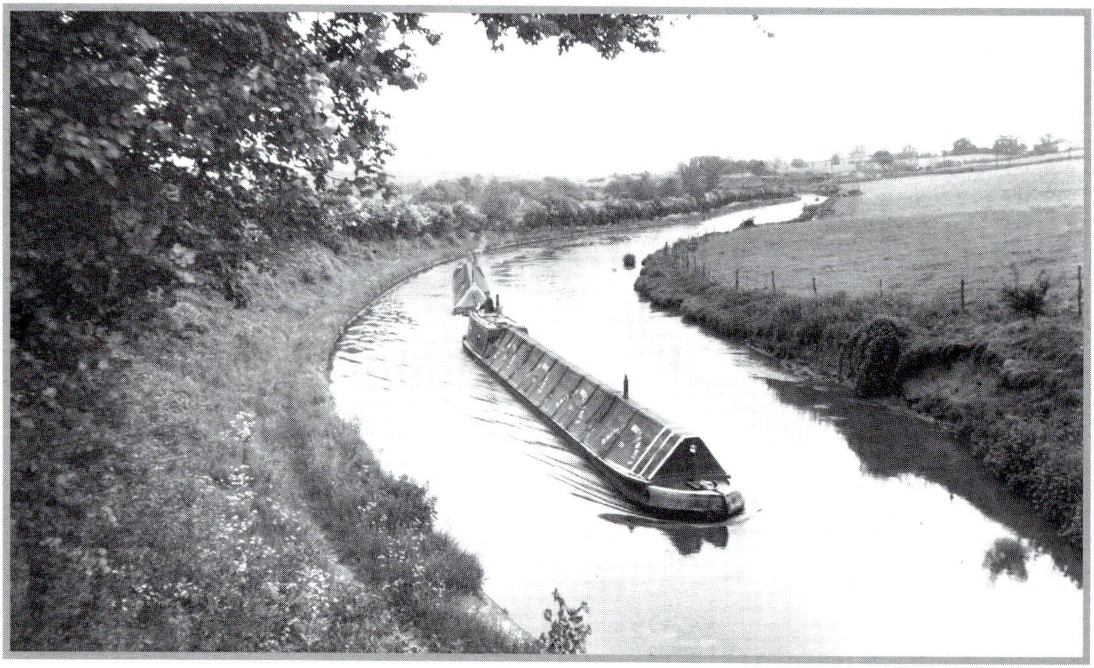

LEIGHTON BUZZARD, THE GRAND UNION CANAL c1955 L211049
Two loaded narrowboats head north on the Grand Union Canal, their cargo concealed from both weather and prying eyes by careful sheeting. This spot is only a mile or so from where the Great Train Robbery took place in 1963.

Blisworth
The Canal c1955
A strange-looking craft heads southwards towards Blisworth Tunnel on the Grand Union Canal. The pretty tower of the 14th-century church is clearly visible here. The tunnel, 3057yds long, is the longest currently open to all boats.

Daventry
The Canal Tunnel c1955
This is the entrance to Braunston Tunnel on the Grand Union Canal. This is 2049 yards long, and it leaks quite appreciably; boaters must wear waterproofs when transiting. Inside, there are several small stalactites forming, together with extensive and brightly coloured salt deposits where water runs into the canal.

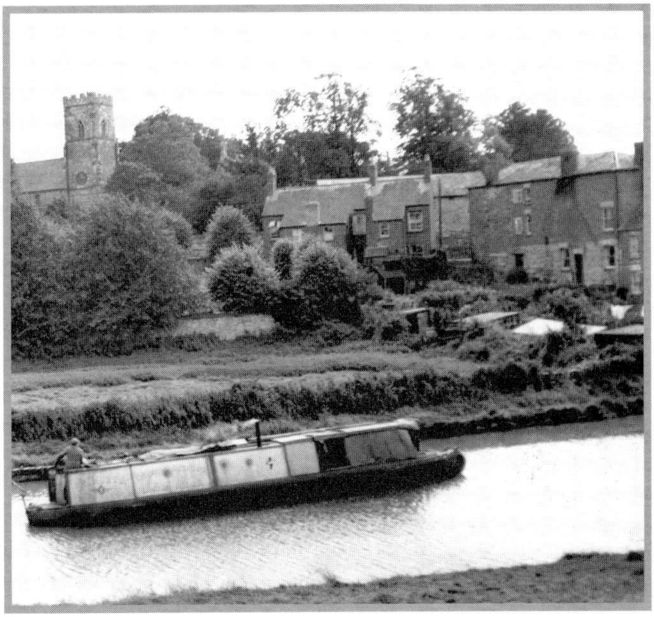

Blisworth, The Canal c1955 B283391

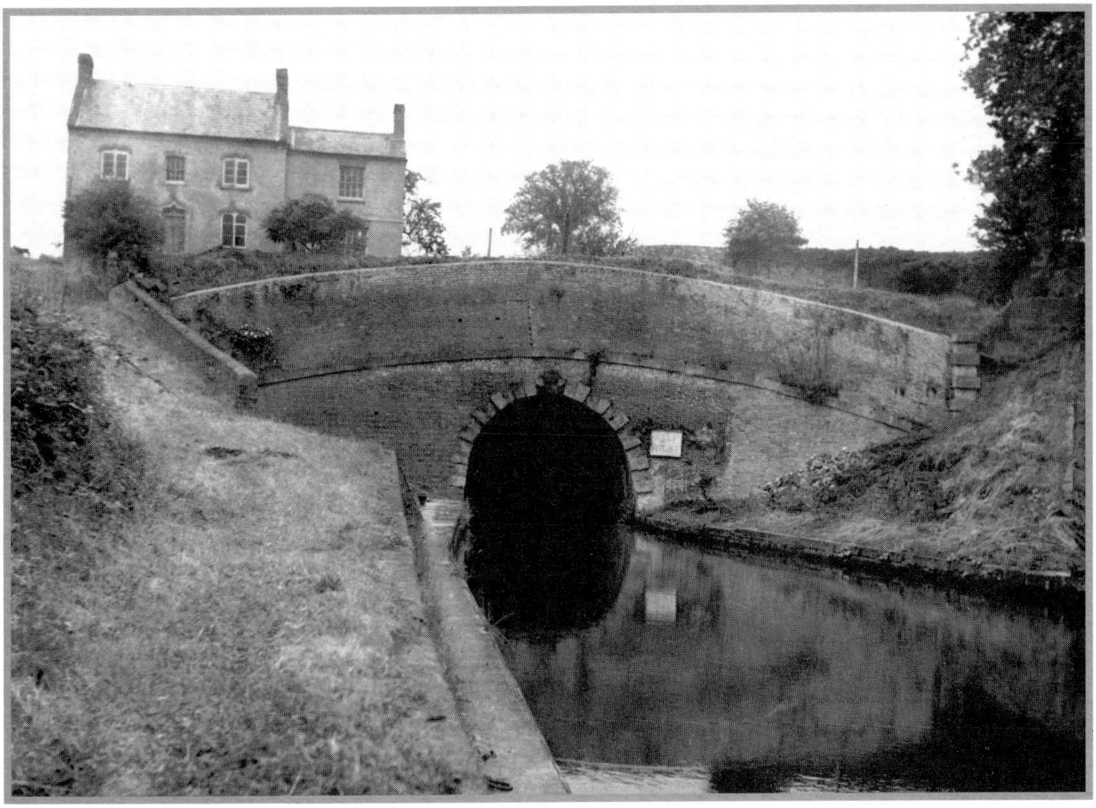

Daventry, The Canal Tunnel c1955 D83014

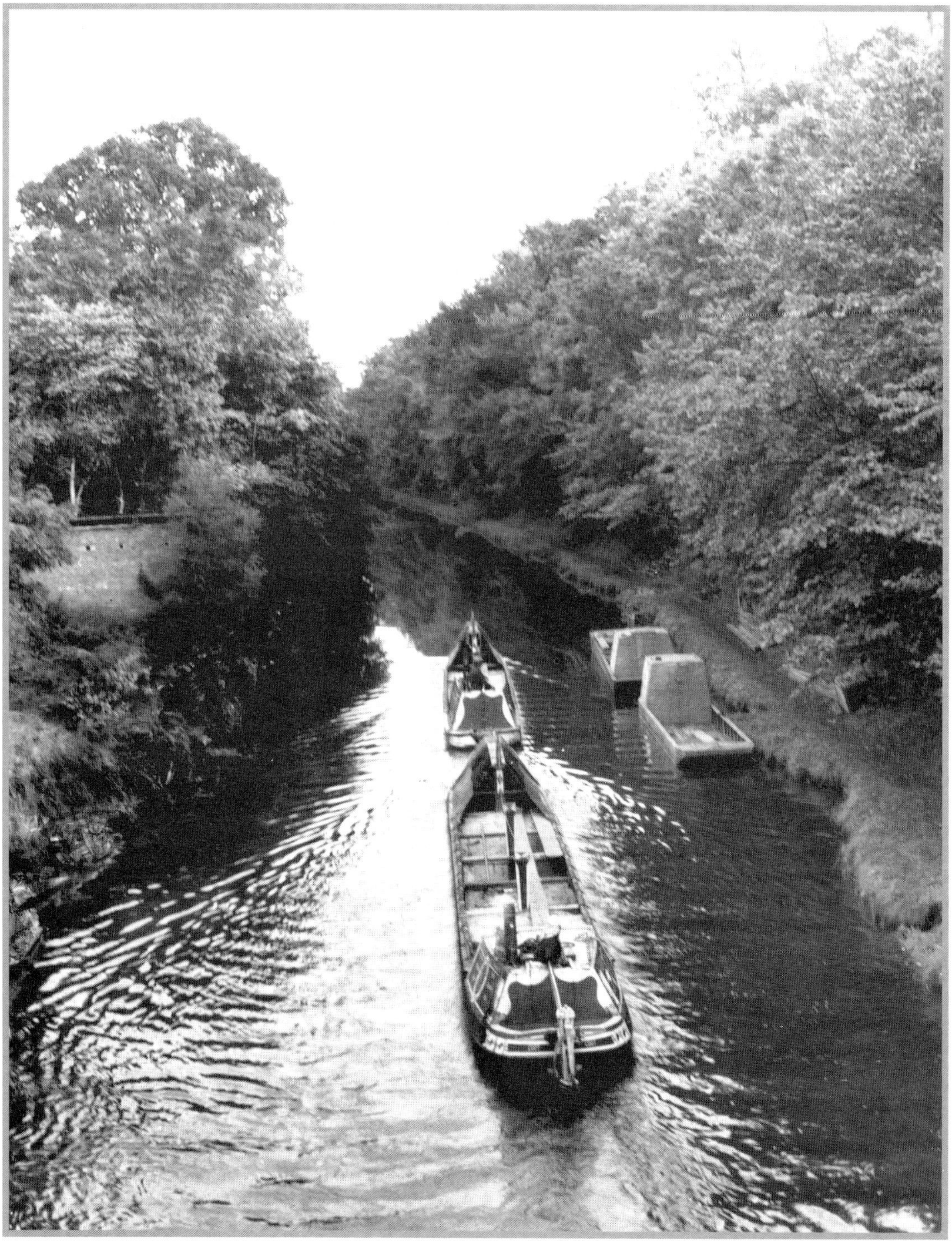

DAVENTRY, THE CANAL c1965 D83042

A pair of loaded working boats head south on the Grand Union Canal from Braunston Tunnel. The somewhat precarious towing path seen here has been reinstated now, and forms part of the long-distance London to Birmingham footpath.

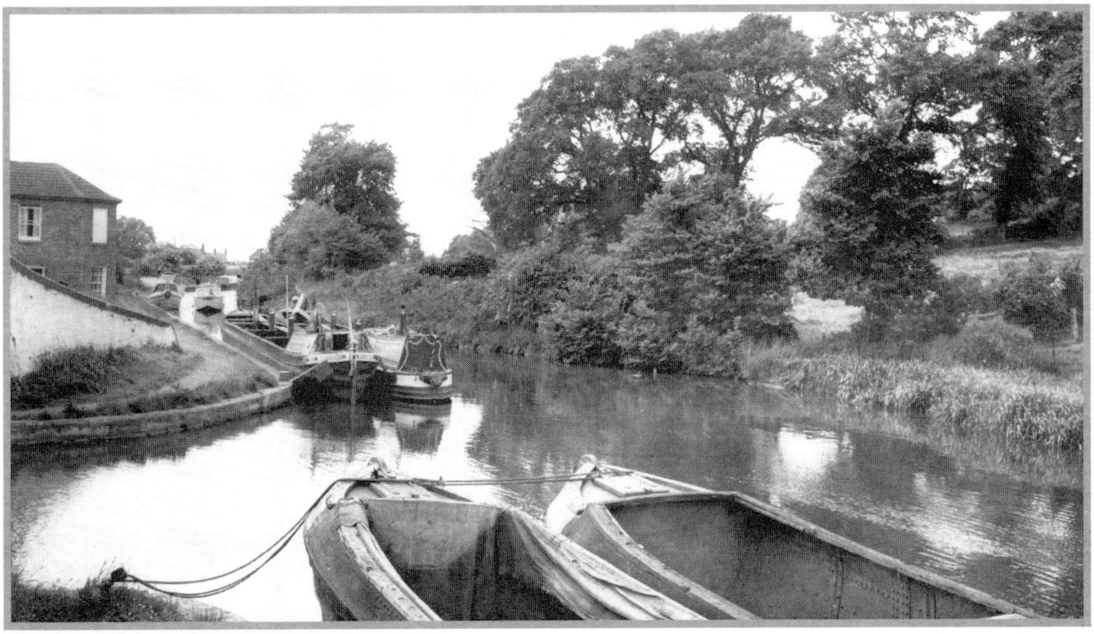

Braunston, The Canal c1965 B778014
A major boating centre to this day, Braunston was the northern end of the Grand Junction canal. At this point it met the Oxford Canal; there used to be a small lock outside the house. This building is now British Waterways offices. The number of empty boats tied up indicates that trade was poor at this time.

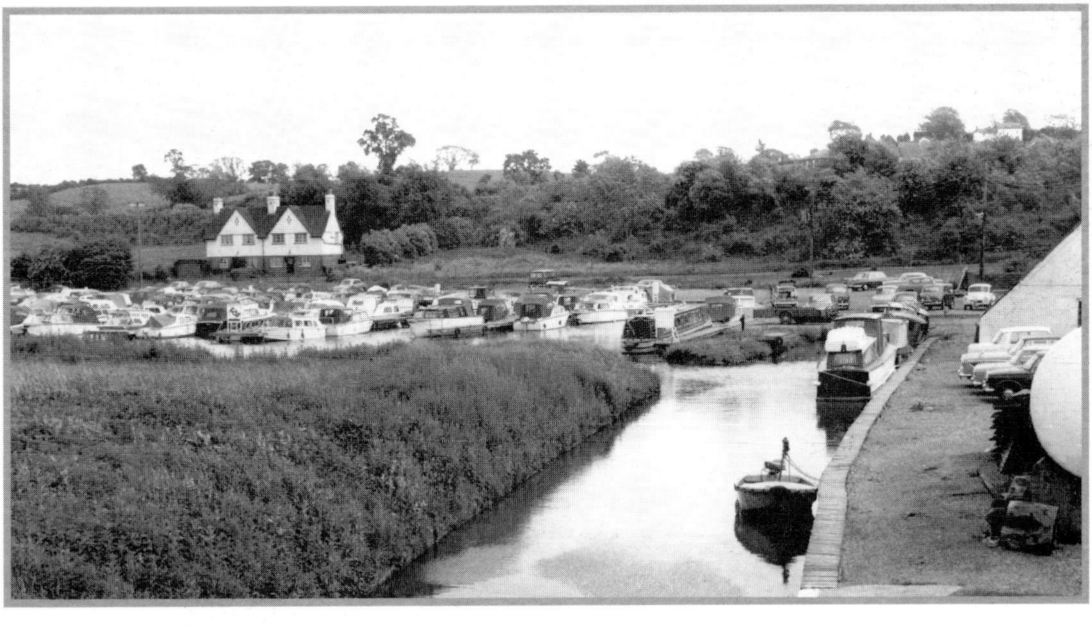

Braunston, The Canal c1965 B778015
What is now a short arm and extensive marina moorings was once the main line of the Oxford Canal. The white building to the right is original, built in the 1780s, whilst the land to the left has been excavated to make more room for boats. The house in the distance has been demolished, and rather picturesque town houses now surround the back of the marina.

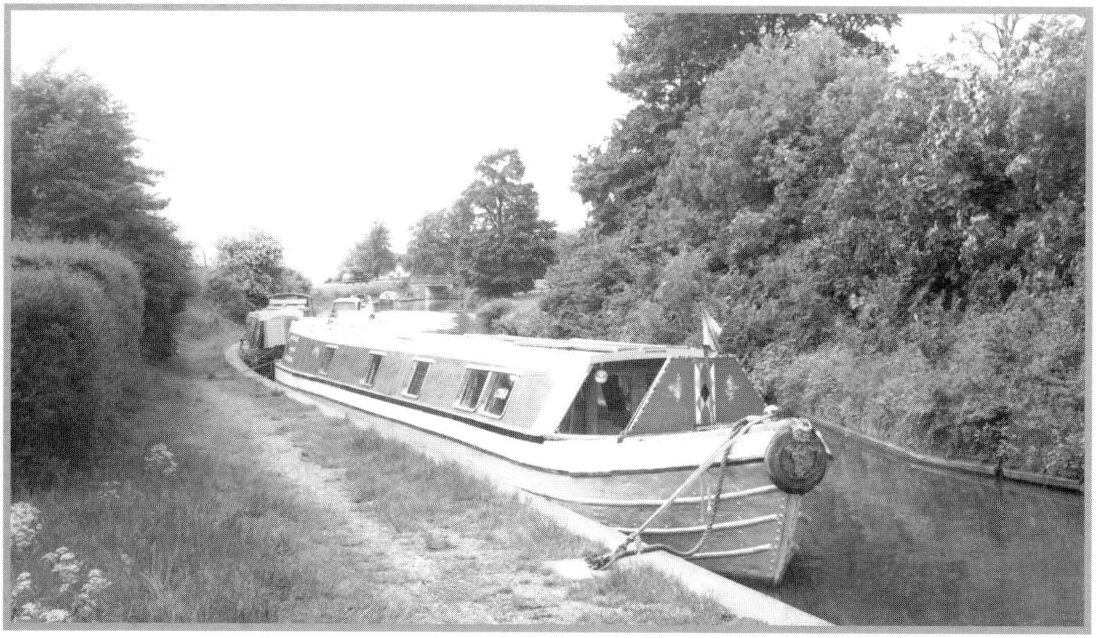

BRAUNSTON, THE CANAL c1965 B778016

Early holiday boats like this were often converted from old working boats. In the distance beyond the bridge is a pub. At the time of this view, it would have been called the Rose and Castle. Since then, it has undergone massive refurbishment and changes of name before becoming The Mill House.

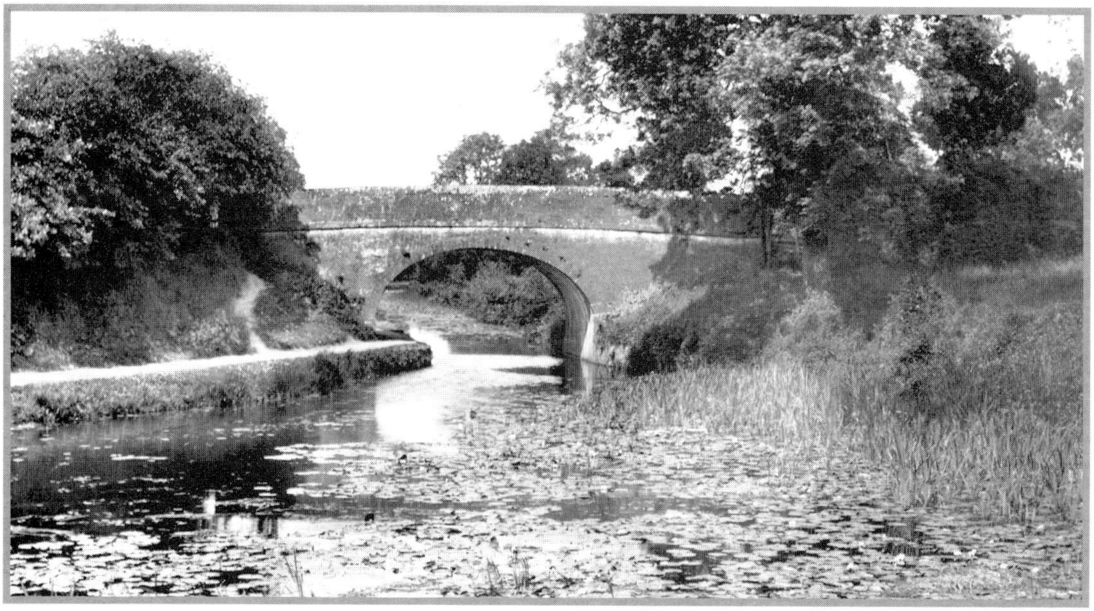

TIVERTON, ON THE CANAL 1903 49613

The Grand Western Canal was a 19th-century dream, planned to run from Taunton to the river Exe near Exeter. In the event, the main line from Taunton was built as a tub boat canal with a very short life, and an 11-mile stretch from Loudwells to Tiverton was built as a barge canal. Tiverton was actually a branch from the main line. Today, you can take a trip on this section aboard a horse-drawn barge from Tiverton.

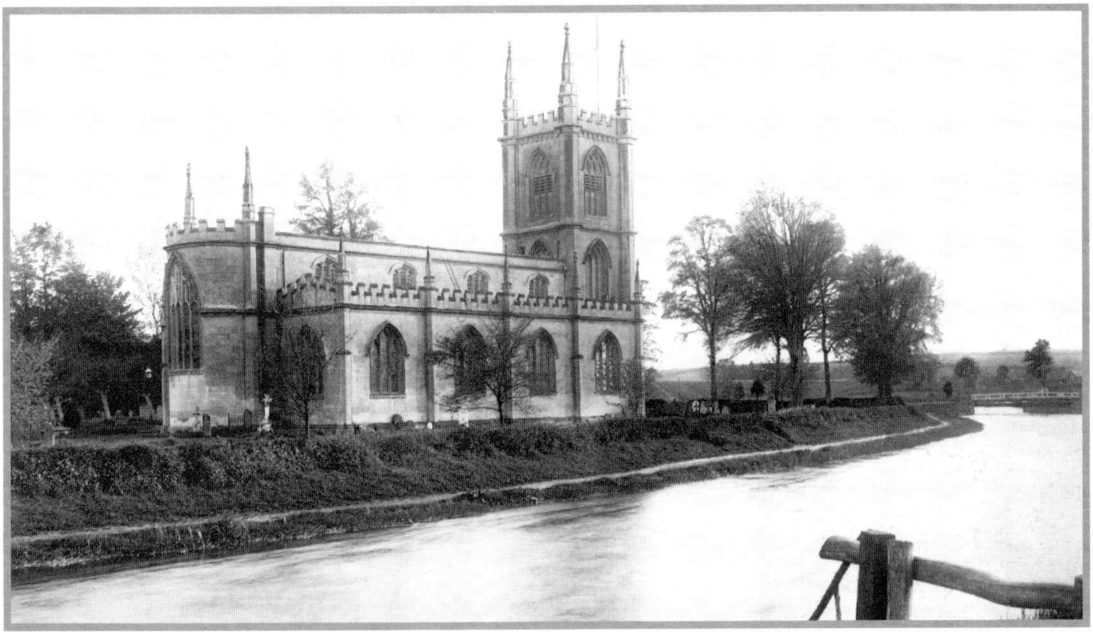

HUNGERFORD, THE PARISH CHURCH 1903 49389
The church of St Lawrence is right alongside the Kennet & Avon Canal. This view today, a century later, is almost unchanged. The flagpole is still in place, and only the trees have grown, creating a much more rustic scene than is evident here.

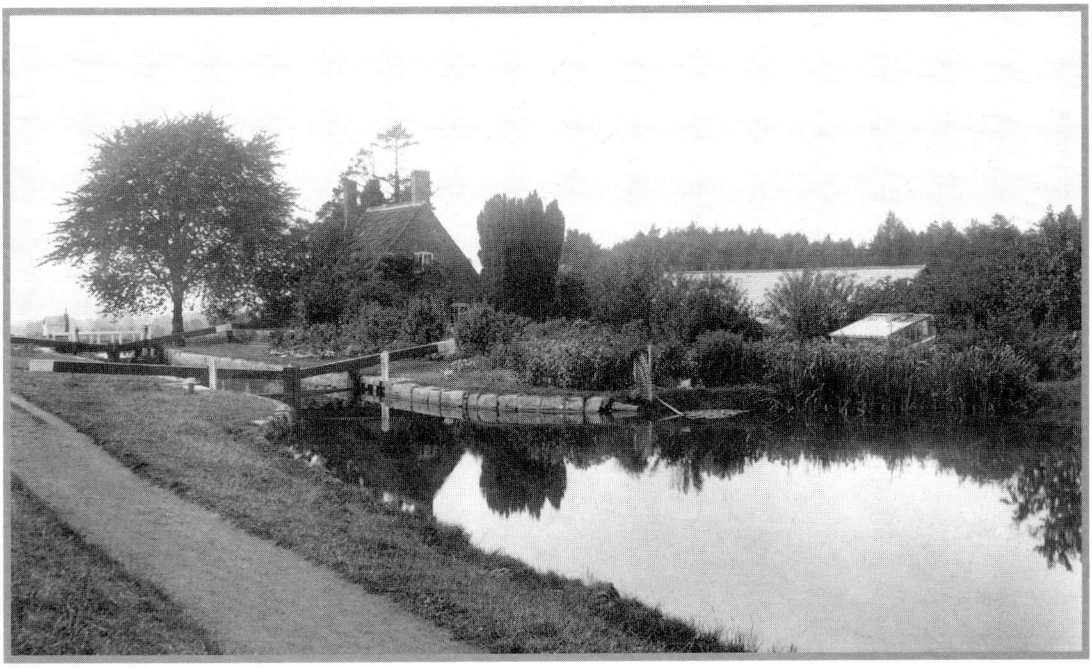

DEVIZES, ON THE CANAL 1898 42318
Devizes is perched on the top of a hill overlooking the Avon valley. From there, the Kennet & Avon Canal plunges down 29 locks to the valley below. This one is on the edge of town, close to the old prison.

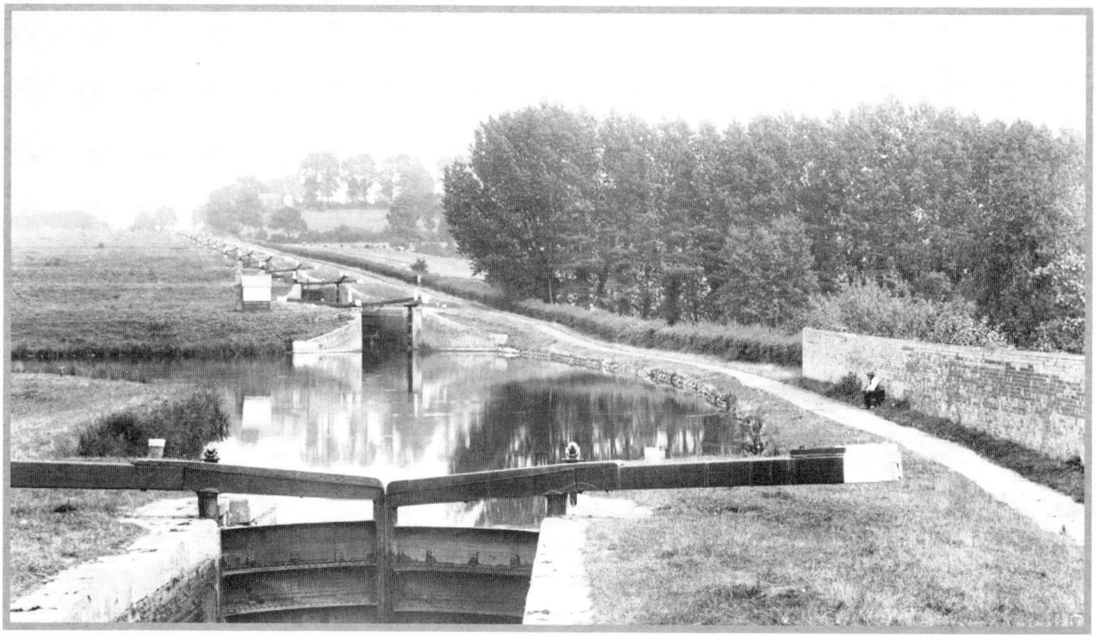

DEVIZES, THE CANAL BRIDGE & LOCK 1898 42320

Part of the Devizes 29 is this set of 16 locks at Caen Hill. These locks are so close together that in order to maintain a satisfactory supply of water, it was necessary to extend the canal at the left-hand side above each chamber. These are known as side ponds.

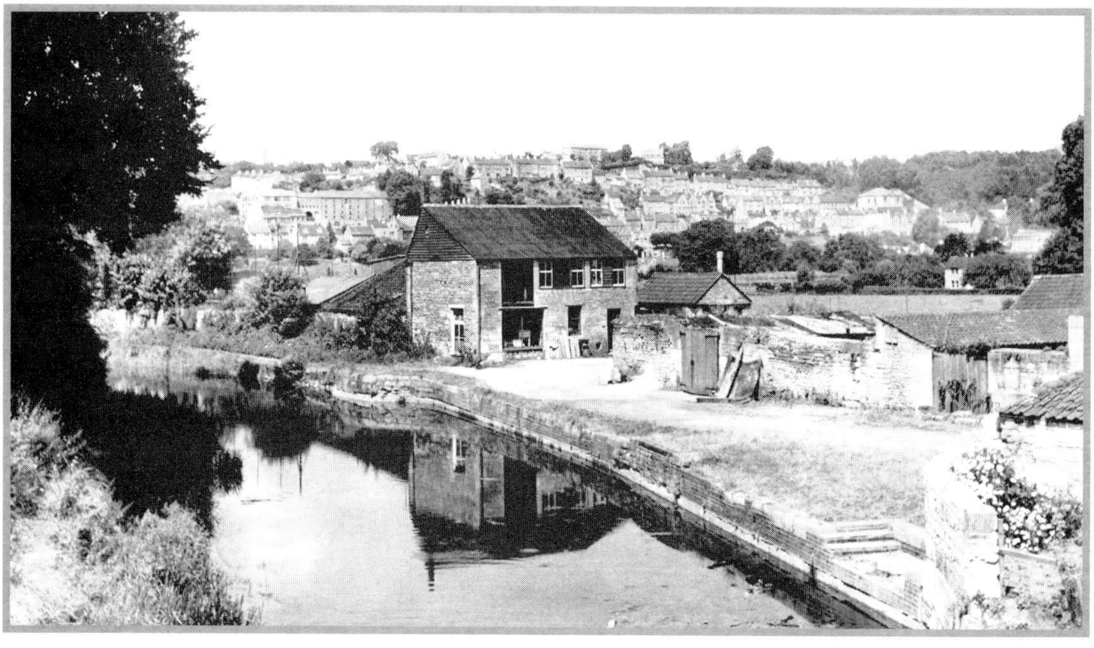

BRADFORD-ON-AVON, THE CANAL c1955 B174039

This area below the town's lock has been enormously improved since the Kennet & Avon Canal was re-opened throughout: boats now tie up here. The town of Bradford-on-Avon can be seen in the distance clinging to the valley side.

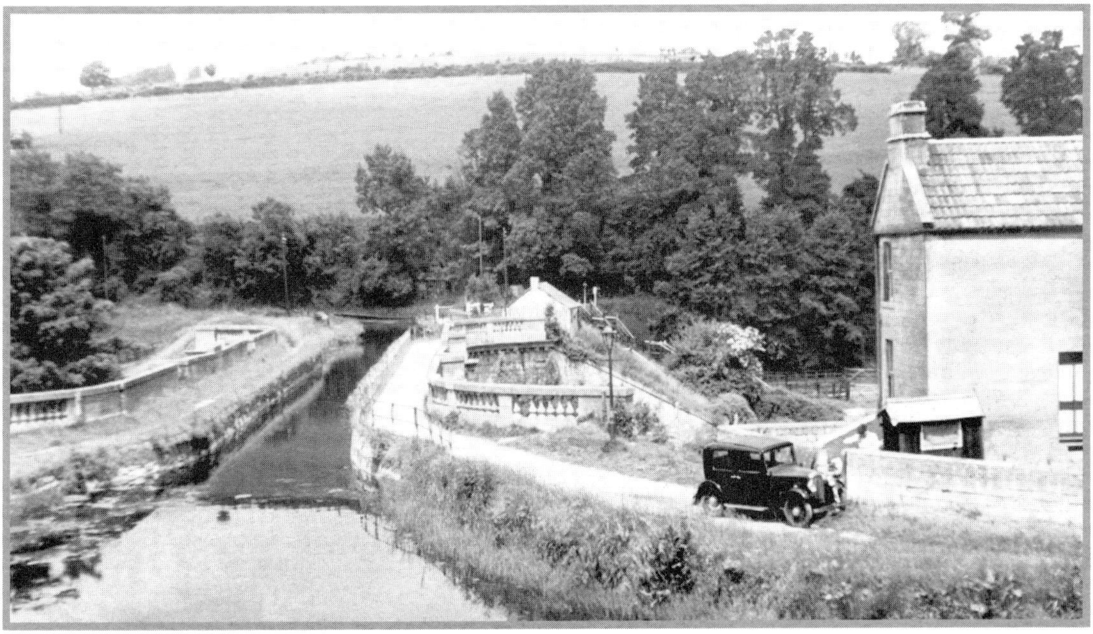

Avoncliffe, The Aqueduct c1955 A329012
On this section of the Kennet & Avon Canal, the river Avon is crossed twice. This aqueduct at Avoncliffe is the first. Although the infrastructure is essentially unchanged, much tidying up of both bank and water has taken place in recent years.

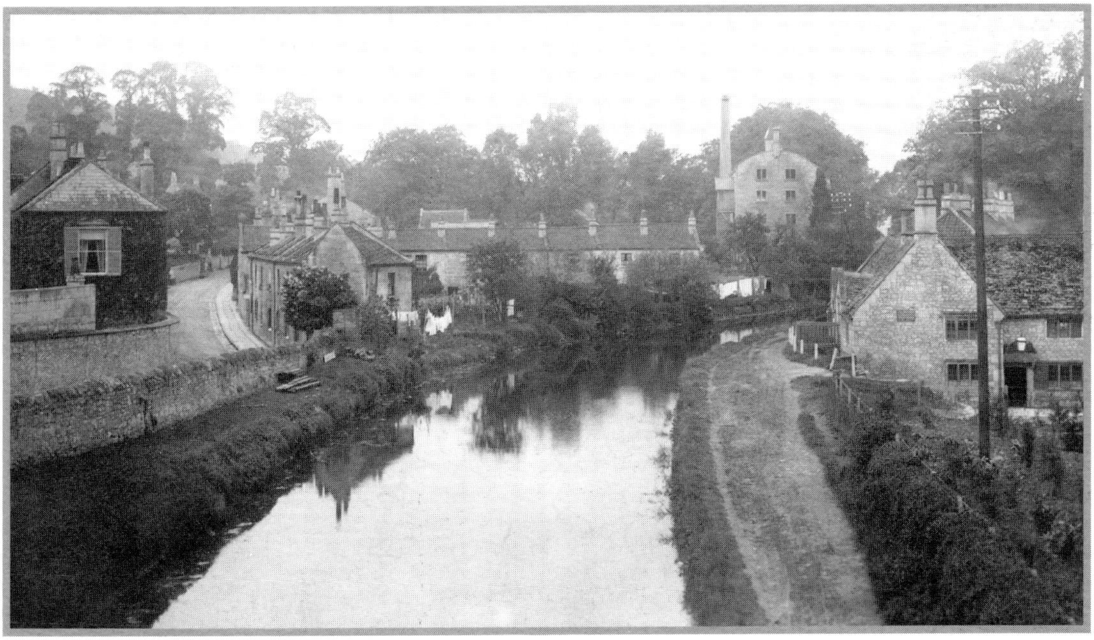

Bathampton, The Canal and the George Inn 1907 57749
The Kennet & Avon was a working canal when this picture was taken. Today, the only boats you will see are recreational ones. The George (the pub on the right) still exists, and is a popular local watering-hole. The towing path is in excellent condition now, and is used for walking and cycling.

CARNFORTH

The Canal 1918 68306

The Lancaster Canal was never connected to the main canal system. Its rugged stone bridges and its proximity to the Pennines make it a most picturesque line. Carnforth is towards the northern end; the top section was abandoned after the M6 motorway was built. Here we see typical barge propulsion, with the animals taking a break as the photographer creates his picture.

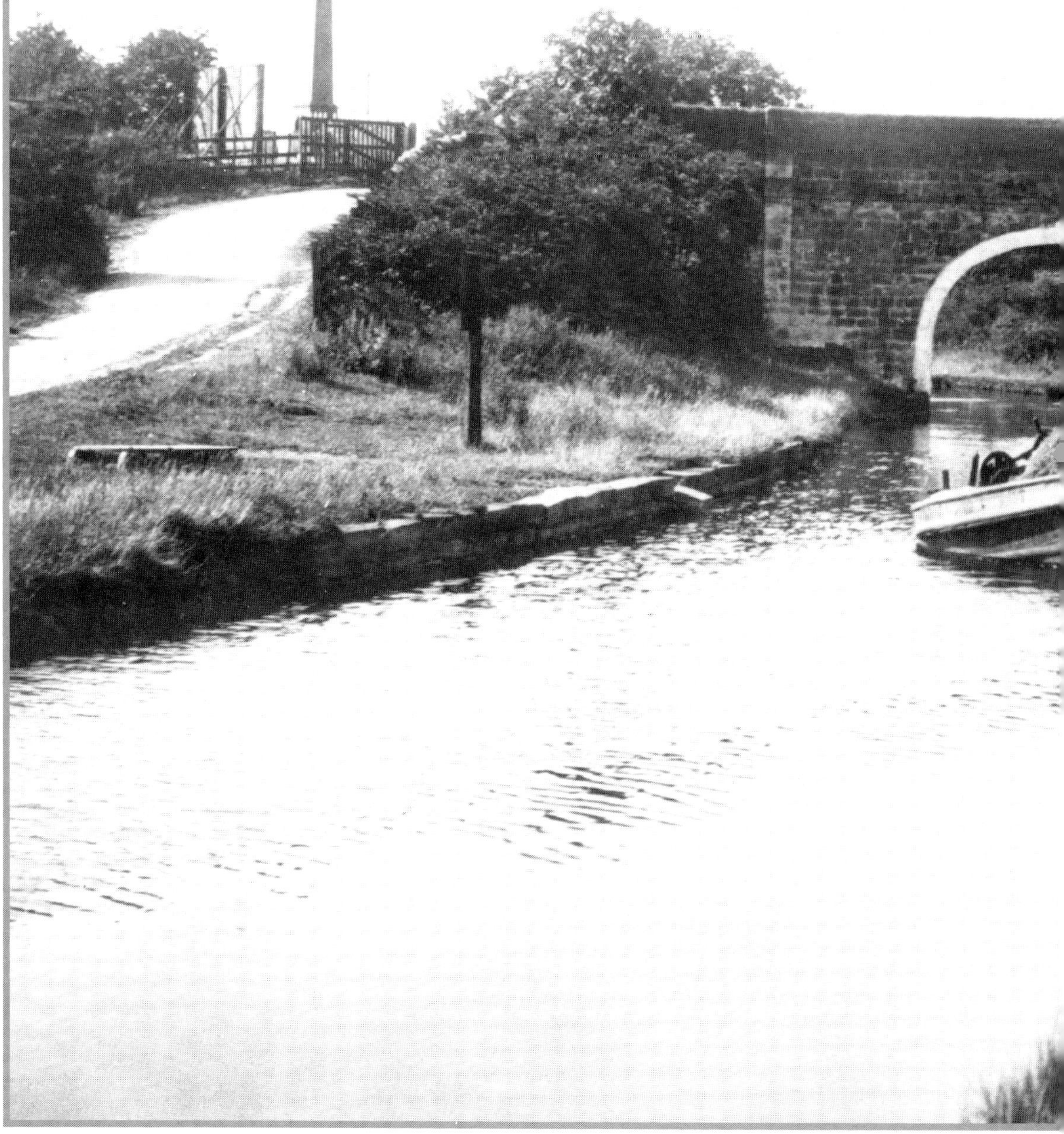

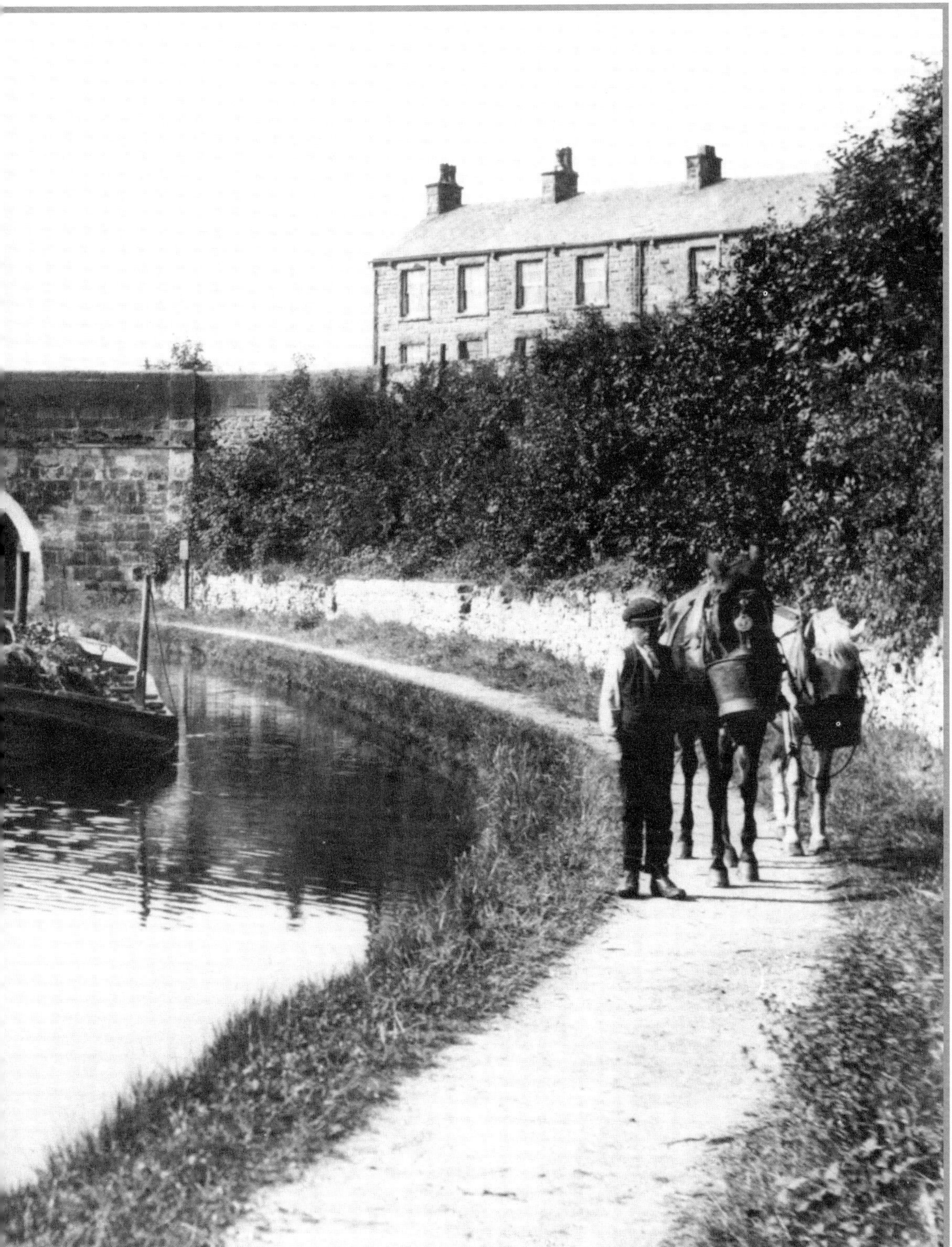

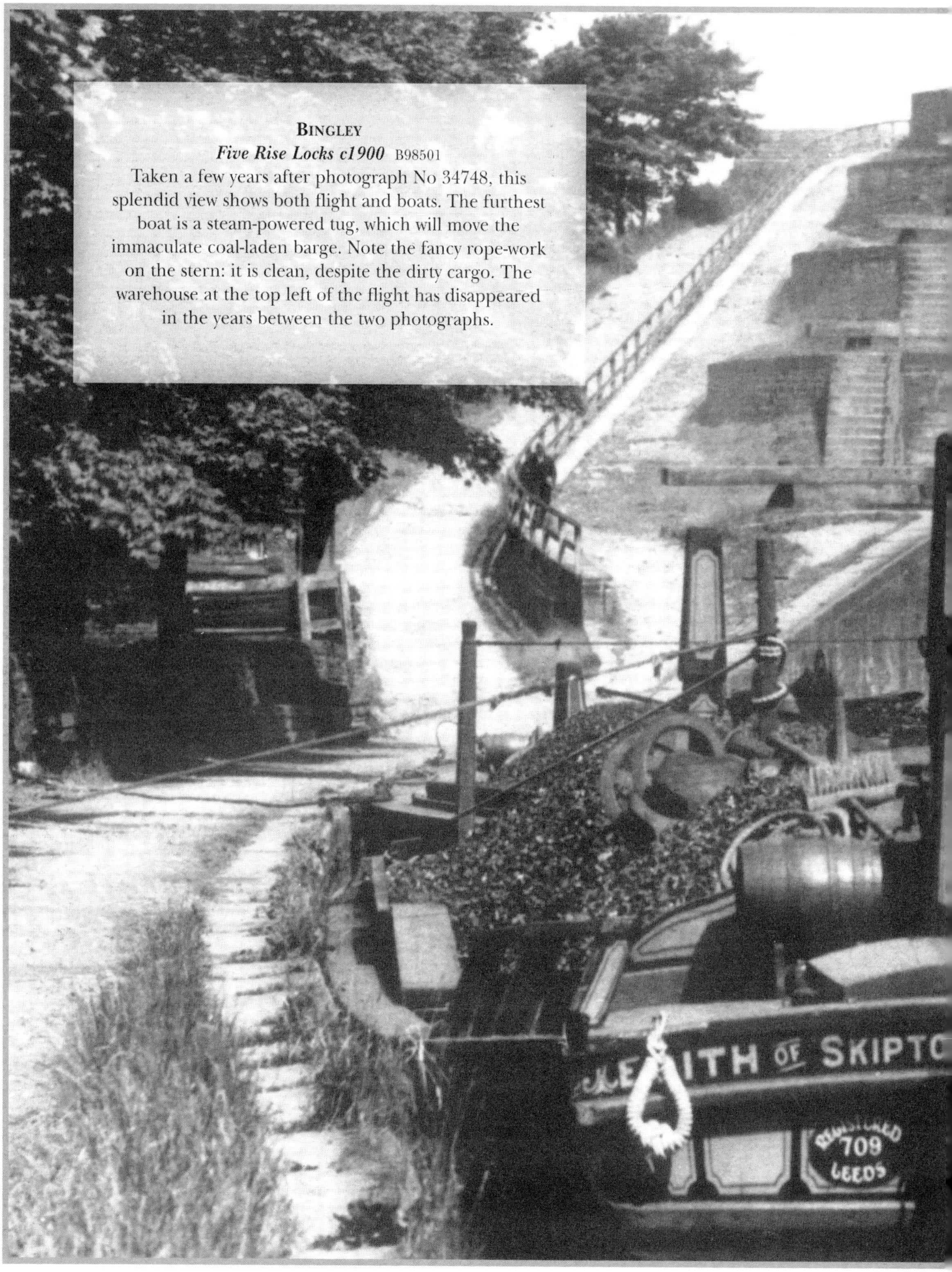

BINGLEY

Five Rise Locks c1900 B98501

Taken a few years after photograph No 34748, this splendid view shows both flight and boats. The furthest boat is a steam-powered tug, which will move the immaculate coal-laden barge. Note the fancy rope-work on the stern: it is clean, despite the dirty cargo. The warehouse at the top left of the flight has disappeared in the years between the two photographs.

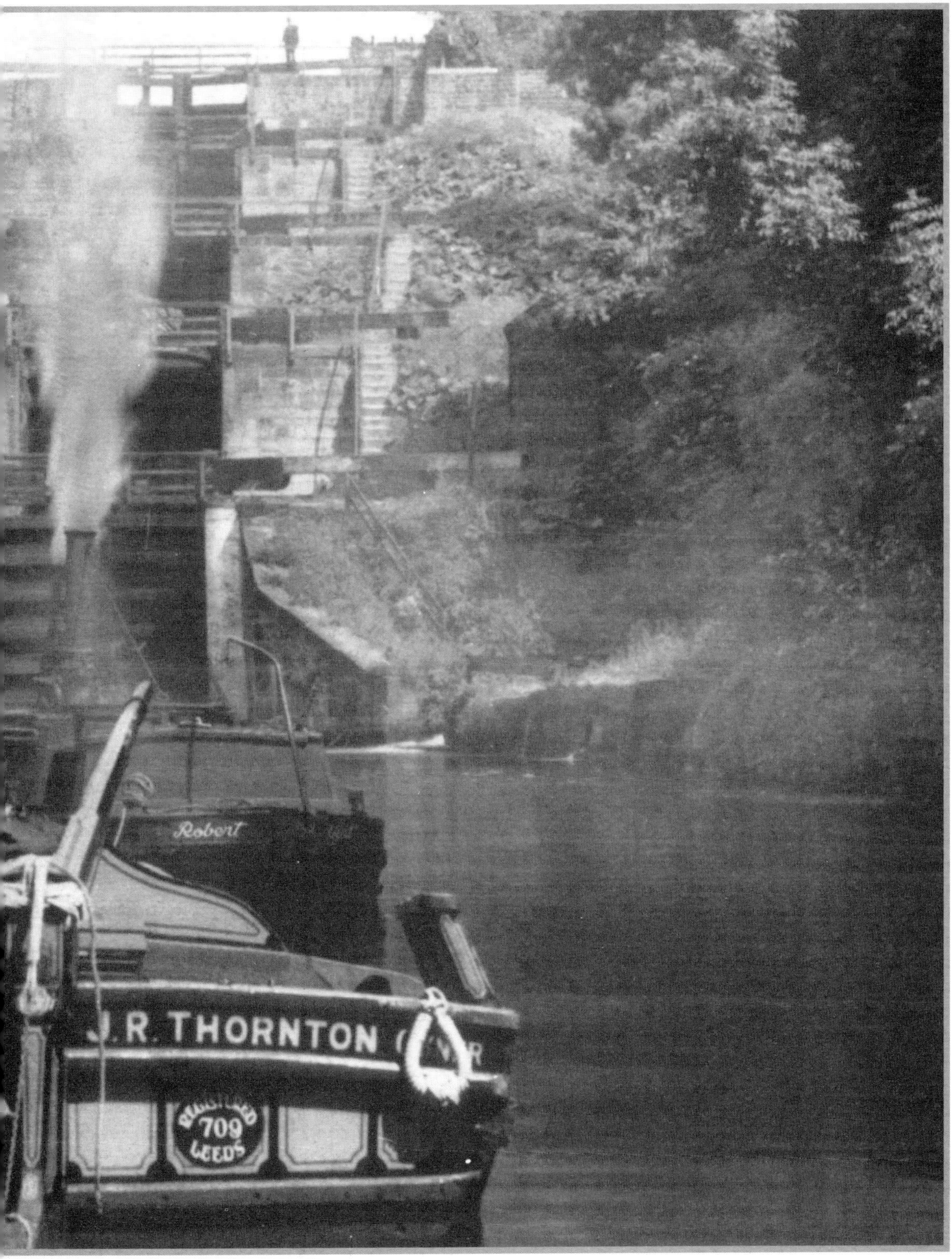
Robert
J.R. THORNTON
709
LEEDS

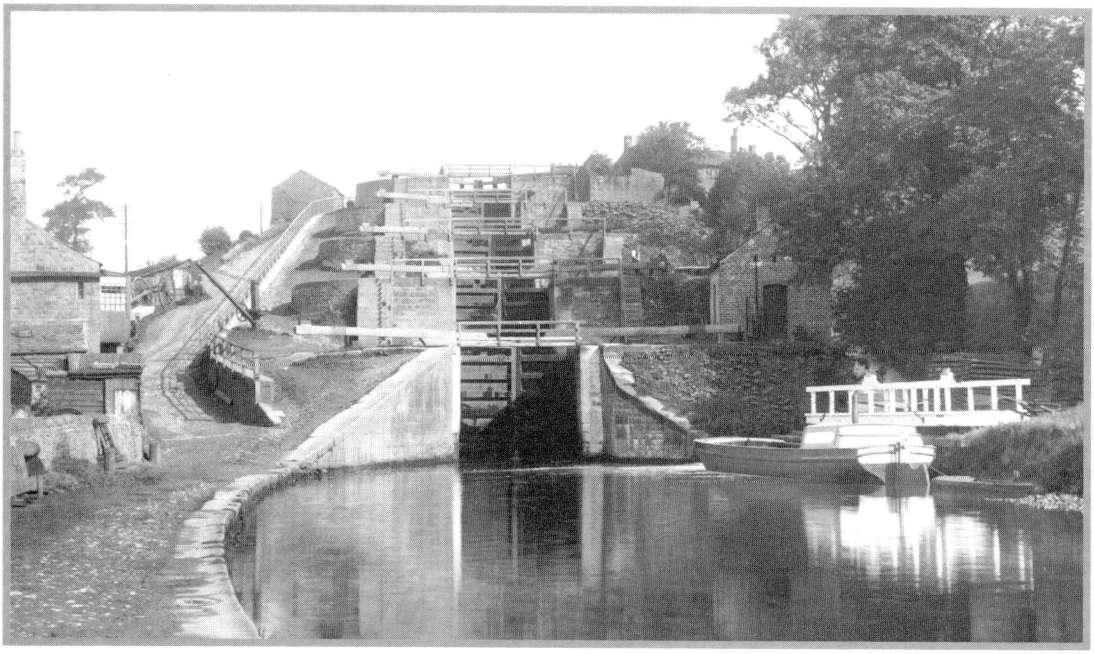

BINGLEY, FIVE RISE LOCKS 1894 34748

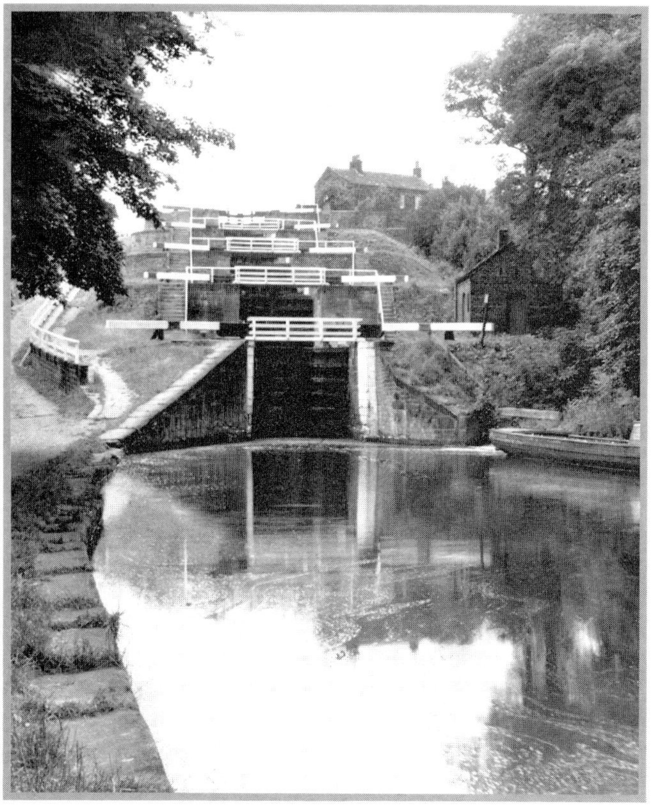

BINGLEY, FIVE RISE LOCKS c1955 B98006

BINGLEY
Five Rise Locks 1894
One of the wonders of the waterway system, the five rise locks at Bingley in West Yorkshire are part of the Leeds & Liverpool canal. They are known as staircase locks, because the top gate of each chamber is also the bottom one of the next: there is no water between the two. A maintenance boat is moored on the right-hand side, and the keeper is working on the right-hand side of the second chamber.

BINGLEY
Five Rise Locks c1955
There is little change here half a century after photograph No B98501 was taken. Today, the house at the bottom left corner is no more, and the grass is kept in bowling-green condition by the resident lock keeper.

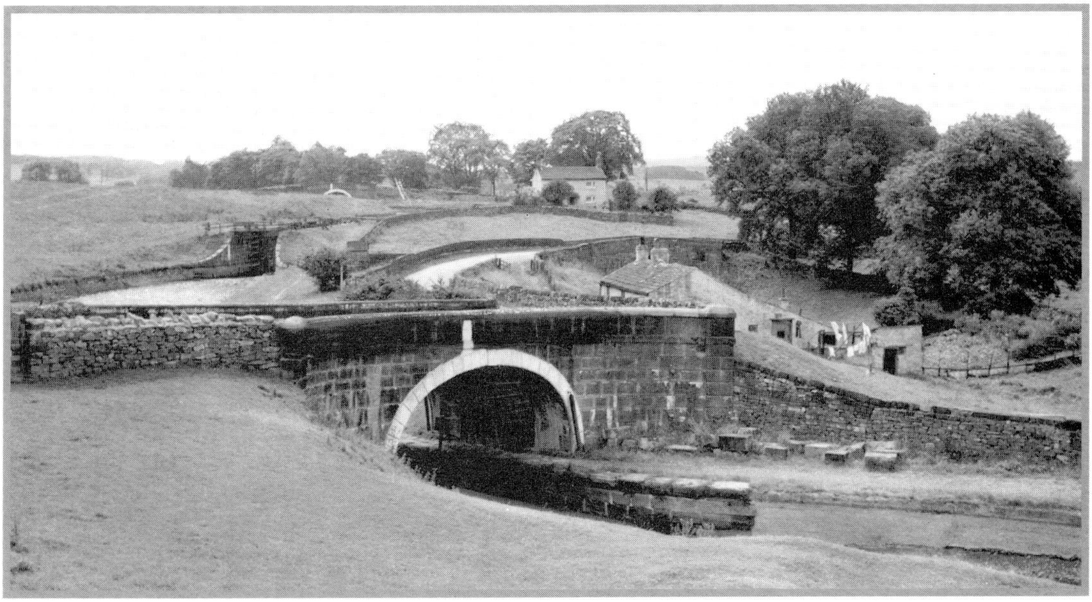

Barnoldswick, The Locks c1955 B589013
The Leeds & Liverpool Canal climbs out of Yorkshire into the Pennines. After these three locks at Greenberfield, there is a short summit and a tunnel before the canal descends into Lancashire. Beyond the house is the site of a three lock staircase. This was built when the canal was opened; the present locks replaced them in an effort to speed up passage.

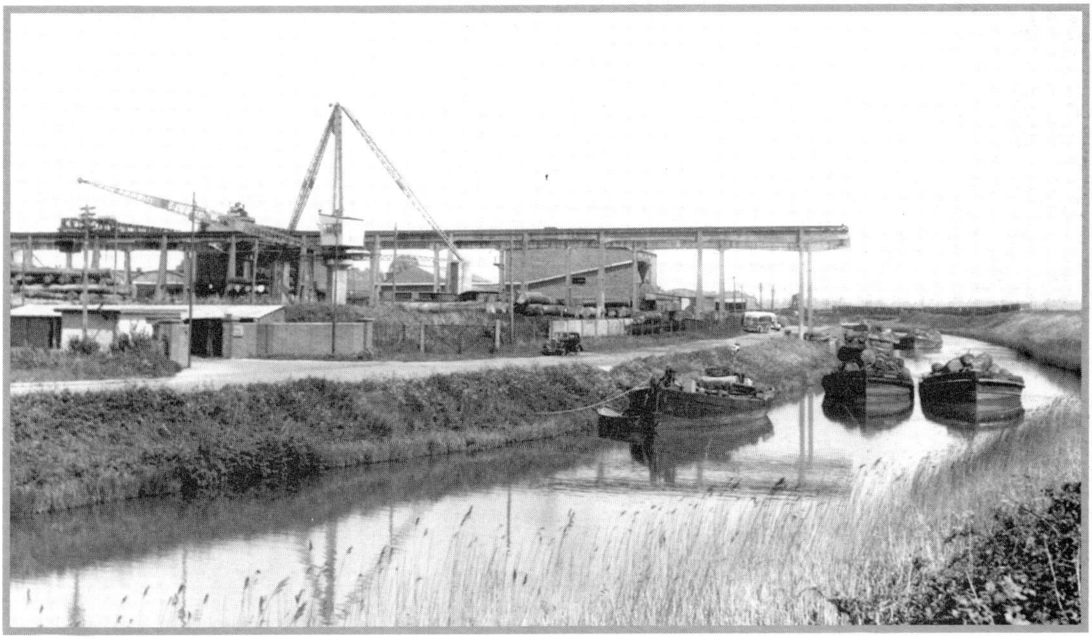

Lydney, Pine and the Works c1960 L200036
This is a view now firmly consigned to the history books. The Lydney Canal in Gloucestershire was about a mile in length, and carried trade up to the mid 1970s. A plywood mill imported timber from Africa, which came to the canal from Avonmouth docks by barge, as we can see here. The area has since been sold for development.

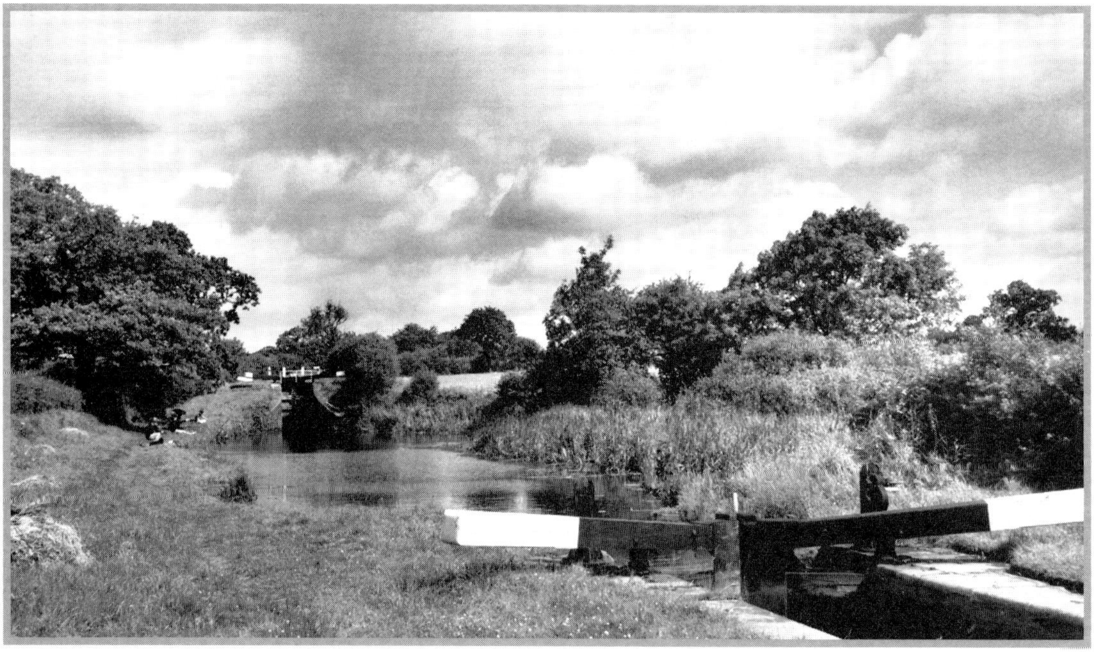

CONGLETON, THE CANAL c1960 C151101

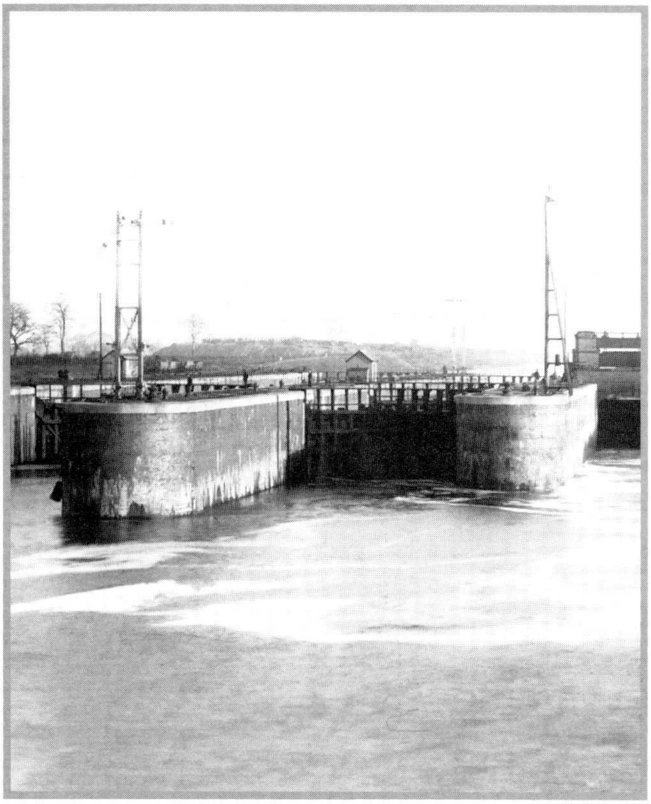

MANCHESTER, THE SHIP CANAL 1894 33696

CONGLETON
The Canal c1960
The Bosley flight of 12 locks on the Macclesfield Canal is located in simply superb scenery. The locks are unique in narrow canal construction in that the top gates are doubles, rather than the singles found elsewhere. This canal never closed, and is eternally popular with leisure boaters.

MANCHESTER
The Ship Canal 1894
This must be a very early photograph of the navigation, for the canal did not open until 1 January 1894. 36 miles long, and many years (and financial crises) under construction, it linked Manchester to the sea, allowing ocean-going ships to trade right into the city.

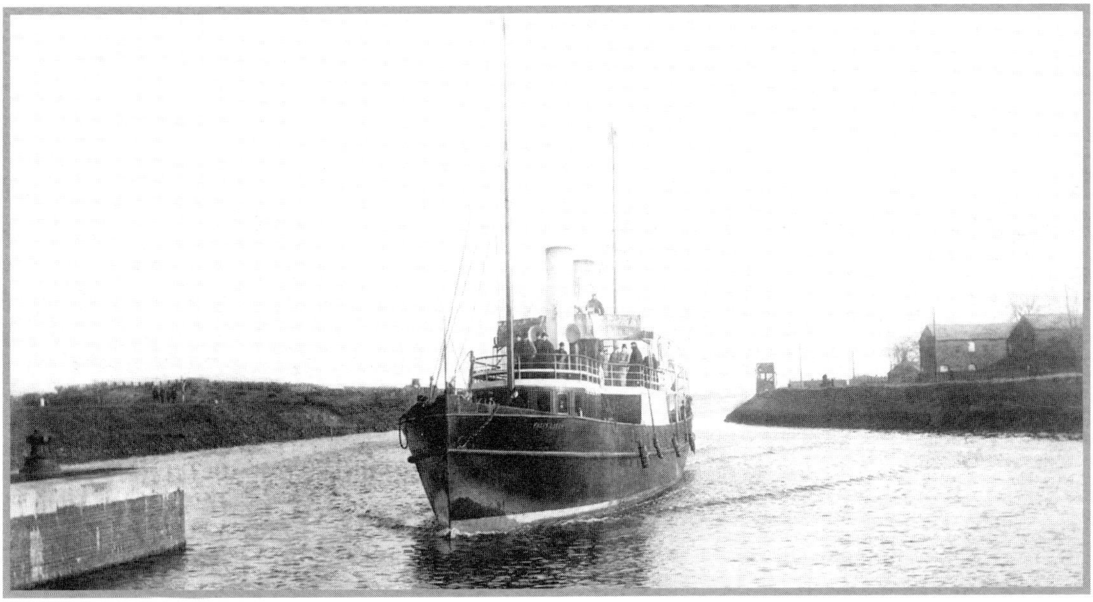

MANCHESTER, THE SHIP CANAL 1894 33697A
The 'Fairy Queen', a passenger-carrying vessel, is seen on the Manchester Ship Canal during the early months after its opening. Ships of 12,500 tons deadweight can travel the full length of the canal, and its construction encouraged industry along its banks. Oil refineries and many household consumer-goods names had or have premises along this canal.

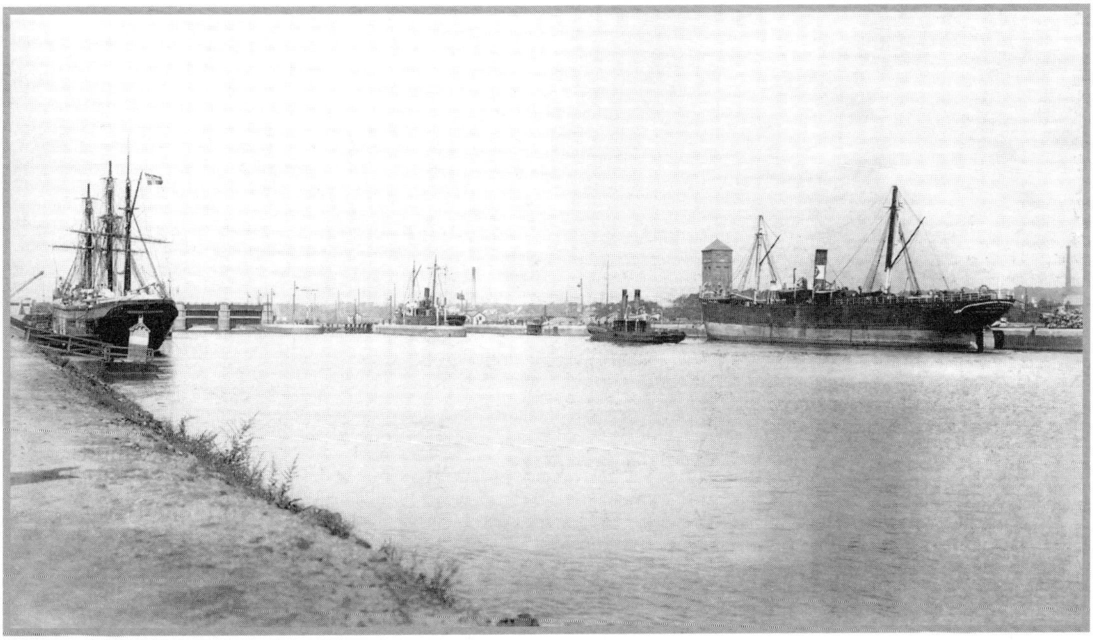

MANCHESTER, THE SHIP CANAL 1895 36396
This view shows the range of shipping that could once be seen on the MSC. The steamer to the right is the 'Alverton' from West Hartlepool. Up to 17m tons of cargo was being handled at one stage, but trade is now severely curtailed, and some of the docks at the far end are undergoing redevelopment.

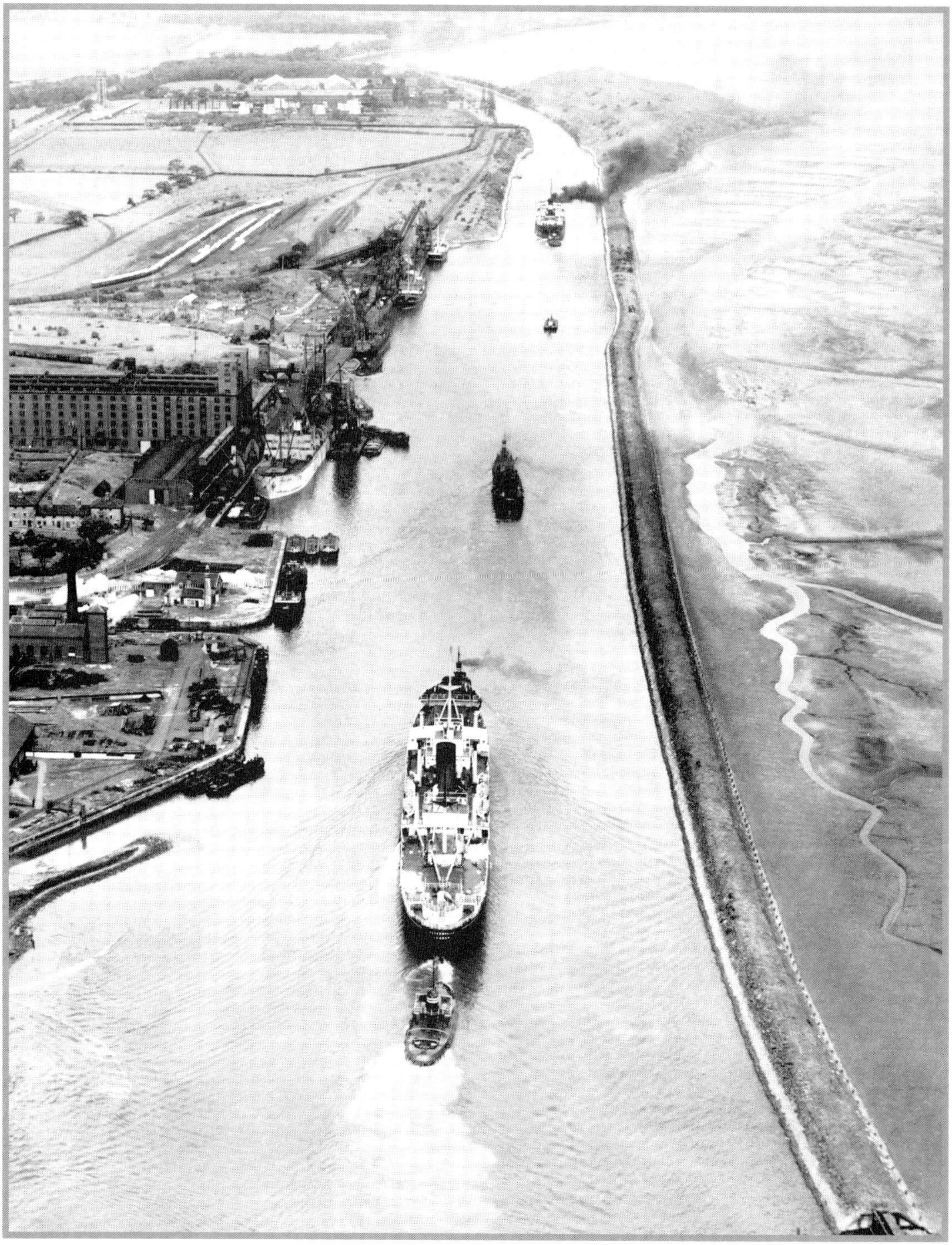

MANCHESTER SHIP CANAL, ELLESMERE PORT 1947 M340501
Two steamers head for the tidal lock at Eastham on their way out of the Manchester Ship Canal. On the right is the river Mersey, and to the left, by the building with a tall chimney, is the entrance to the Shropshire Union Canal. This area, partially redeveloped, is now home to The Boat Museum.

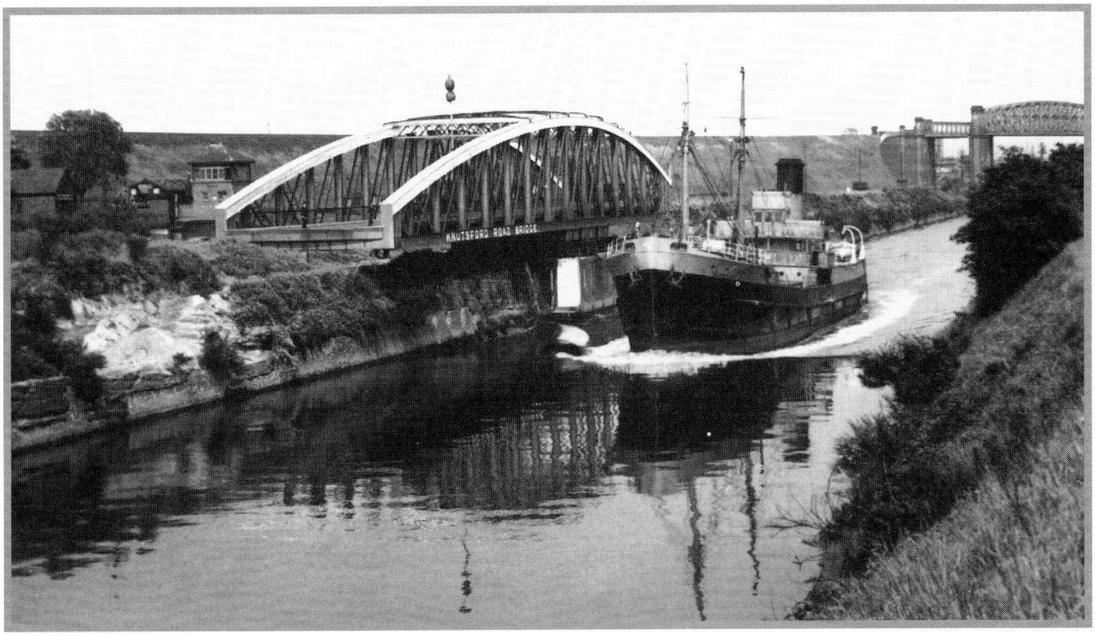

GRAPPENHALL, THE CANAL c1955 G200001

A steamer heads away from Manchester Docks, passing the swinging Knutsford Road bridge near Warrington. Beyond, Latchford Viaduct takes the railway high over the canal. A long slope is needed for trains to gain the necessary height.

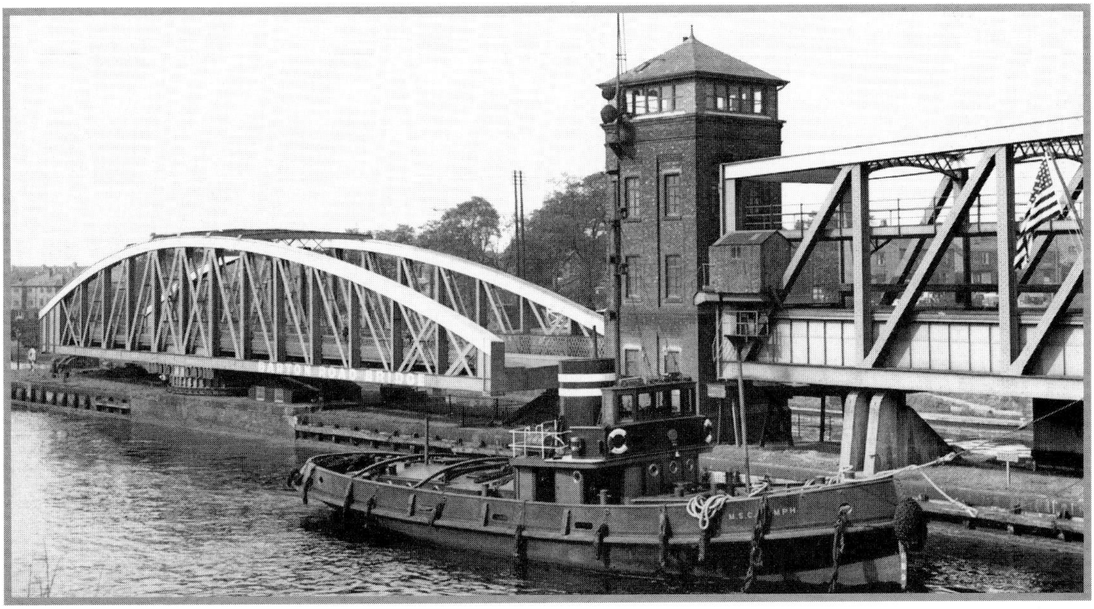

BARTON, TUG GOING DOWN THE SHIP CANAL c1955 B823008

To the right is a magnificent piece of engineering. Barton Swing Aqueduct is actually the Bridgewater Canal crossing the MSC. It is 234ft long and 19ft wide; shutters close off the water, allowing the aqueduct to be swung. In total this weighs 1500 tons, but it is so perfectly balanced that it requires only a very small motor to move it. The MSC tug 'Nymph' is seen here attached to the stern of an American-registered ship.

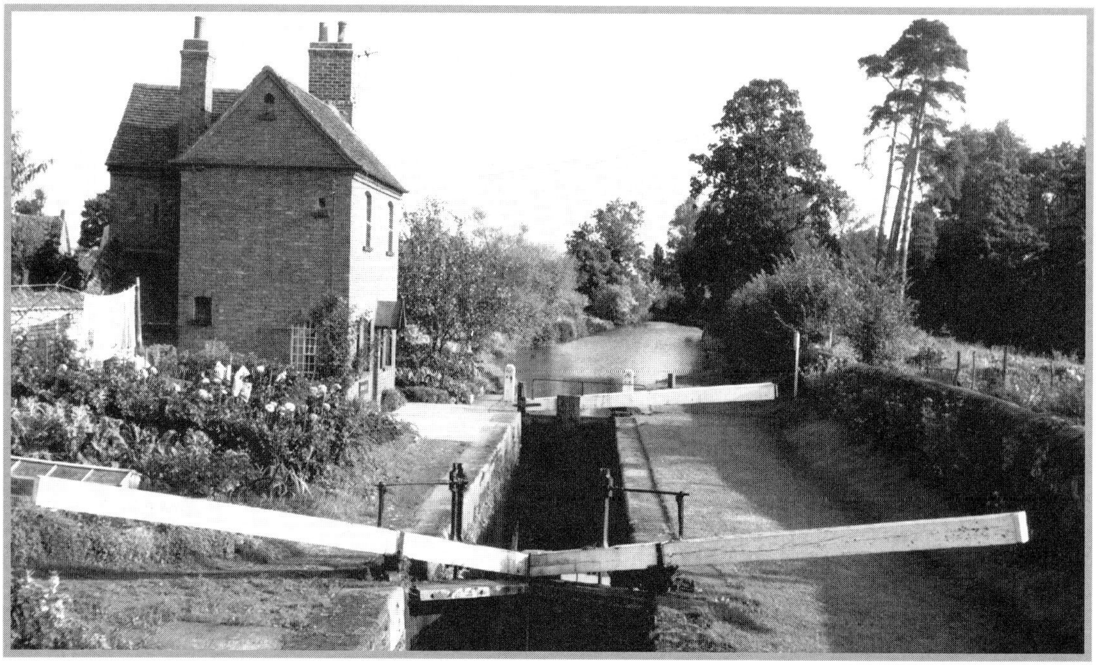

CROPREDY, THE LOCK c1960 C291015
The Oxford Canal is a pretty, meandering line, very popular with holidaymakers. And locks such as this one help to create the rustic atmosphere. The scene today is instantly recognisable.

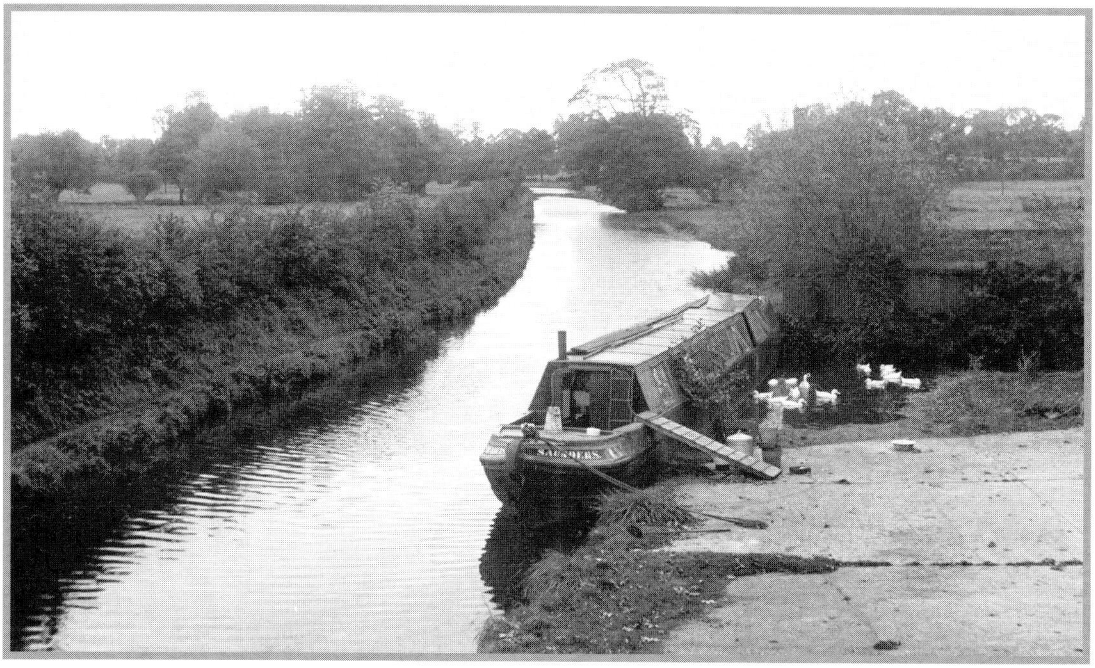

CROPREDY, THE CANAL c1960 C291006
This view shows an early example of a houseboat on the Oxford Canal. As an inexpensive home, converted narrowboats are still popular, especially closer to Oxford where there are dozens to be seen.

Banbury
The Canal 1921
This is a typical Oxford Canal drawbridge. You may be surprised to learn that they are quite easy to operate, for they are very well-balanced. The two gentlemen in the picture are enjoying a lazy afternoon's fishing, whilst their female companion appears to be absorbed in a book and utterly oblivious to our photographer.

Banbury
The Canal 1921
Here we see another peaceful scene taken at the same time as photograph No 70592. The boat is a disused butty, and makes a fine perch for the anglers. The peace and quiet they are obviously enjoying has gone now: it is shattered by the construction of the M40 motorway close by.

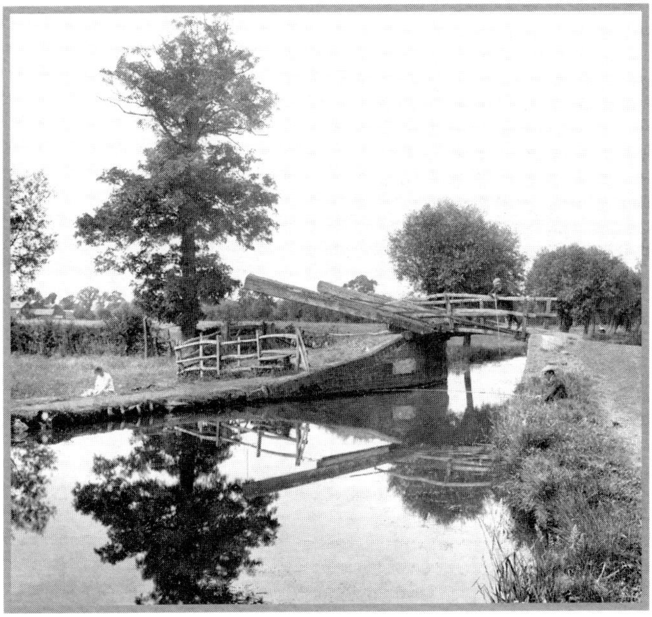

Banbury, The Canal 1921 70592

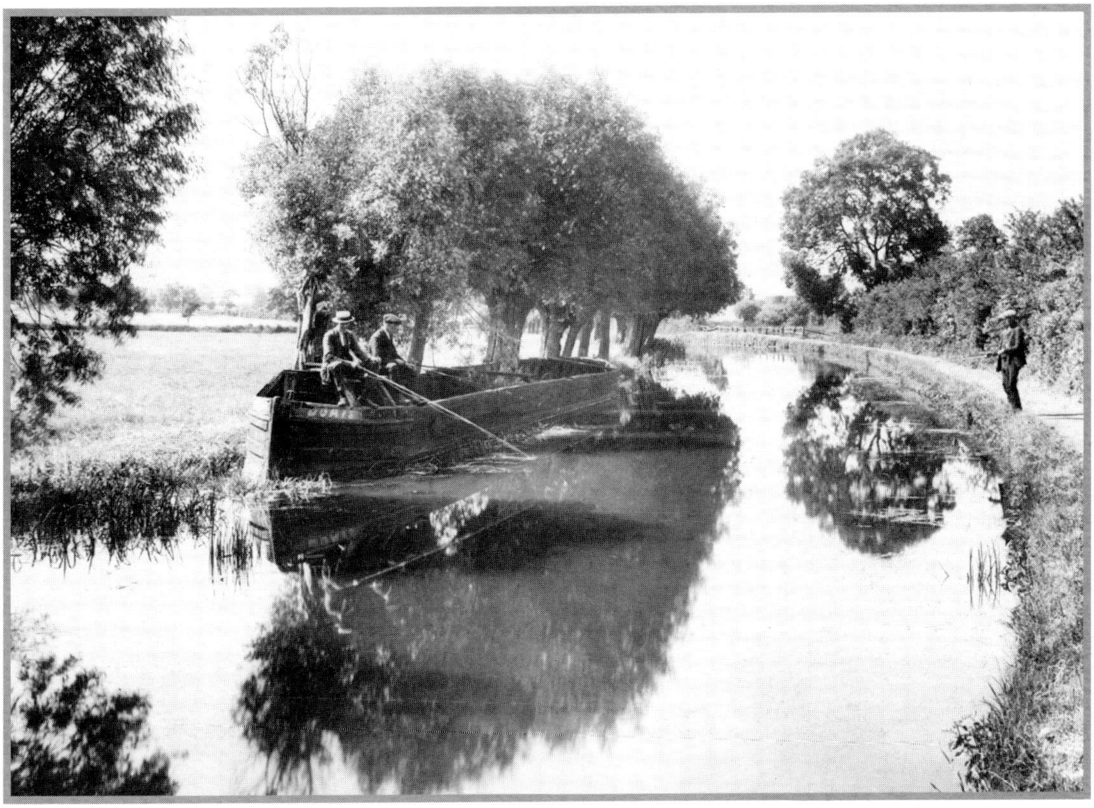

Banbury, The Canal 1921 70593

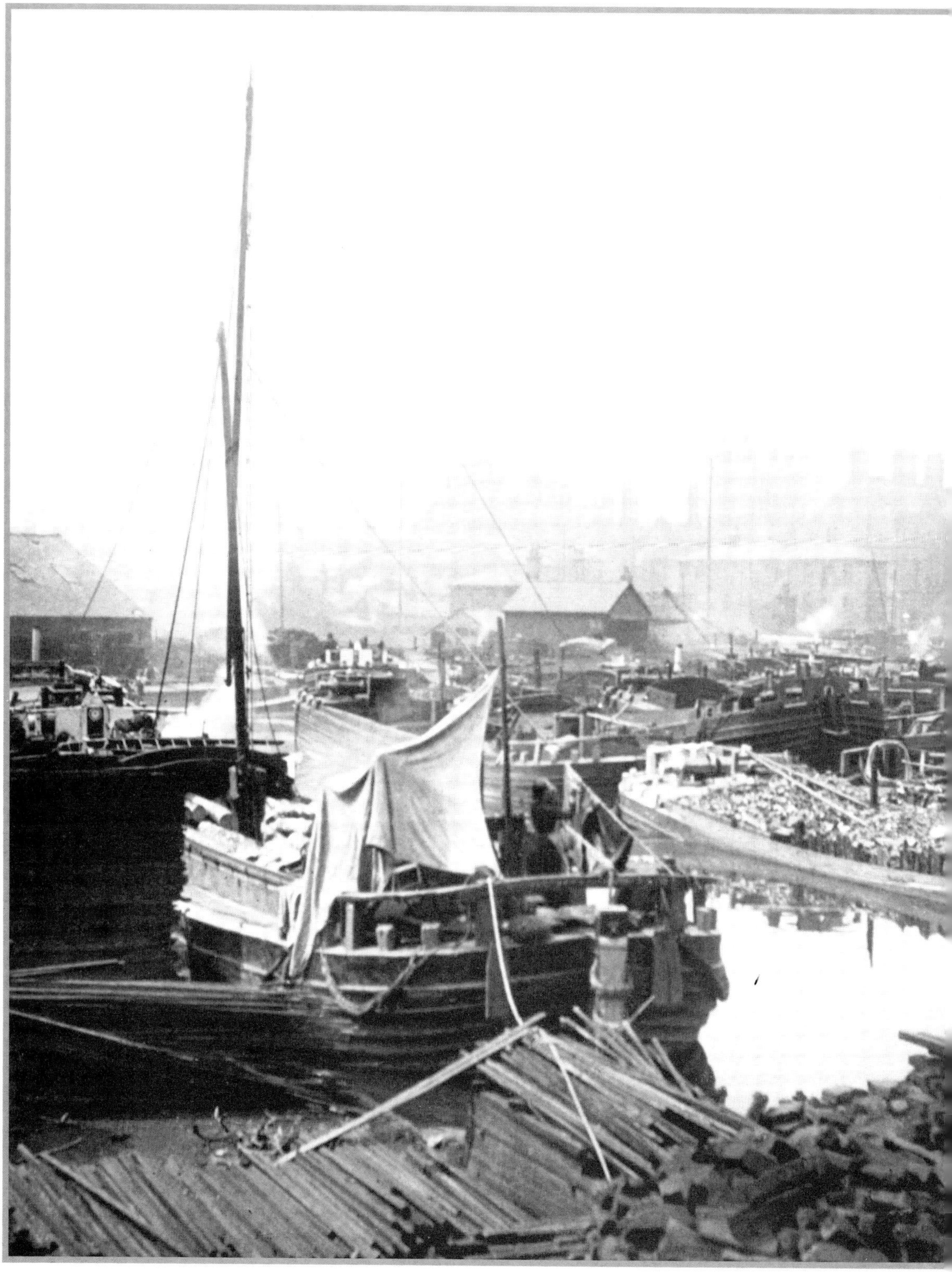

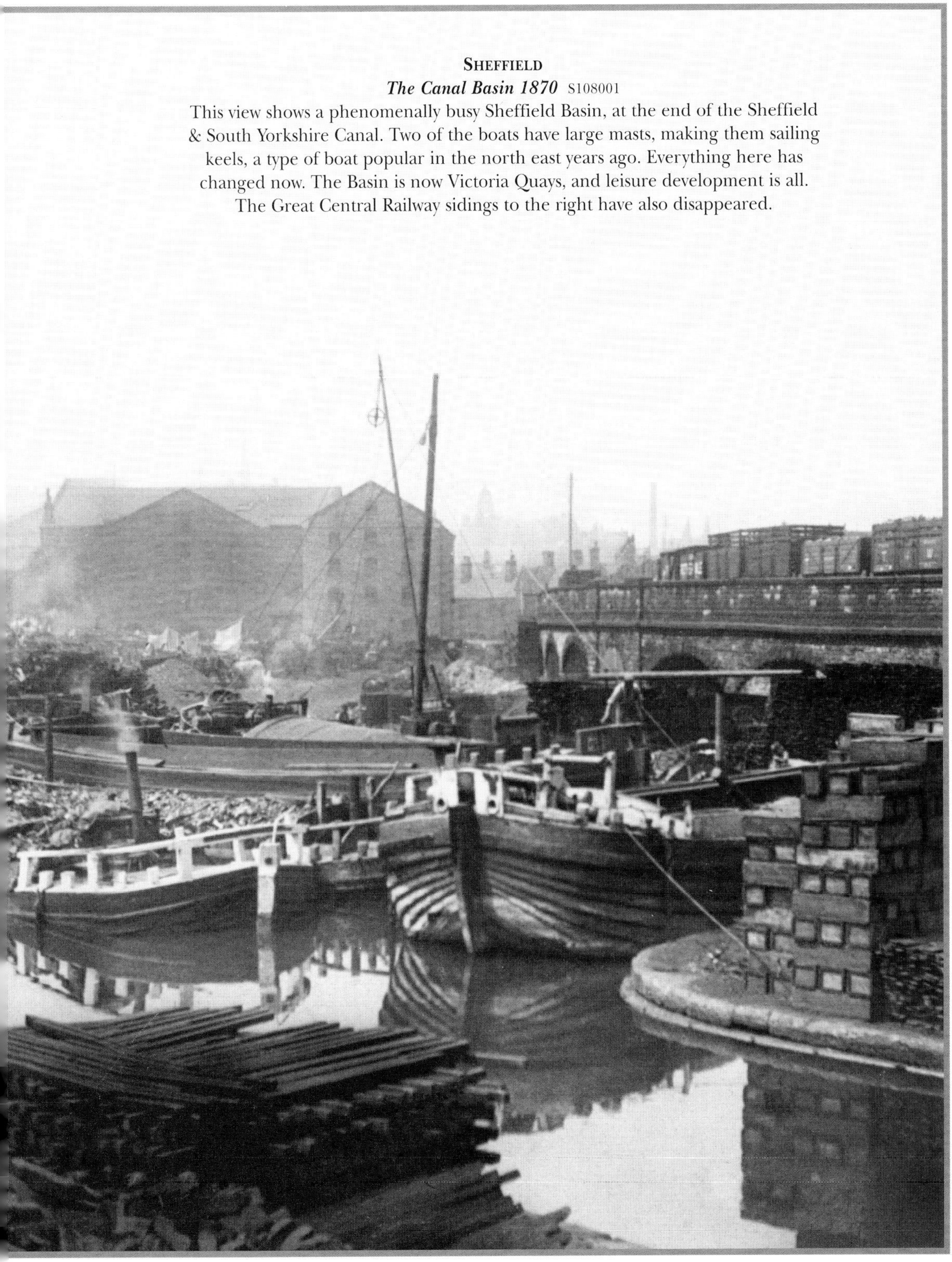

SHEFFIELD

The Canal Basin 1870 S108001

This view shows a phenomenally busy Sheffield Basin, at the end of the Sheffield & South Yorkshire Canal. Two of the boats have large masts, making them sailing keels, a type of boat popular in the north east years ago. Everything here has changed now. The Basin is now Victoria Quays, and leisure development is all. The Great Central Railway sidings to the right have also disappeared.

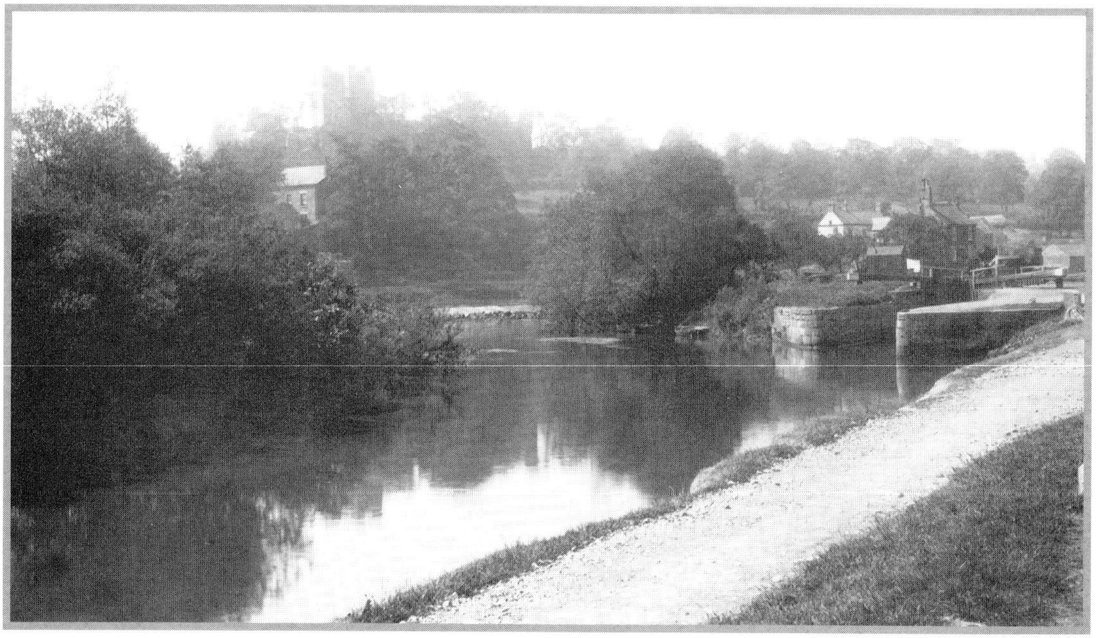

CONISBOROUGH, THE CASTLE FROM THE RIVER 1895 35317

This view no longer exists. When the Sheffield & South Yorkshire Canal was modernised in the early 1980s, several locks were re-sited and enlarged, and this was one of them. Note the English heritage-run Conisborough Castle in the background.

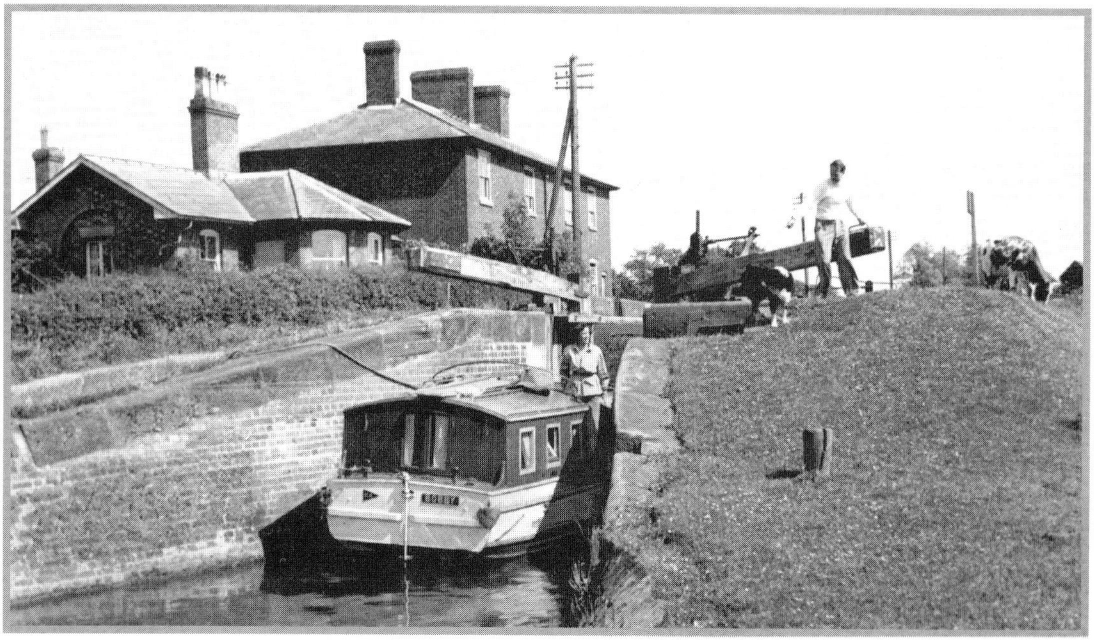

WHEATON ASTON, THE LOCK c1955 W286009

The Shropshire Union canal runs between Wolverhampton and Ellesmere Port. A narrow canal, it passes through delightful countryside, especially around the Wheaton Aston area. The lock keepers cottage (left) is now a private house, and the large building behind has gone.

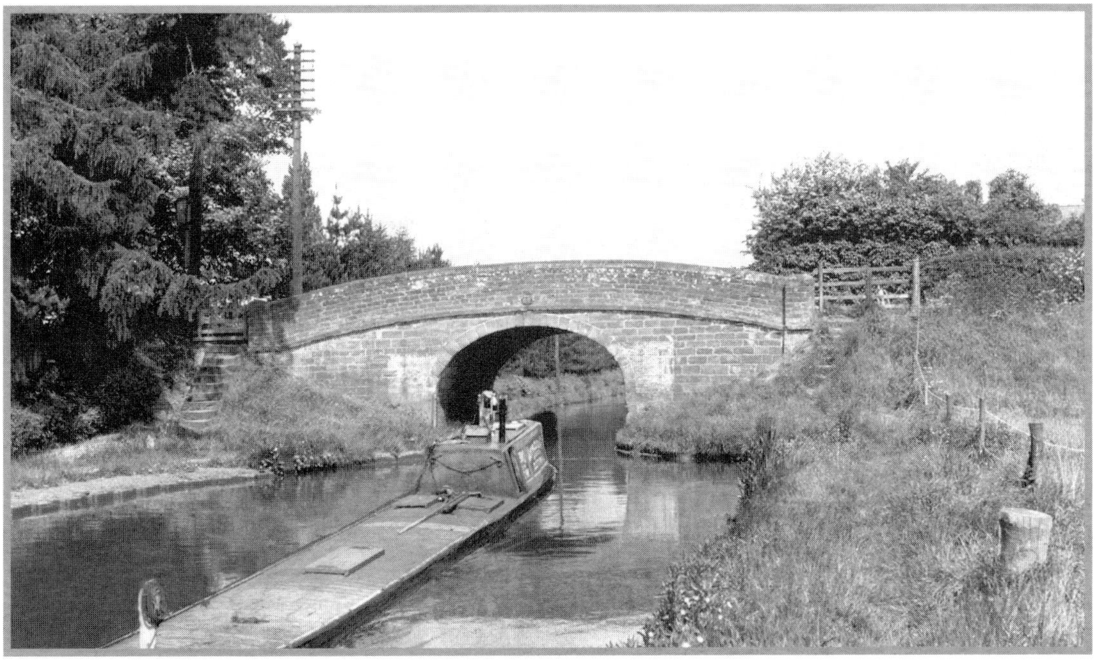

MARKET DRAYTON, THE CANAL BRIDGE c1955 M32031R
Heading south on the Shropshire Union Canal is what appears to be a tank boat belonging to Thomas Clayton of Oldbury. These boats carried Shell oil from Ellesmere Port from 1924 until shortly after this picture was taken.

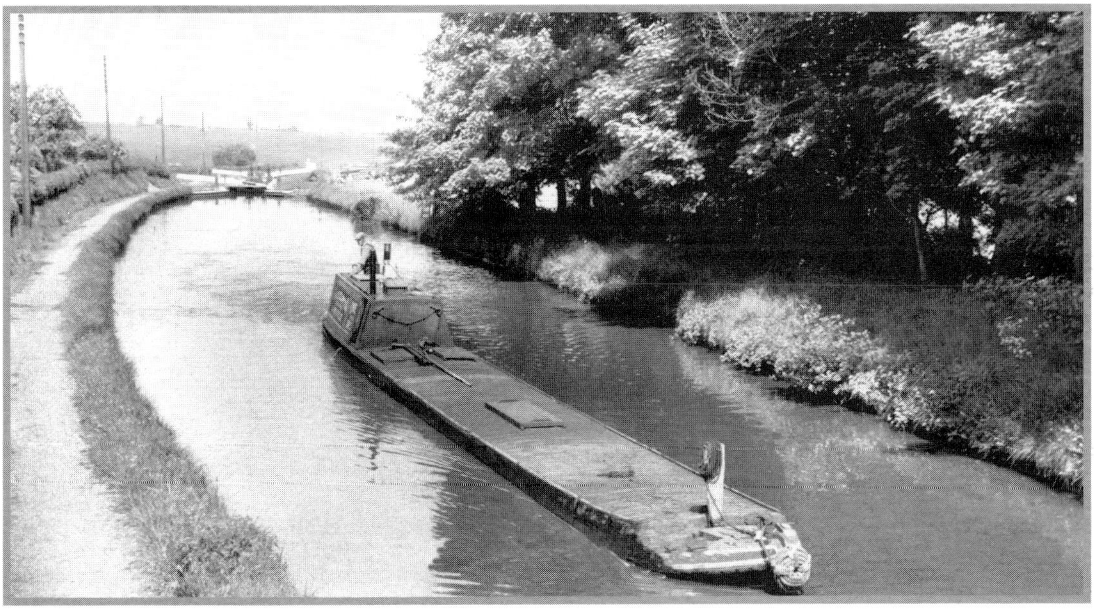

MARKET DRAYTON, TYRLEY LOCK c1955 M32035
The boat we saw in photograph No M32031R is now seen climbing the 5 locks at Tyrley. From here, there was a lock-free run all the way to the edge of Wolverhampton - apart from the one at Wheaton Aston which we saw earlier. After that, there was a flight of 21 before a short dash to the company's base, where the cargo would be pumped out. The boats used to take a week to do the round trip of some 160 miles.

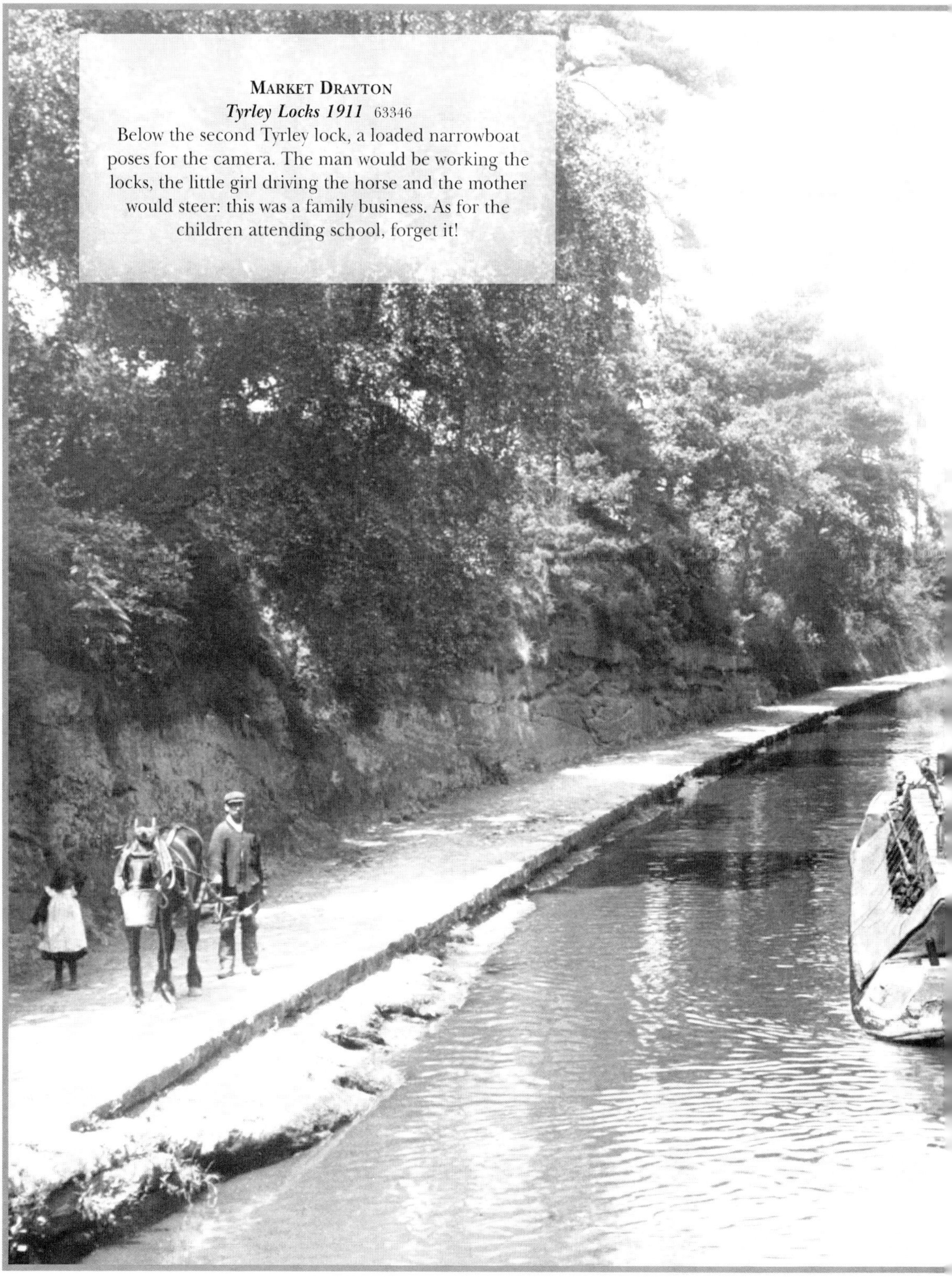

MARKET DRAYTON
Tyrley Locks 1911 63346
Below the second Tyrley lock, a loaded narrowboat poses for the camera. The man would be working the locks, the little girl driving the horse and the mother would steer: this was a family business. As for the children attending school, forget it!

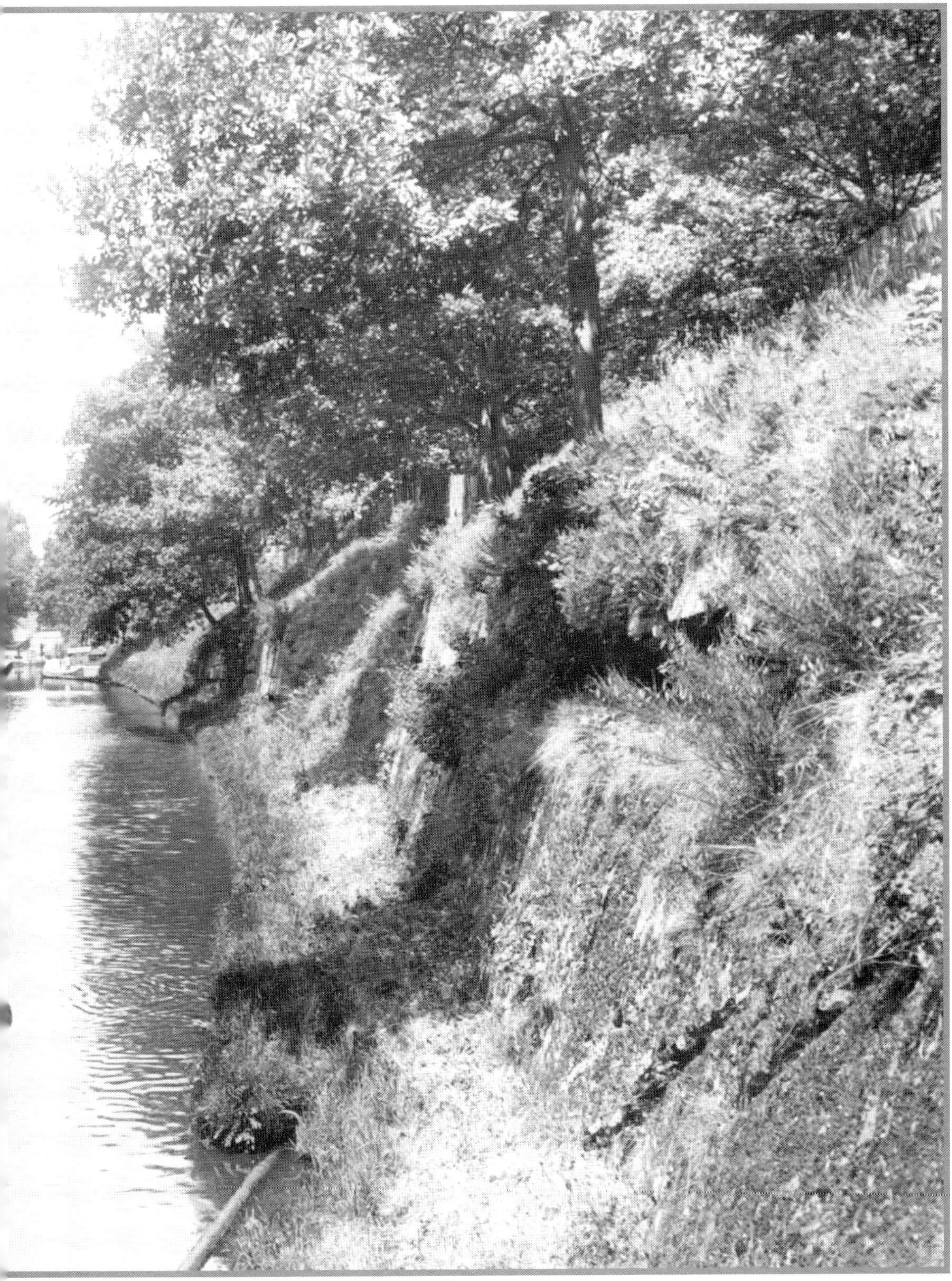

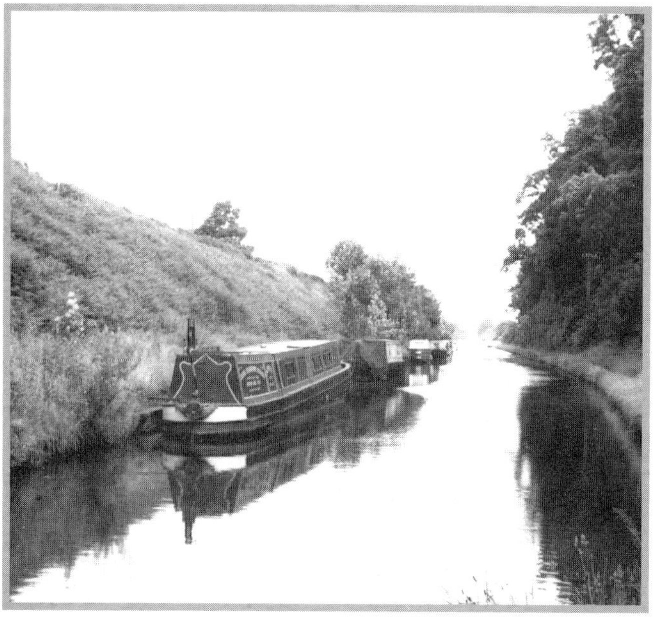

BREWOOD, THE CANAL C1965 B680003

BREWOOD

The Canal c1965

The long straight character of the Shropshire Union canal is plain to see here. The builder, Thomas Telford, believed in cutting through hills and bridging valleys. The boats to the left are early examples of leisure boating.

GREAT HAYWOOD

The Canal c1955

At the northern end of the Staffs and Worcester Canal, an unusual pleasure boat conversion heads towards Wolverhampton. The narrow section is a solid aqueduct over the river Trent. Shugborough Hall, Lord Lichfield's house, is behind the trees to the left; the small building on the towing path is now a craft shop.

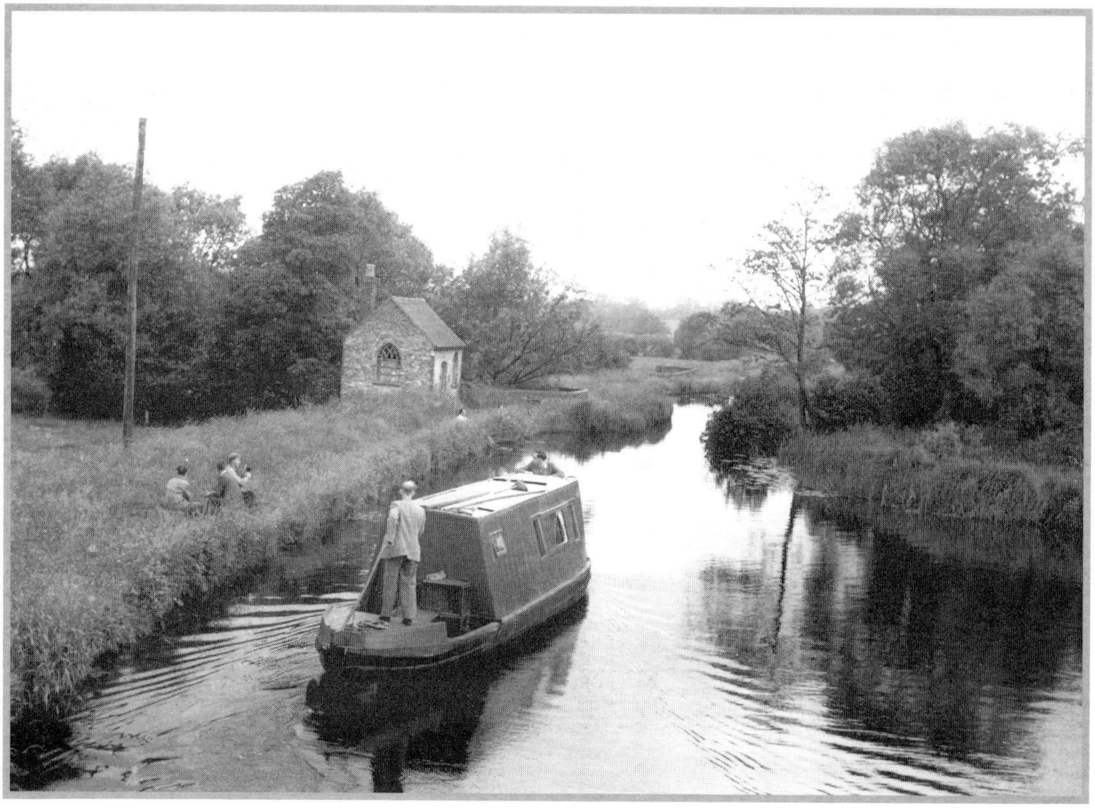

GREAT HAYWOOD, THE CANAL C1955 G303010

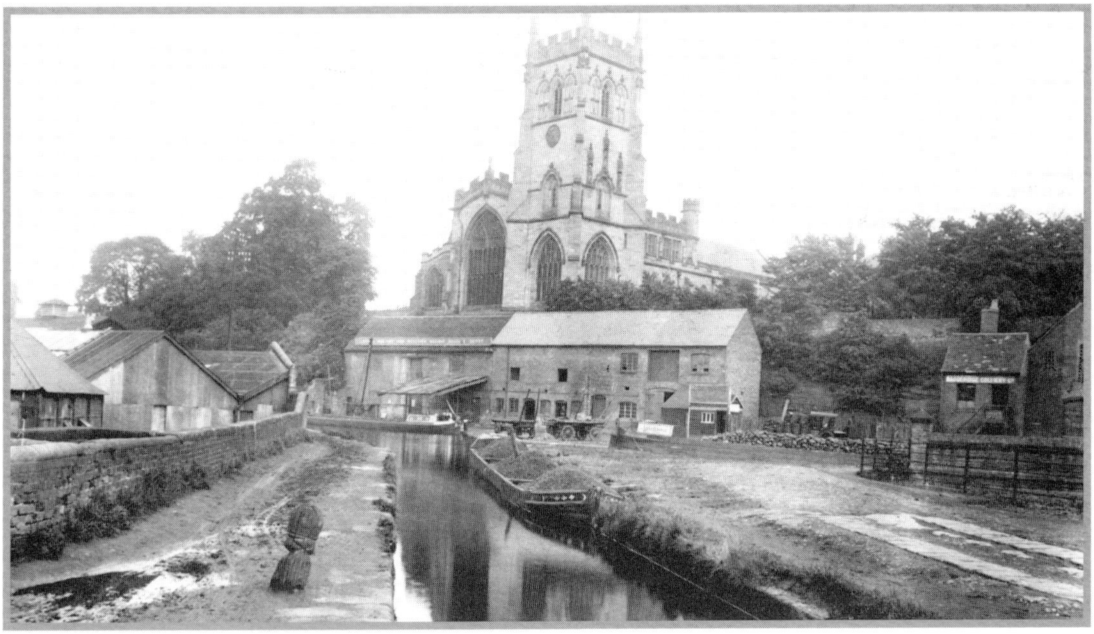

Kidderminster, The Church and the Canal 1931 84619
This is the Staffs and Worcester Canal. St Mary and All Saints church looks delightful, and is built from local red sandstone. The warehouse beneath is owned by the London Midland and Scottish Railway Company; one of their boats is moored close by. To the right, an ancient lorry is just visible, loading coal from the Baggeridge Colliery yard.

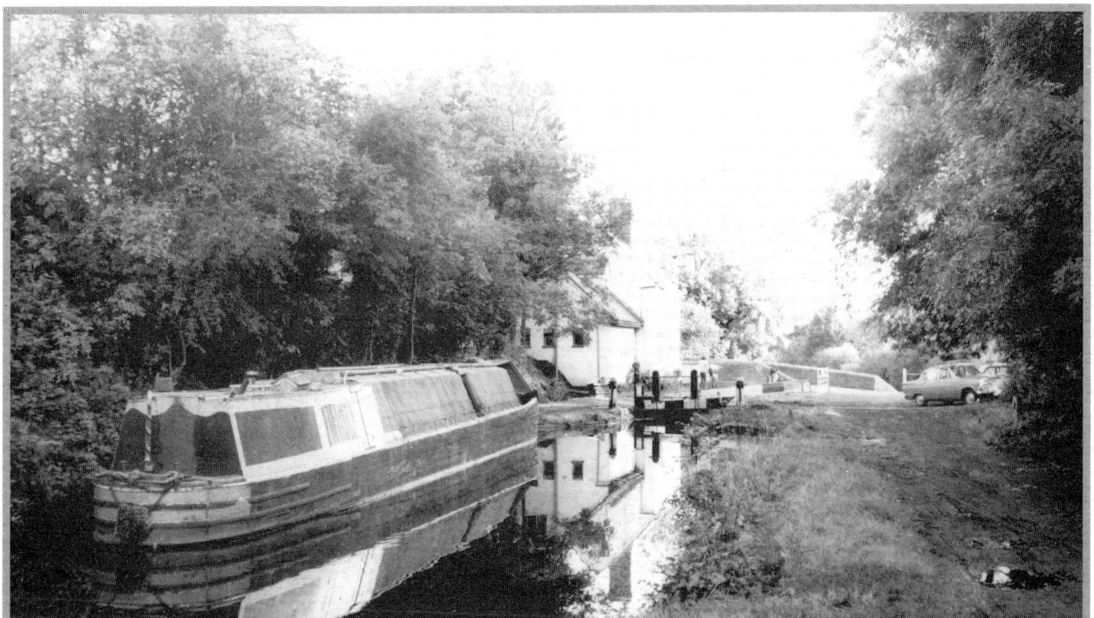

Kinver, The Canal c1965 K37144
The Staffs and Worcester Canal is extremely rural in this length. There are sandstone rocks overhanging the canal and bosky slopes, which all add to the sheer beauty.

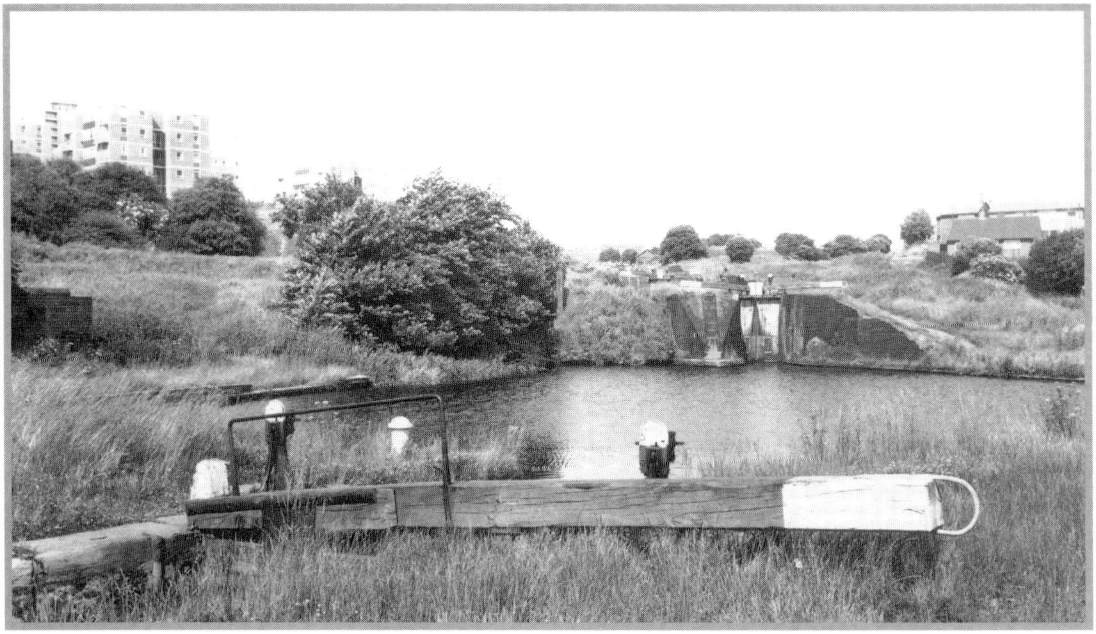

BRIERLEY HILL, THE CANAL LOCKS c1965 B355004
These are the Delph Locks at Brierley Hill on the Dudley No 1 Canal. They are universally known as 'The Nine', despite the fact that there are only 8. The confusion arose after the flight was rebuilt with one fewer. To say the locals have a long memory is putting it mildly: the rebuilding took place in 1850!

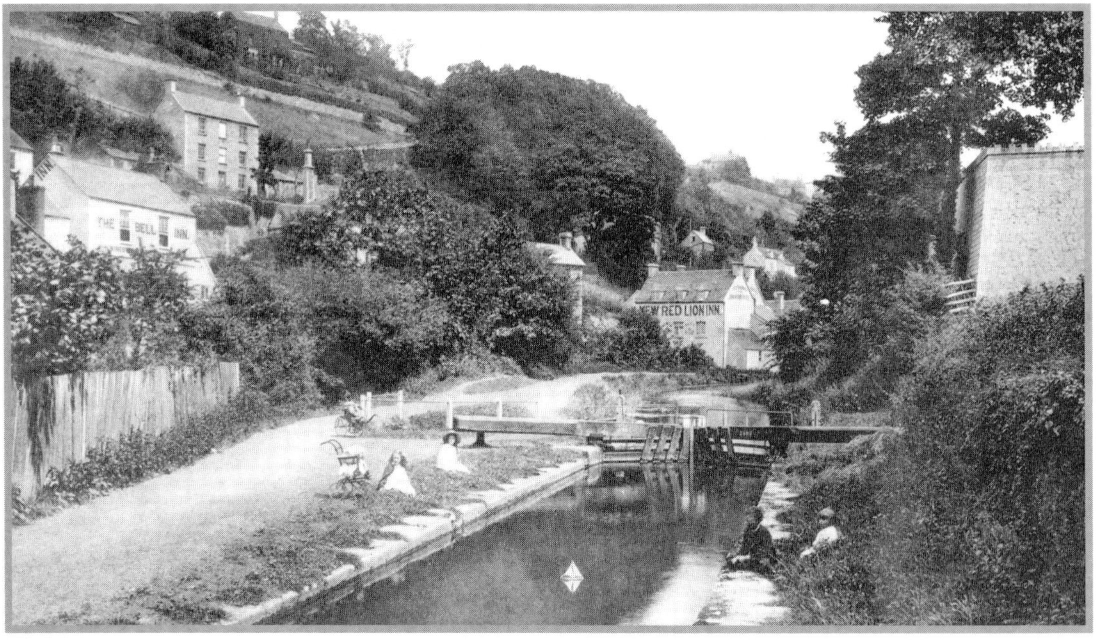

CHALFORD, ON THE CANAL 1910 62711
This is the now-derelict Thames and Severn canal which linked the two rivers. As it climbs the area known as Golden Valley, the scenery is magnificent. This is the Bell Lock near Chalford: the lock around the corner is known (unsurprisingly) as the Red Lion. The children play with dolls and boats, unfettered by today's safety police.

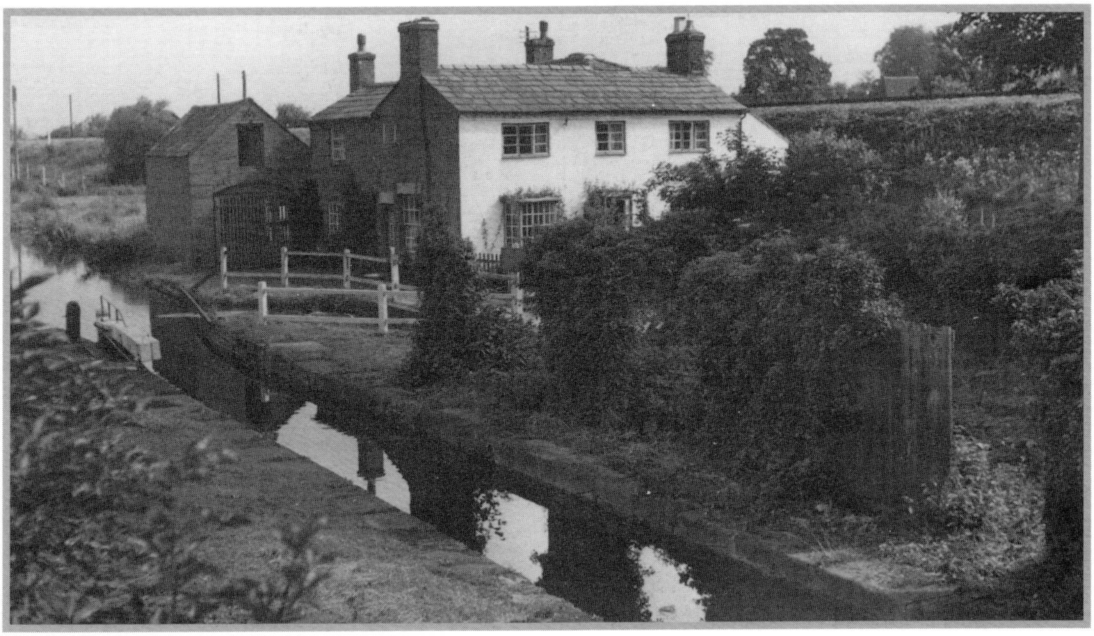

GREAT HAYWOOD, THE LOCK c1955 G303005
The Trent and Mersey Canal never actually linked to the Mersey, but it did make a connection with the Bridgewater Canal in Cheshire which did. Here, close to the junction with the Staffs & Worcester Canal, is Haywood Lock. The railway behind the house is now electrified.

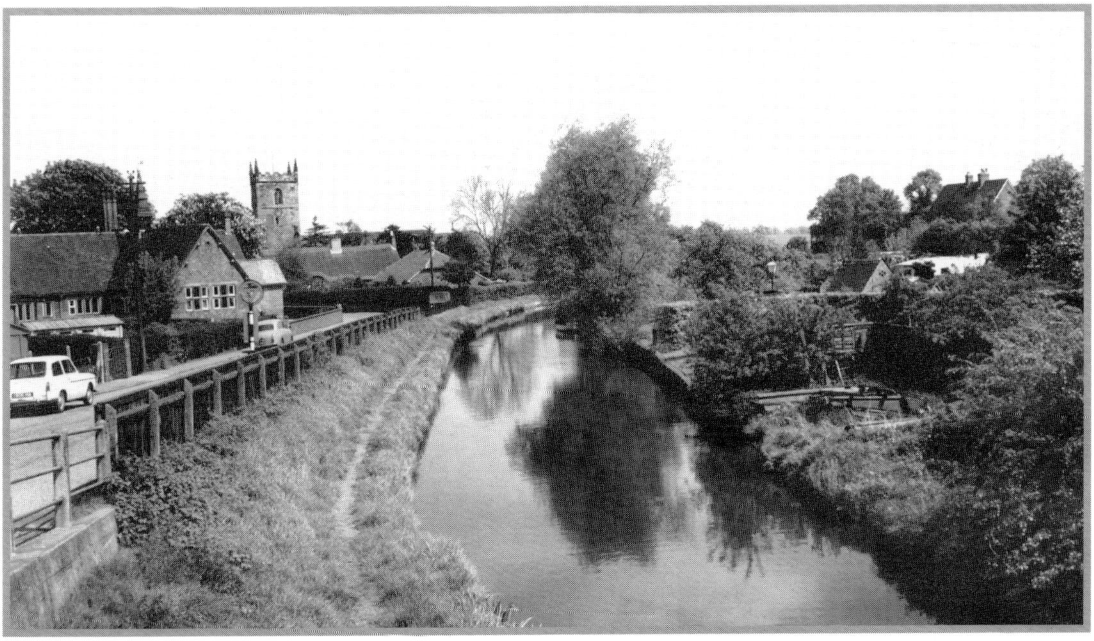

ALREWAS, THE CANAL c1955 A318001
This pleasant village on the Trent & Mersey Canal was a popular stop-off point for old boatmen: the pubs in the village were the main attraction. The church is mainly 13th- and 14th-century. The Austin A40 and Standard 10 cars on the left are a reminder of a more gentle motoring age.

CANAL BOATS c1930 O128501

The Frith archive records this photograph as being taken at Oldbury, but this is patently not so. The boat on the right is wide beam: that narrows the area for consideration somewhat. The best guess is that we are just below Copper Mill Lock at Harefield on the Grand Union Canal. The pair of horse boats, of which the 'Blyth' is the left hand one, are heading towards the bank, where the man in the bow will heave his line to the shore for the horse to be re-attached.

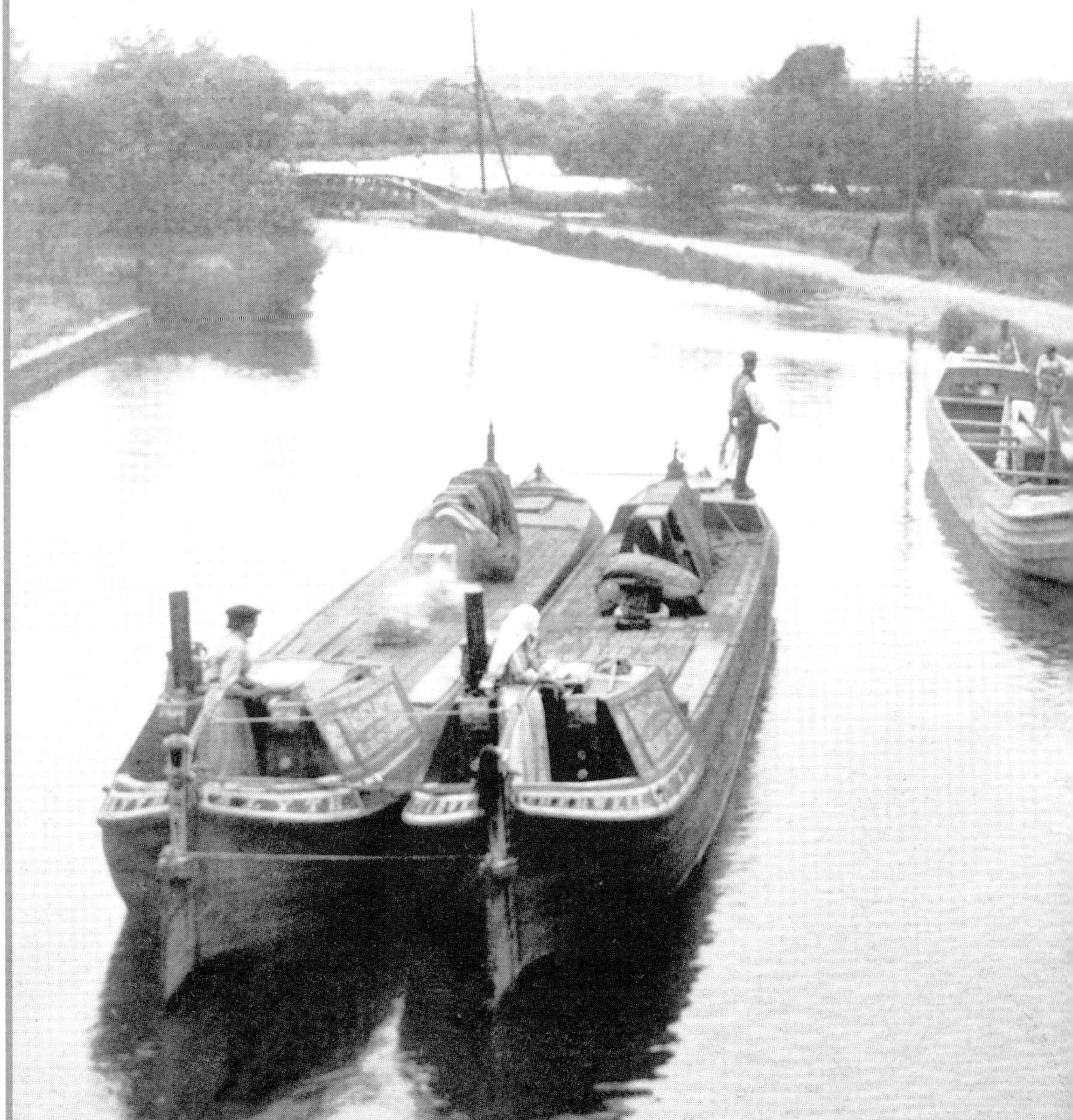

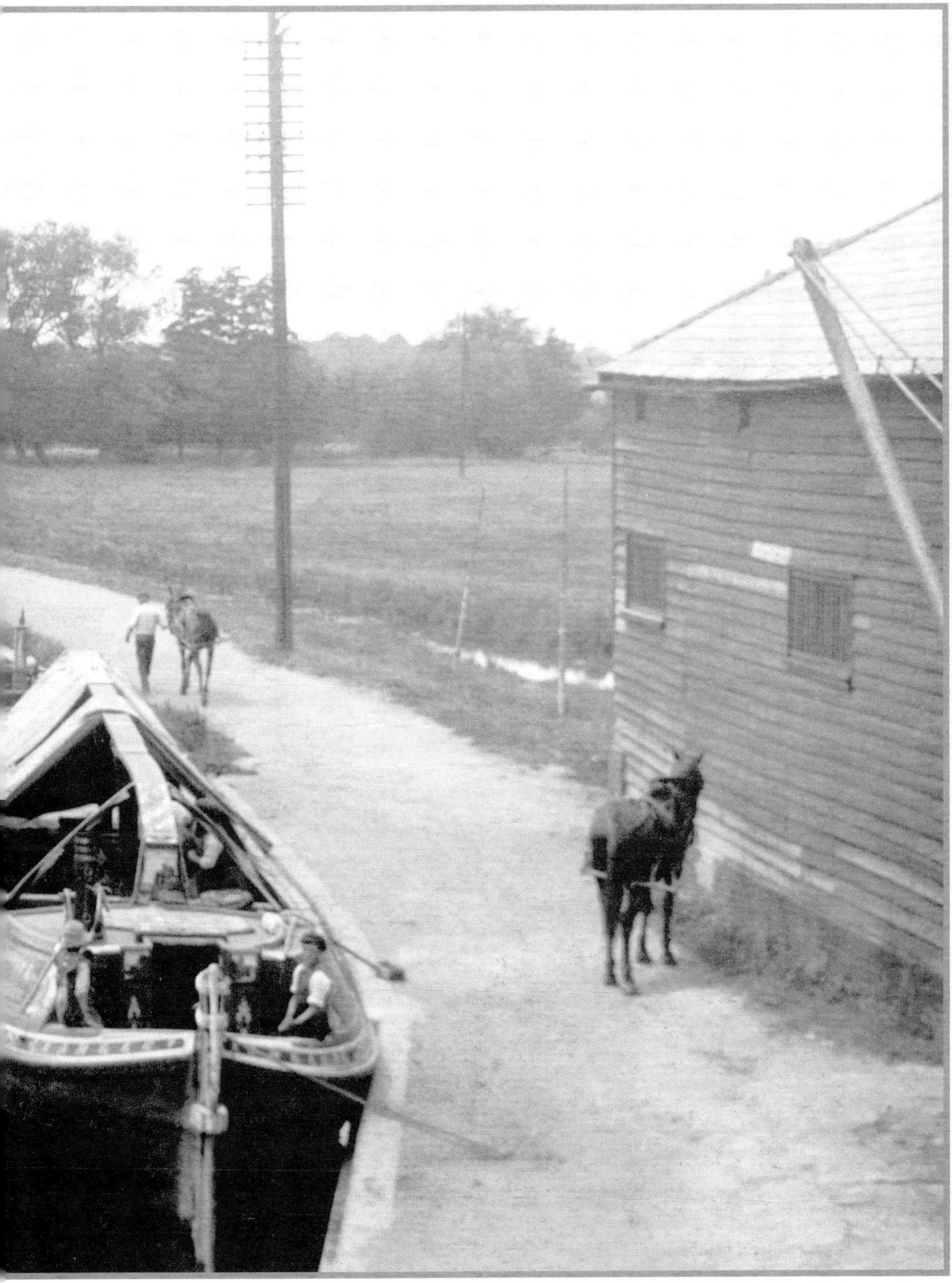

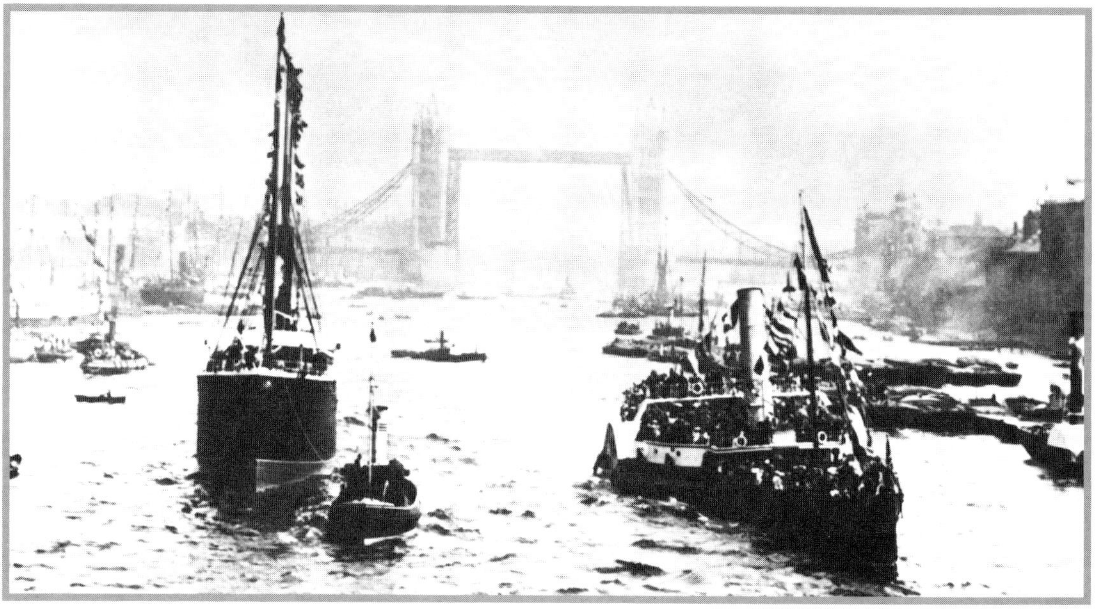

LONDON, THE OPENING OF TOWER BRIDGE 1894 L130019

This is a truly historic photograph, which shows the lowest crossing of the river Thames (except for the new Dartford motorway bridge) on the day it opened in 1894. Every boat carries crowds of people, and bunting abounds. John Wolf-Barry was the Engineer in Charge of the work. An example of his father's skills will be seen further upstream.

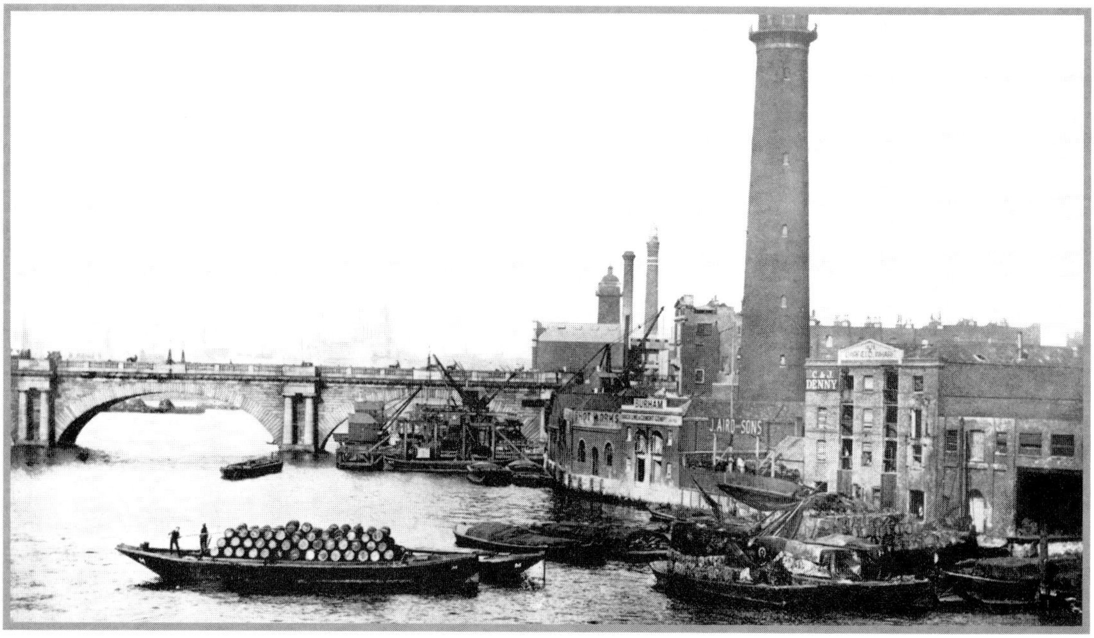

LONDON, WATERLOO BRIDGE c1890 L130281

Except for the dome of St Paul's Cathedral in the distance, this scene is very different today. John Rennie's gorgeous bridge, built in 1817 as both river crossing and monument to the battle, was demolished in 1923. The area around the shot tower on the right became the site of the Festival of Britain in 1951. The river traffic is also history.

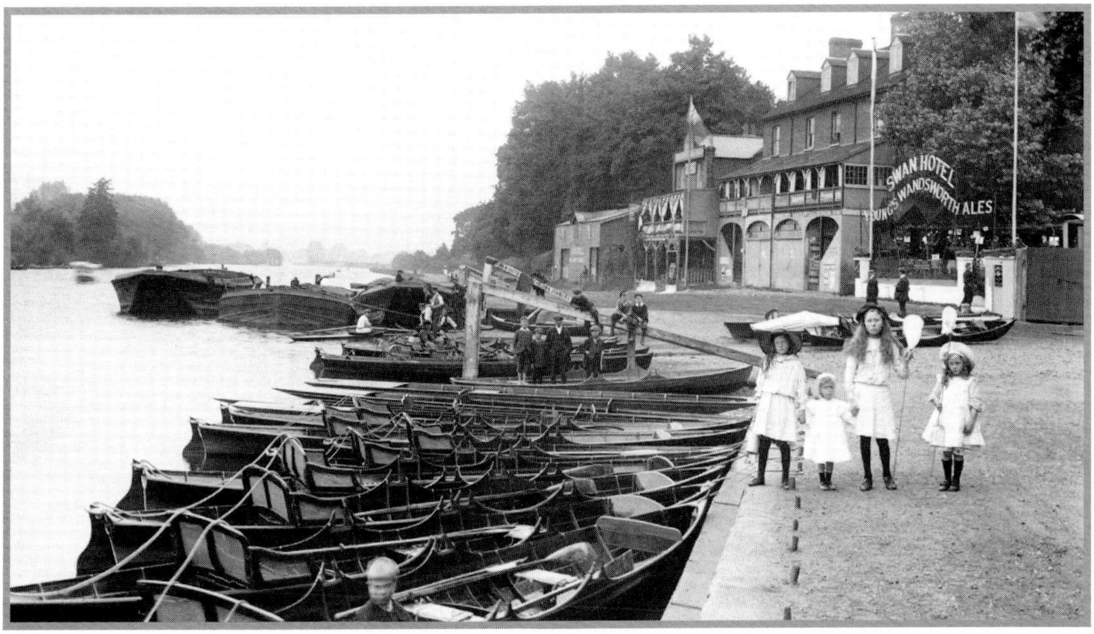

WALTON-ON-THAMES, THE ANGLERS 1908 60037
Here we see girls with fishing nets at a popular Thames-side location. The Swan has been on this spot since 1770. The recreational aspect of the river in the foreground is in stark contrast to the huge lighters tied up beyond.

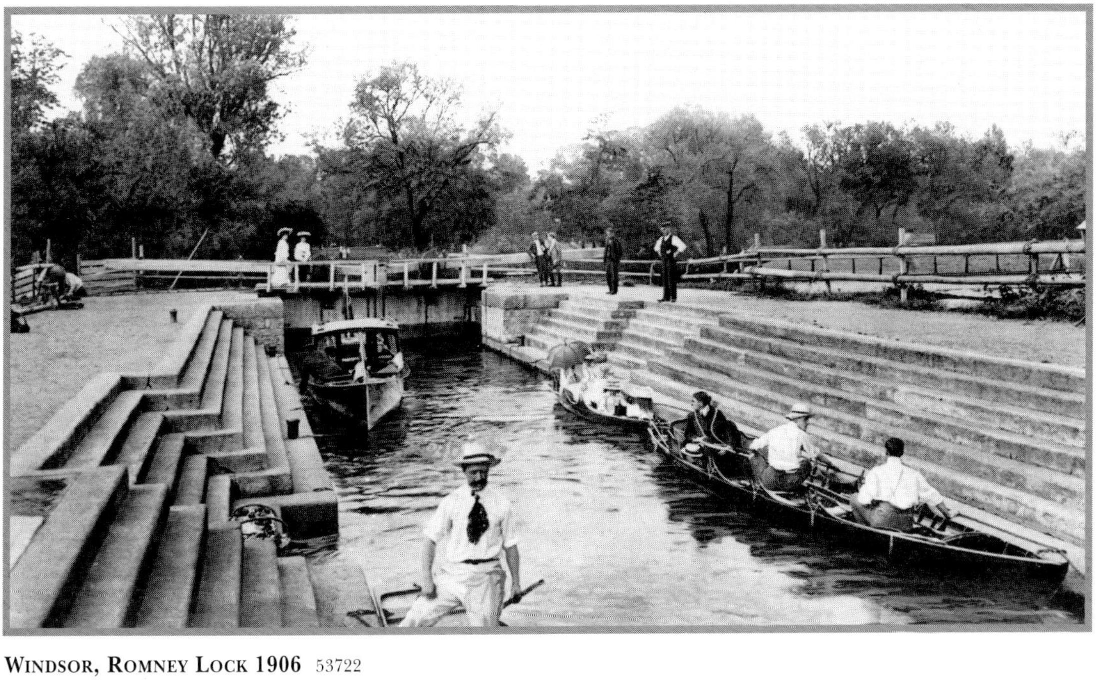

WINDSOR, ROMNEY LOCK 1906 53722
An assorted bunch of pleasure boats patiently wait for the lock to fill on a fine summer's day. A parasol to be seen on the rearmost boat on the right, together with the voluminous dresses, is a reminder that in Edwardian days ladies still stayed firmly covered up.

ETON

The River Thames 1909 61893

At Romney Lock, a Salter Brothers' passenger steamer - the 'Nuneham' - heads towards Windsor Bridge. Judging by the high fashions on display aboard, cruising the river was a popular event, even in those days.

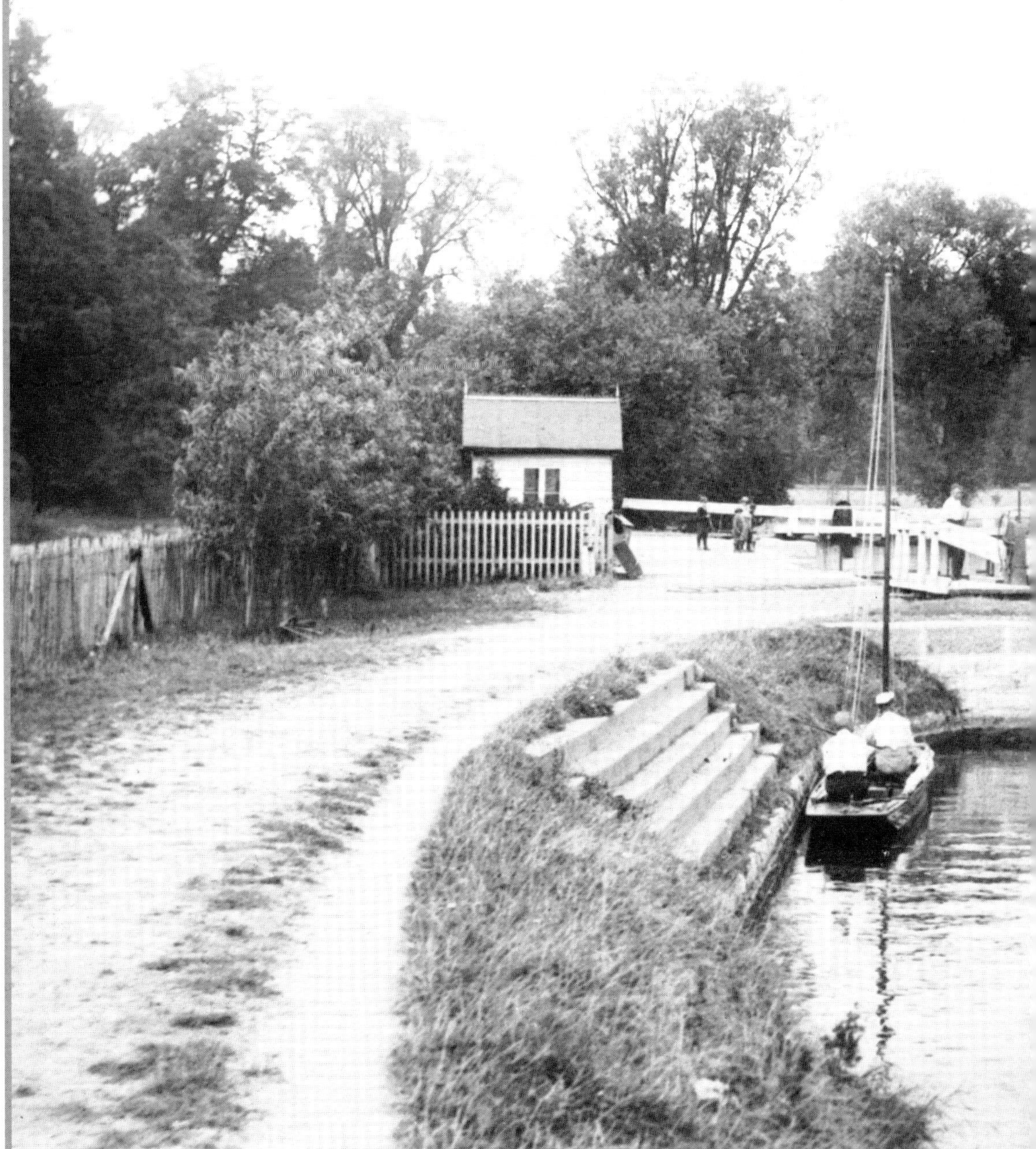

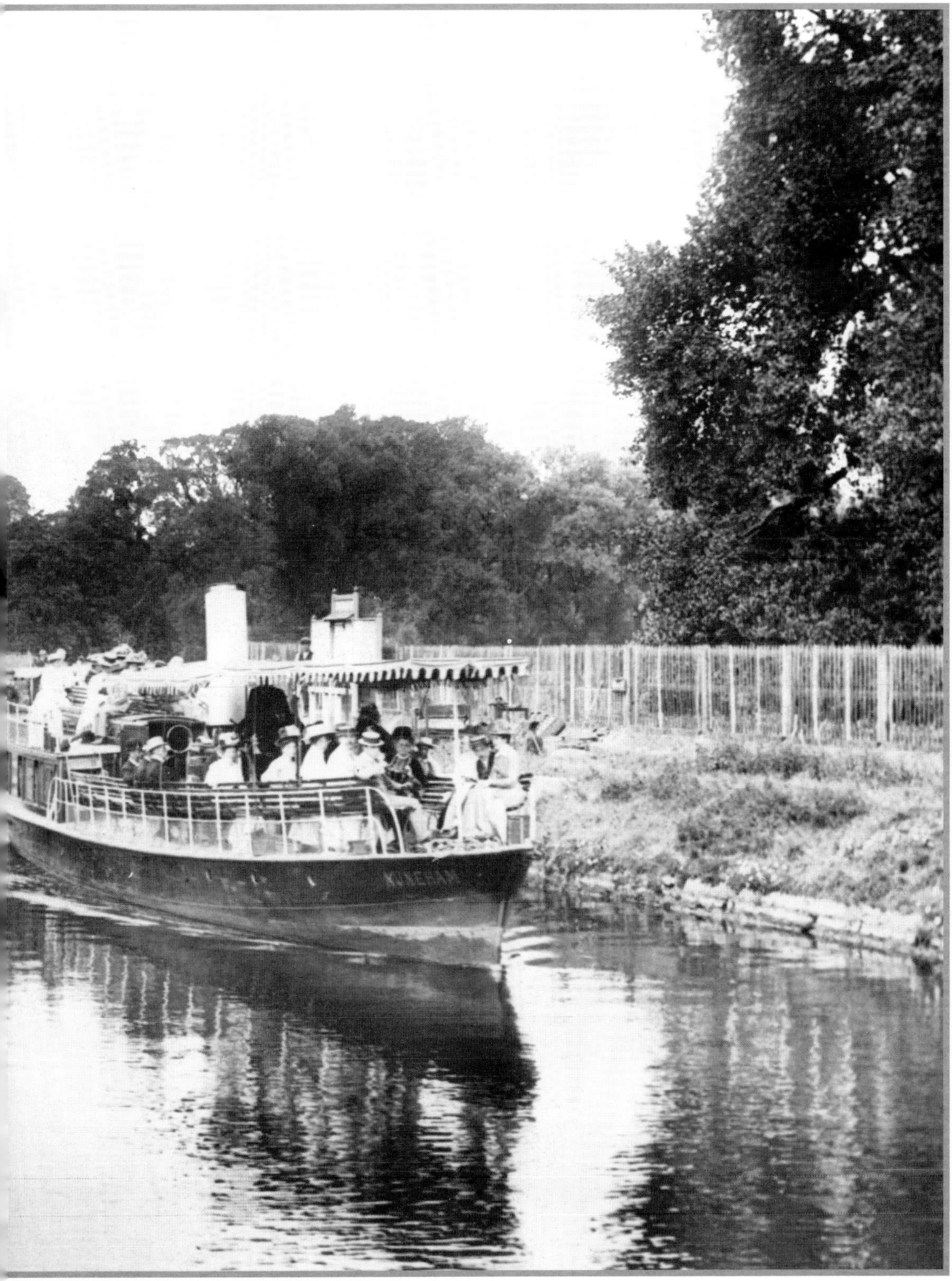

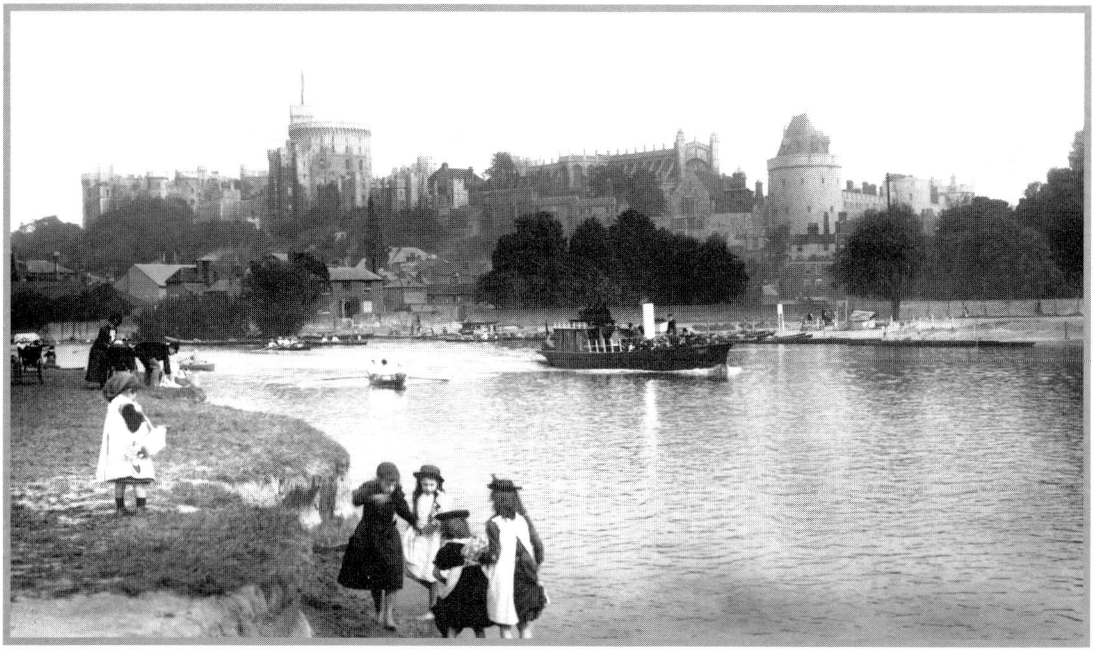

WINDSOR, THE CASTLE FROM THE RIVER 1895 35367A

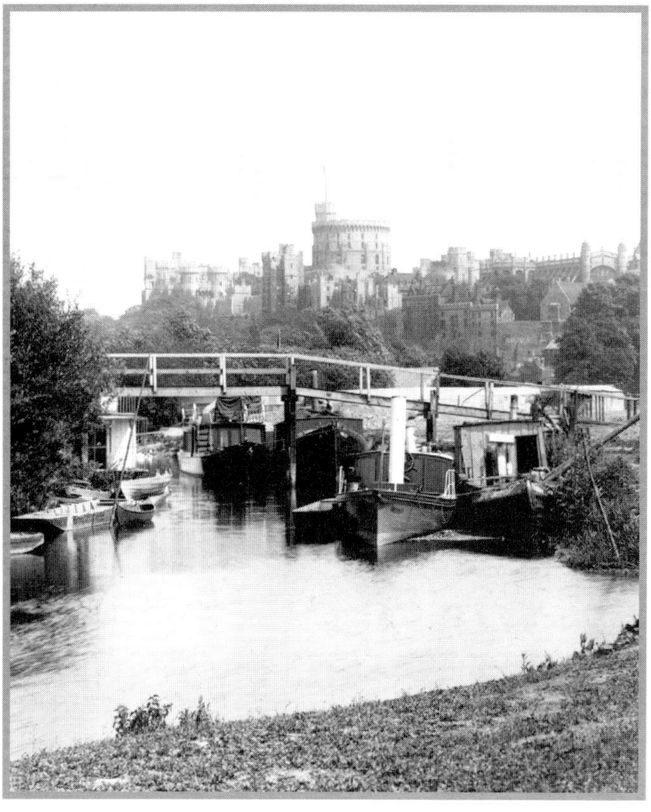

WINDSOR, THE CASTLE FROM THE MEADOWS 1895 35371

WINDSOR
The Castle from the River 1895
Another pleasure steamer ploughs its watery furrow in the shade of Windsor Castle. In the foreground, a group of girls are getting muddy and wet. Their younger sister stands on the bank, clear of trouble.

WINDSOR
The Castle from the Meadows 1895
A collection of pleasure craft are tied up on one of the river's many backwaters. Windsor racecourse is close by here. The Round Tower of the Castle is 12th-century, although the site was selected by William the Conqueror. Most of what can be seen from the river was built during the reign of George IV (1820-1830).

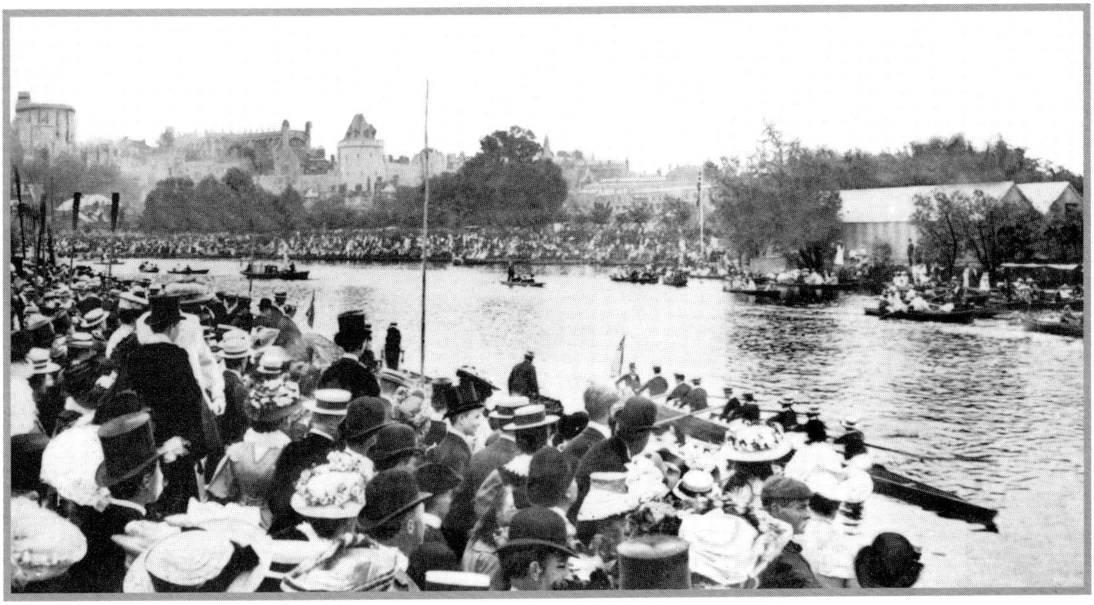

ETON, THE FOURTH OF JUNE PROCESSION OF BOATS 1906 53724
Our cameraman was standing quite close to the place where photograph No 35371 was taken as he captured the excitement of this riverside party, organised by Eton College. This celebration marks the monarch's official birthday, and has been held for centuries. The top hats sported by the boys can still be seen, even if they are no longer generally worn for the rest of the year.

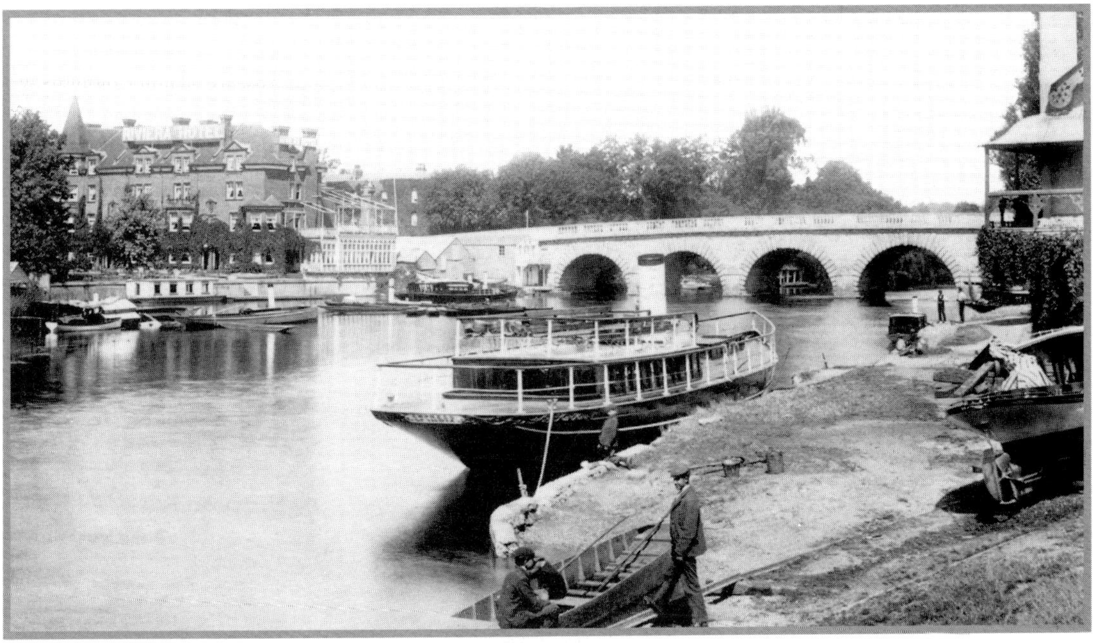

MAIDENHEAD, THE BRIDGE AND THE RIVIERA HOTEL 1899 43031
Here we see the town bridge in Maidenhead with an elegant steamer - the 'Empress of India' - tied up in the foreground. The slipway to the right no longer exists, but the hotel across the water does, now trading as the Thames Riviera and River Bar.

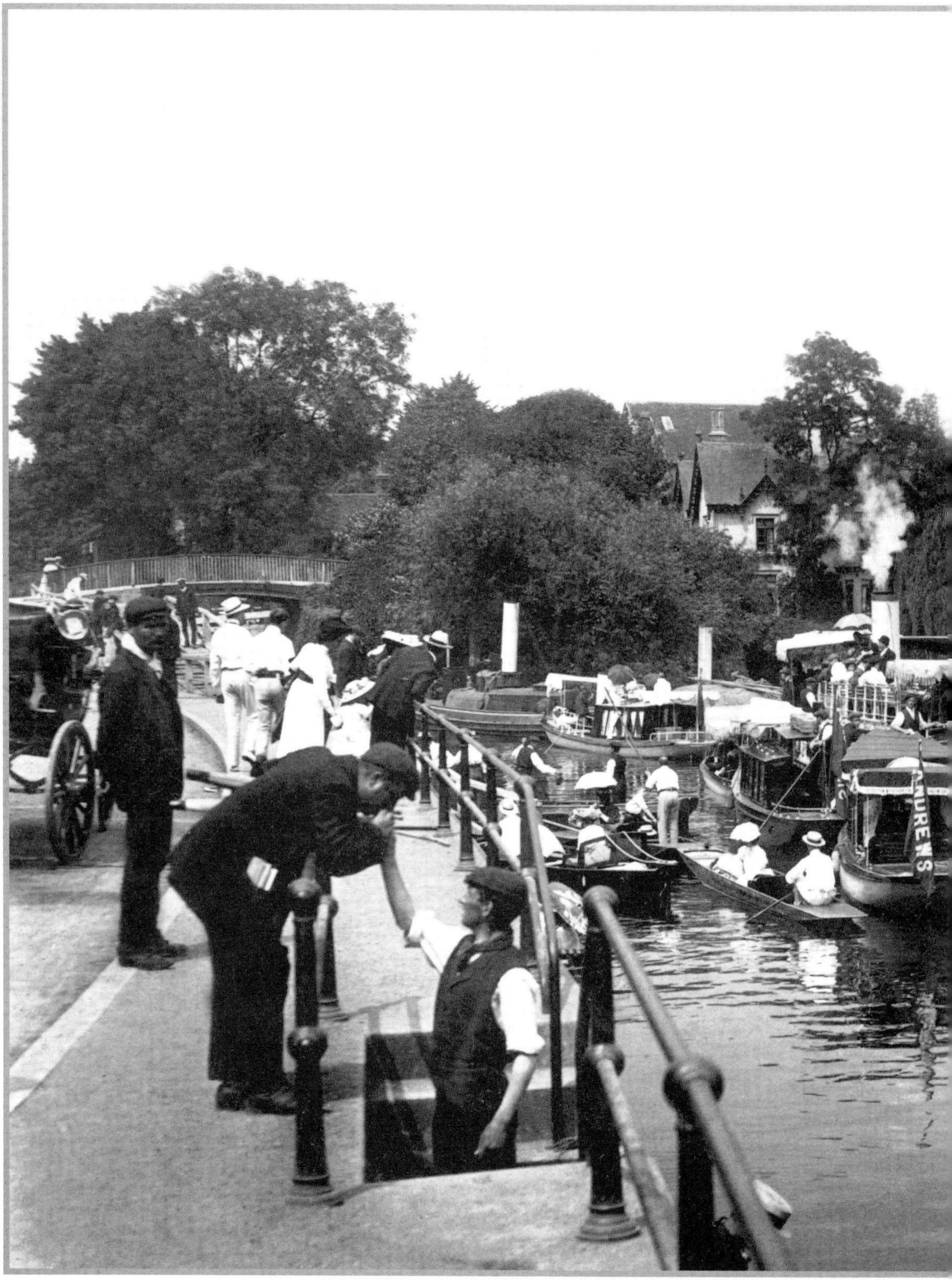

Maidenhead

Boulters Lock 1906 54083

This frantically busy scene is below Boulters Lock. In the melee, the nearest boat to the camera appears to be flying the Stars and Stripes of the USA, which might not be a common sight on England's premier river in those days. The large wicker hamper on the stern would indicate an extended cruise. Is the man bending over (left) lighting a cigarette or chewing the other man's finger nails?

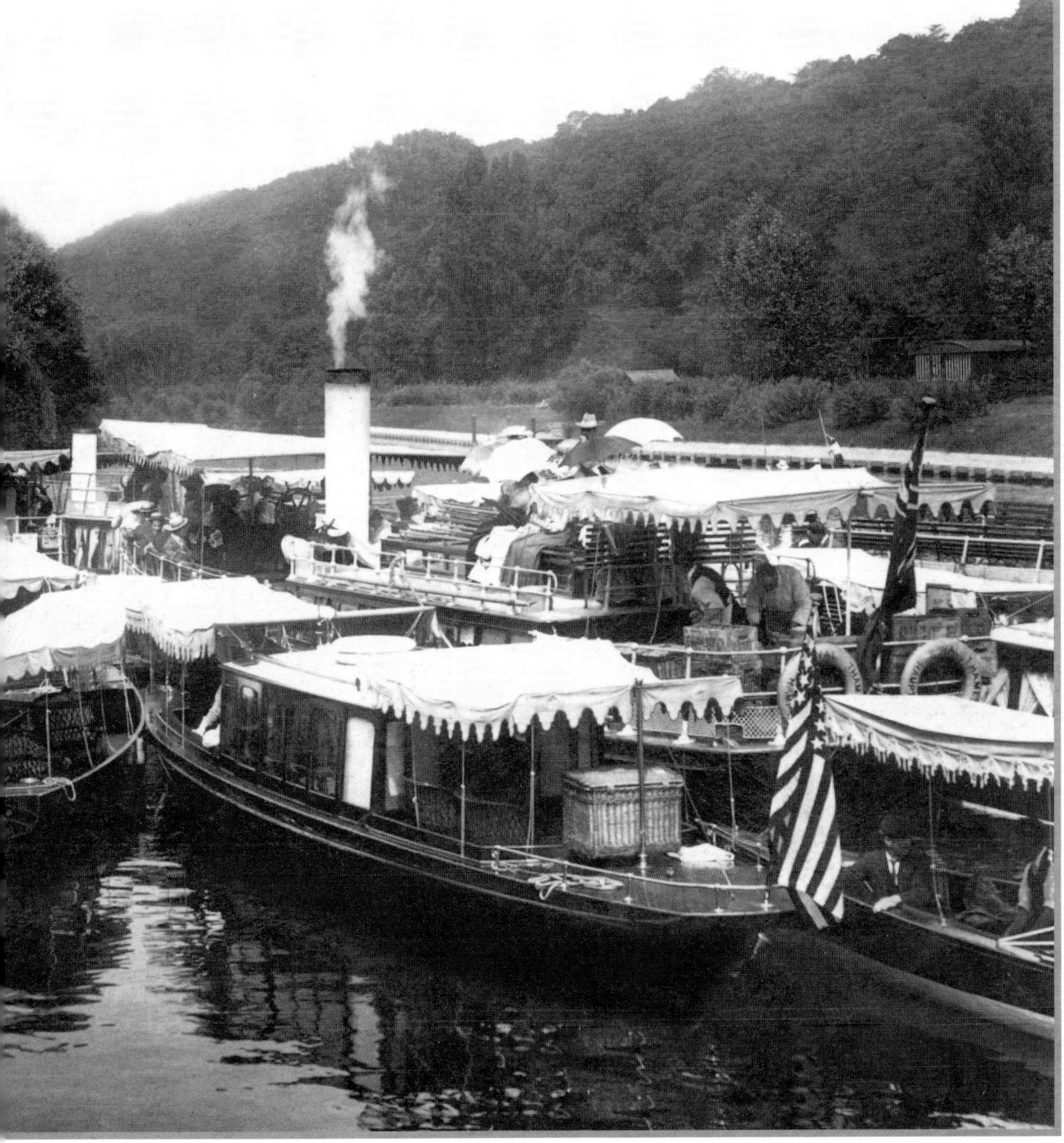

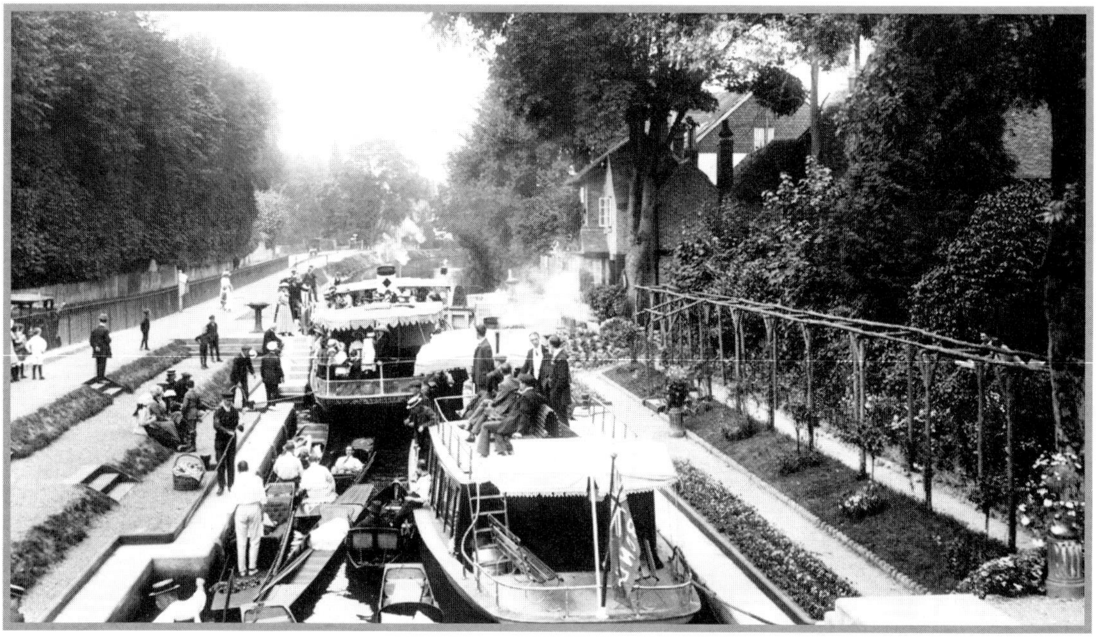

MAIDENHEAD, BOULTERS LOCK 1913 65542
Here we see the lock itself, another busy scene. Only a few years earlier, every head would have been be-hatted. As the reign of Queen Victoria receded, a slightly more laid-back atmosphere was staring to take hold. The Great War - only a year away - would change things for ever.

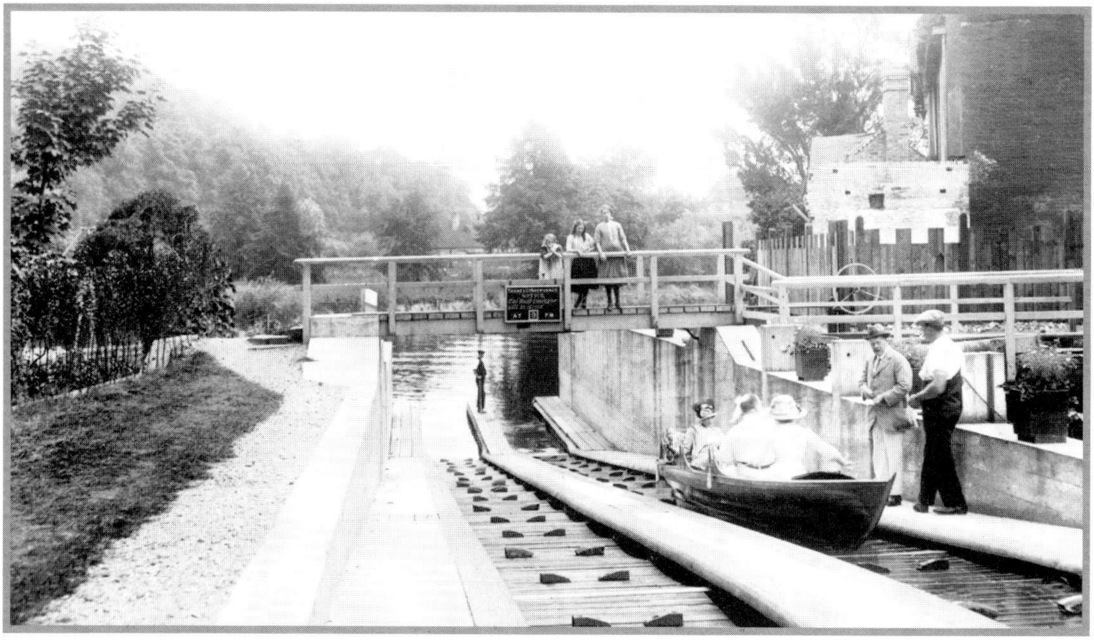

MAIDENHEAD, BOULTERS LOCK, THE ELEVATOR 1913 65545
Whilst the lock alongside is teeming with boats, a small skiff makes its way up the elevator to the upper river level. The sign indicates that this will close at 9pm. The authority who placed the board was the Thames Conservancy, established in 1857.

MAIDENHEAD
Clivedon Woods 1925

Three people aboard the punt steady their craft as a passenger boat heads upstream. The large building in the background is Clivedon, built by Charles Barry in 1851 for the Duke of Sutherland. The Astor family once lived there, and it is now owned by the National Trust and let as an hotel. Barry was also responsible for the Palace of Westminster; his son was the engineer who built Tower Bridge.

BOURNE END
The River 1899

An assortment of people are enjoying this wide open stretch of the river. The boat yard on the far bank - now under different ownership - offers 'Launches and Boats Built to Order'. The steam launch in the foreground is a particularly elegant shape.

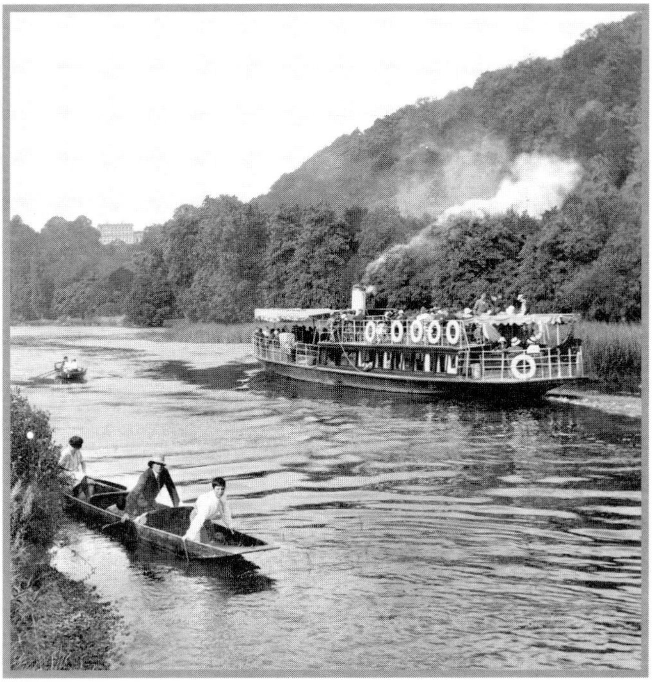

MAIDENHEAD, CLIVEDON WOODS 1925 77613

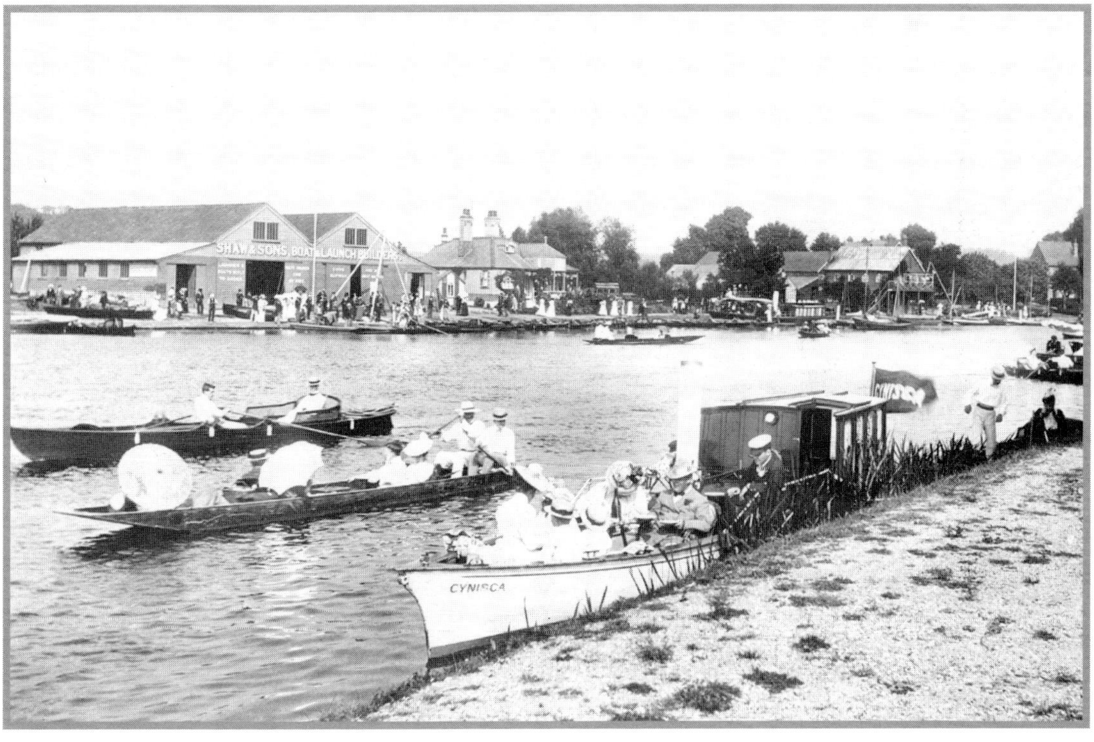

BOURNE END, THE RIVER 1899 43963

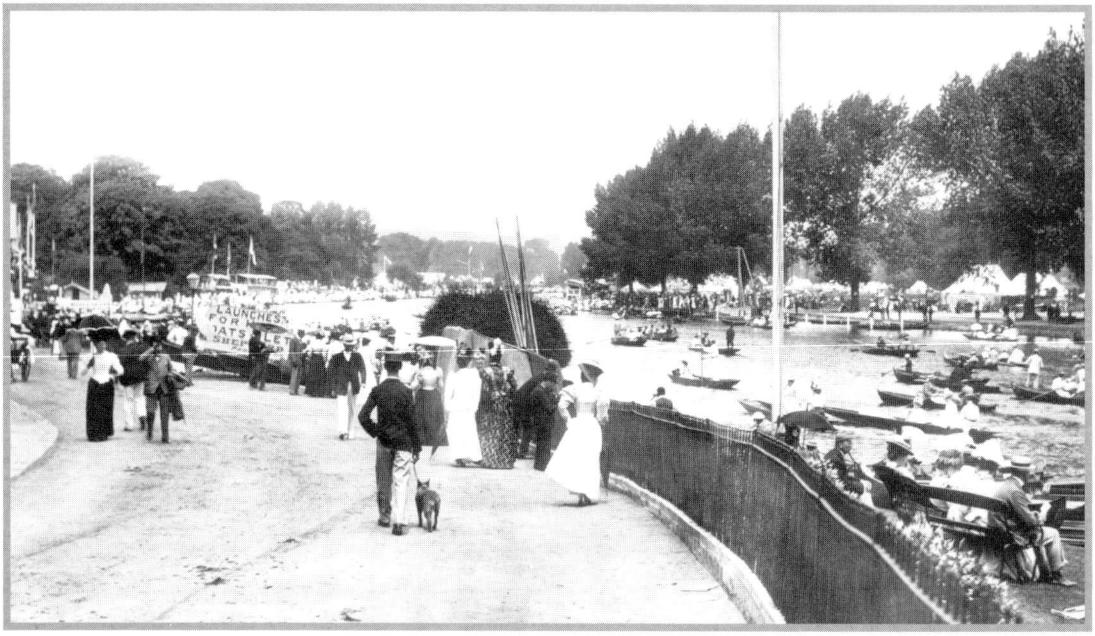

HENLEY-ON-THAMES, REGATTA DAY 1899 43020
To this day, this is the most popular event on the river. A view of the main regatta course is obscured by the bush in the foreground, but there is much other activity to please the eye. The marquees across the water are a small number compared with the acres of tents erected during Regatta Week today.

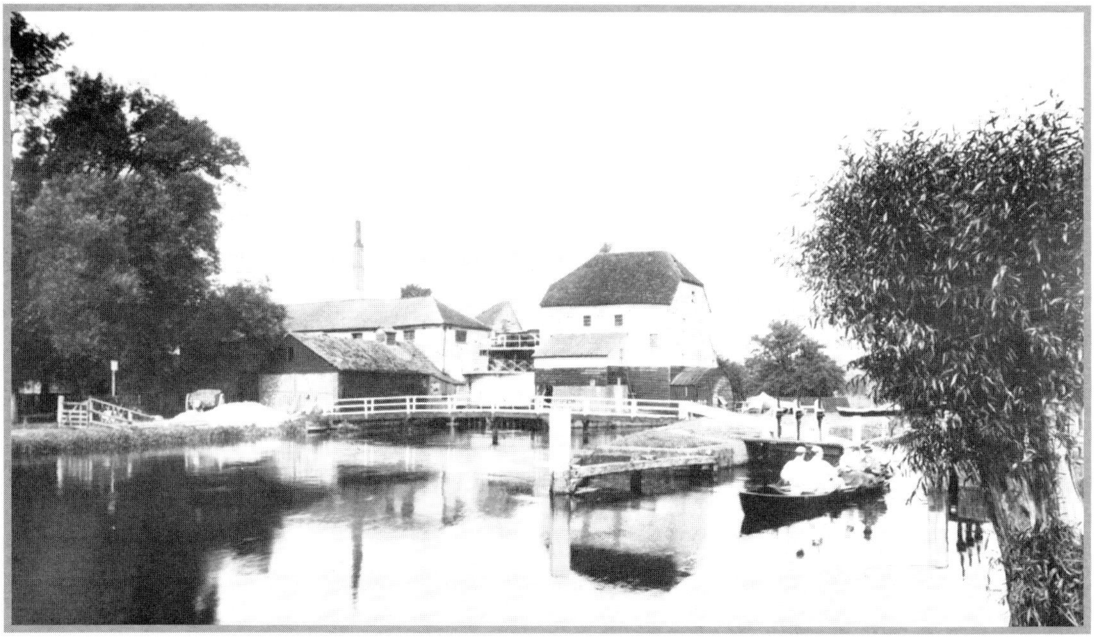

SHIPLAKE, THE MILL AND THE LOCK 1890 27166
This is a wonderful view of the old mill at Shiplake. The top gate of the lock is closed, and the unusual three sluices can be seen as a rowing skiff leaves the chamber. Once, there were mills all alongside the Thames, and over the years disputes over water rights were rife.

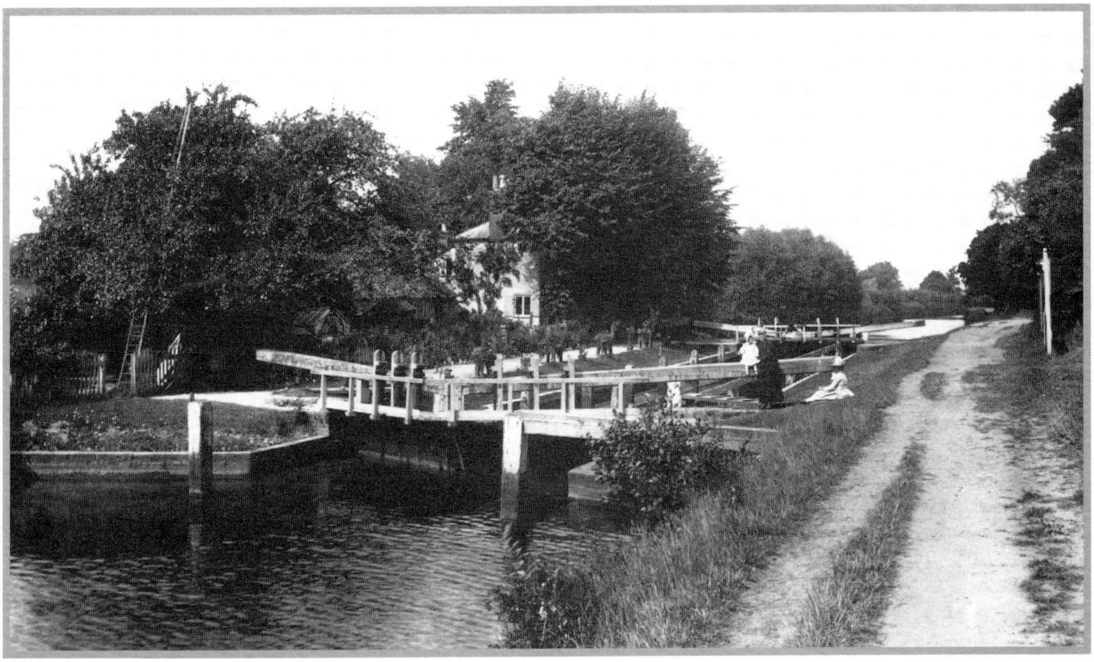

SONNING, THE LOCK 1890 27159
A small child perches precariously on the lock gate balance beam: one wriggle and disaster could follow. To the left, a huge ladder is in place, seemingly to pick the fruit hanging from the branches.

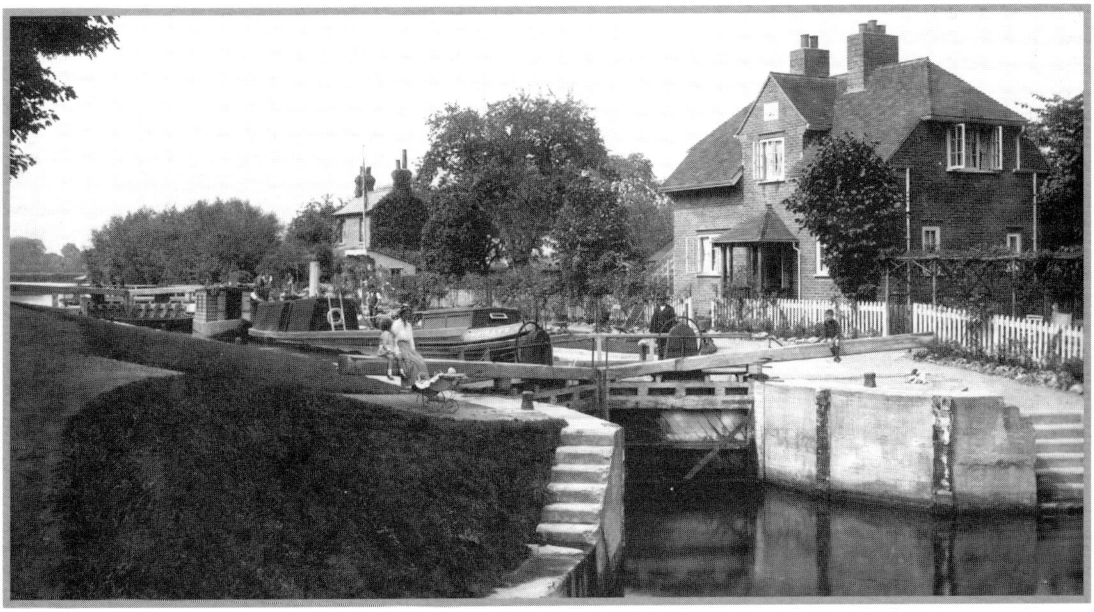

SONNING, ON THE THAMES 1917 67959
27 years after photograph No 27159, the chamber has been rebuilt, new gear fitted to the gate sluices and a house built for the lock-keeper by the Thames Conservancy. Despite the passage of years, the balance beams still have a magnetic attraction as a seat. A deck-chair just behind the lock-keeper is presumably his resting place between operating the lock.

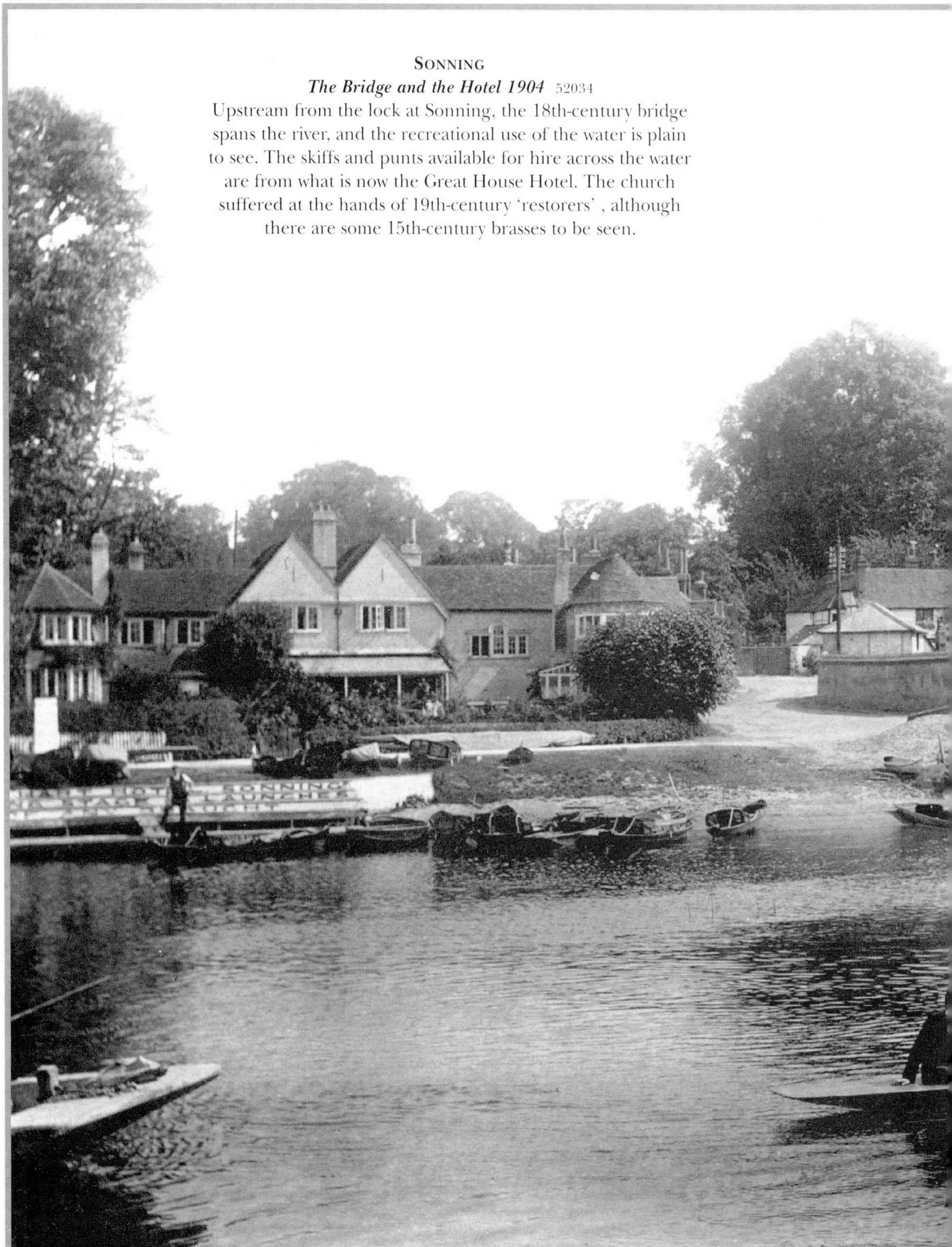

SONNING

The Bridge and the Hotel 1904 52034

Upstream from the lock at Sonning, the 18th-century bridge spans the river, and the recreational use of the water is plain to see. The skiffs and punts available for hire across the water are from what is now the Great House Hotel. The church suffered at the hands of 19th-century 'restorers' , although there are some 15th-century brasses to be seen.

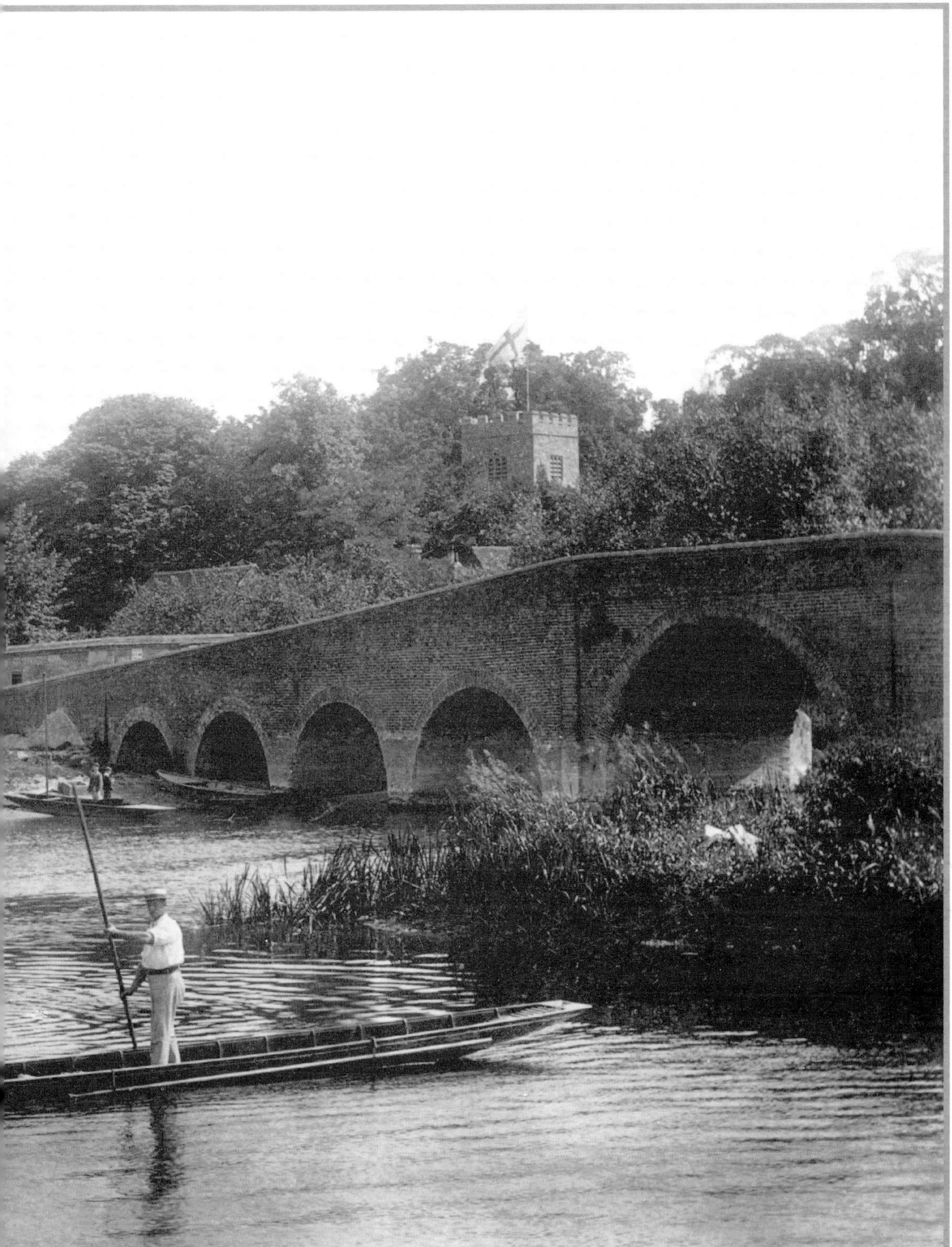

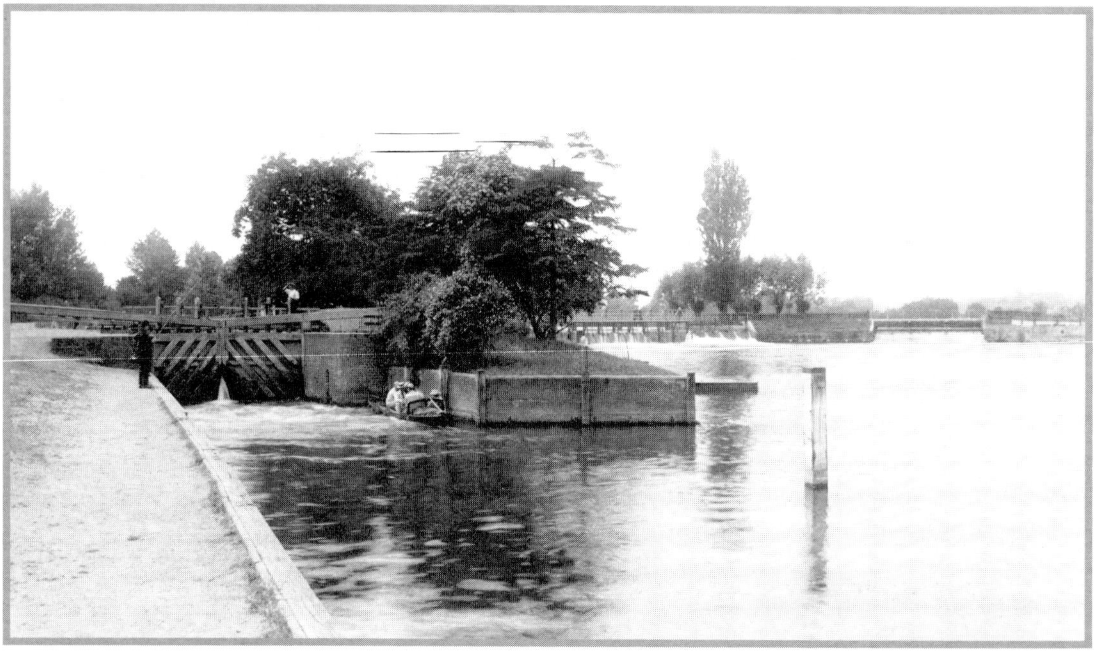

Caversham, The Lock 1890 27108

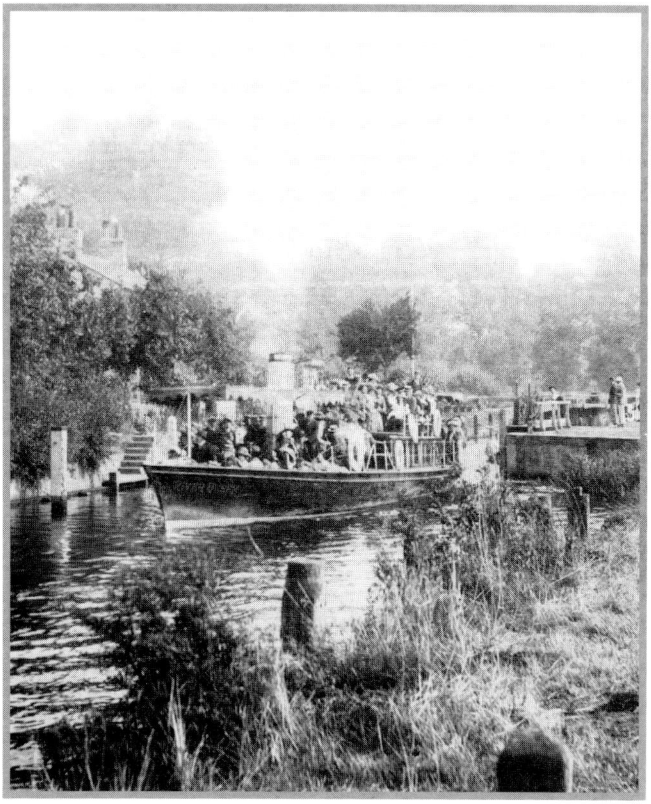

Mapledurham, The Lock 1917 67970a

Caversham

The Lock 1890

On the edge of Reading, a rowing boat hangs on as the lock keeper drains the lock to allow it entry. To the left, a fisherman tries his luck in the turbulent water. This area is known as View Island.

Mapledurham

The Lock 1917

Upstream of Reading is Mapledurham Lock, where a steamer is leaving the chamber. Today's Health and Safety authorities would be in an apoplexy to see the 'River Queen' pack so many passengers aboard. Mapledurham House - behind the trees - has been used as a film set in Inspector Morse mysteries, and also in the film 'The Eagle Has Landed'.

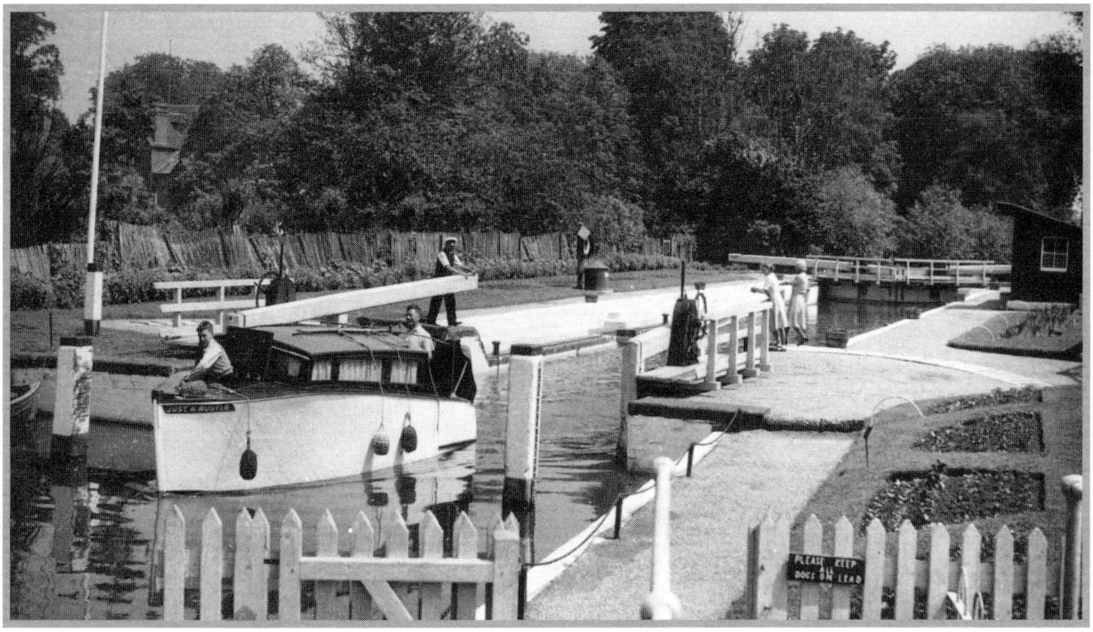

Pangbourne, Whitchurch Lock c1955 P5039

The growth of pleasure cruising on the river can now be seen. This holiday boat has just left the lock, and willing hands are ashore ready to close the gates. The wheels on the sluice gear - and indeed the gates themselves - are now all operated by electricity.

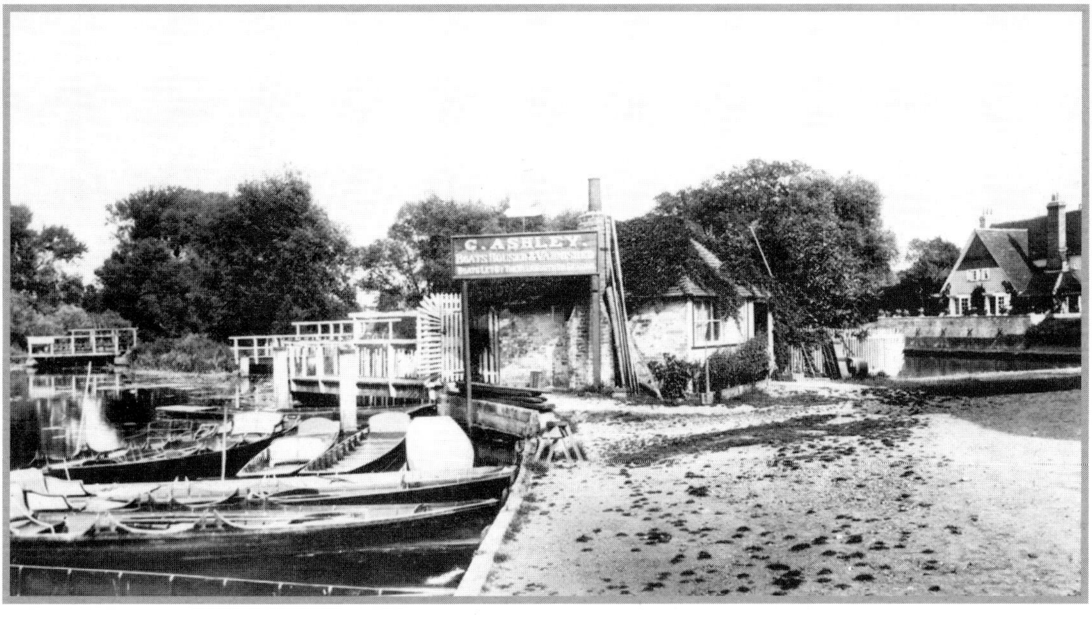

Pangbourne, View from The Swan 1899 43000

This evocative scene at Pangbourne no longer exists, alas. Mr. Ashley no longer lets 'Boats by the Week, Month or Season', nor are they 'Housed and Varnished'. This view is from The Swan pub, still in existence. It was here that Jerome K Jerome, two friends and his shamed-looking dog took a train back to London, having abandoned their journey which was written up as 'Three Men in a Boat'.

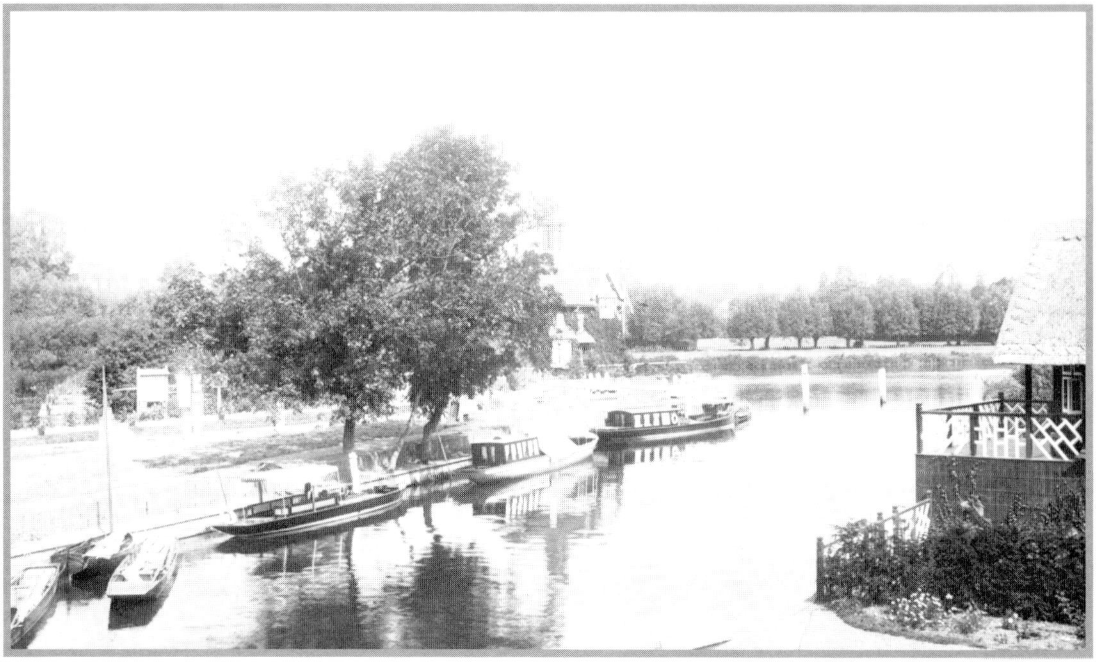

GORING, THE LOCK 1896 38313
The lock chamber is to the left of this historic view, and the house beyond the trees can be seen in photograph No 43000. The boats in the foreground are typical examples of elegant Thames pleasure cruisers.

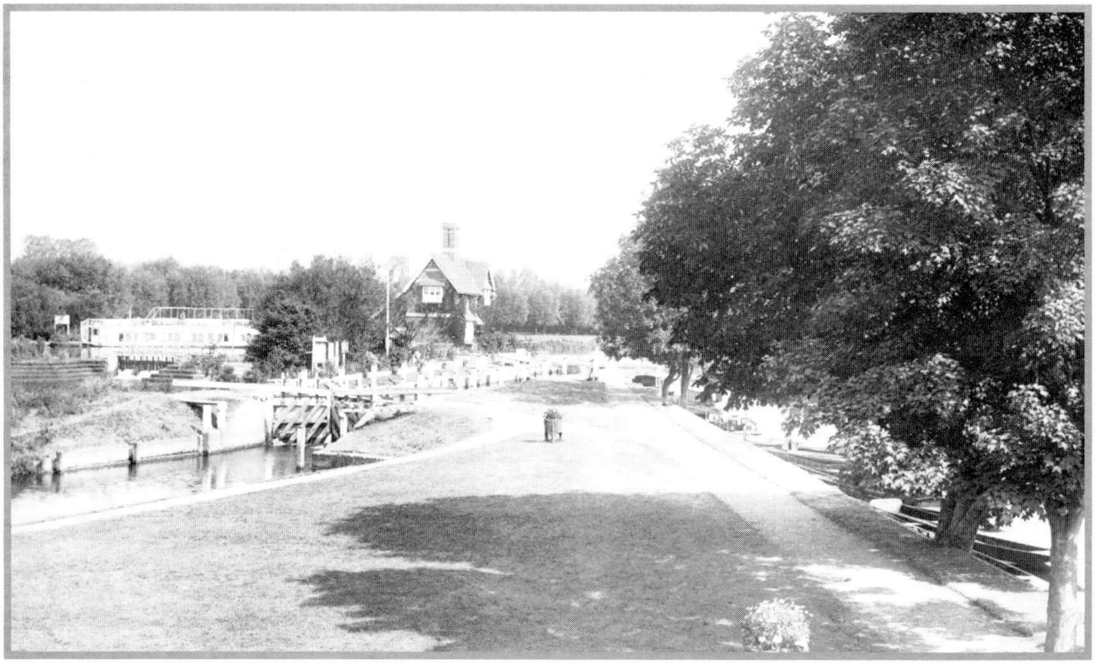

GORING, THE LOCK 1896 38312
The complicated-looking construction in the left distance is the sluice mechanism that controls the flow of the river. In times of heavy rainfall, the excess water runs off here.

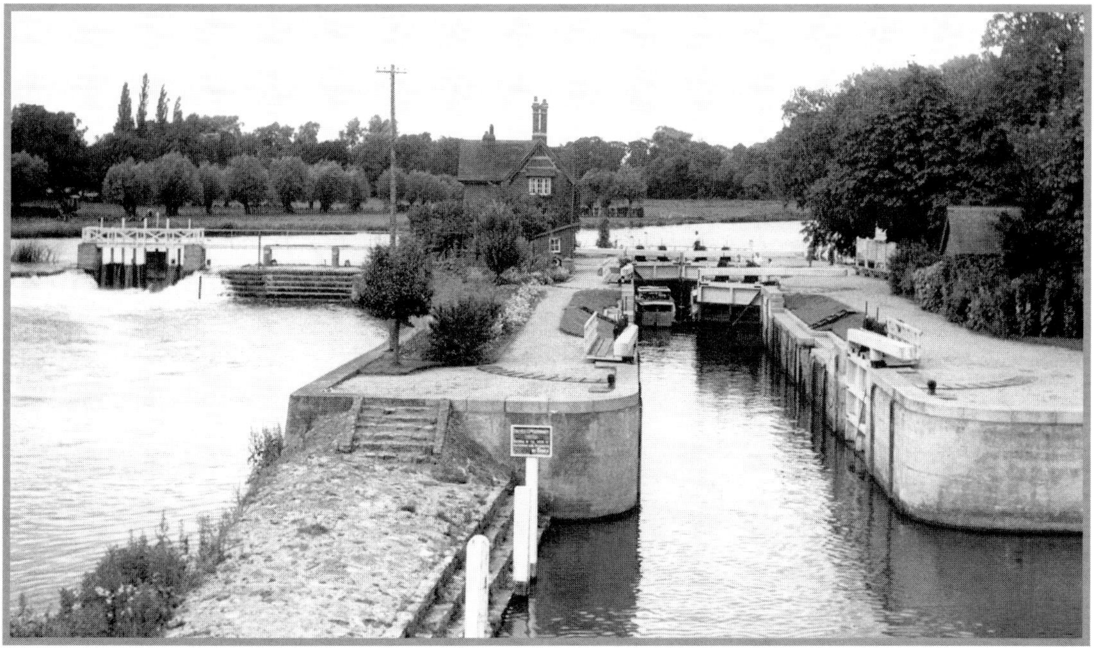

STREATLEY, THE LOCK AND THE WEIR c1955 S221004

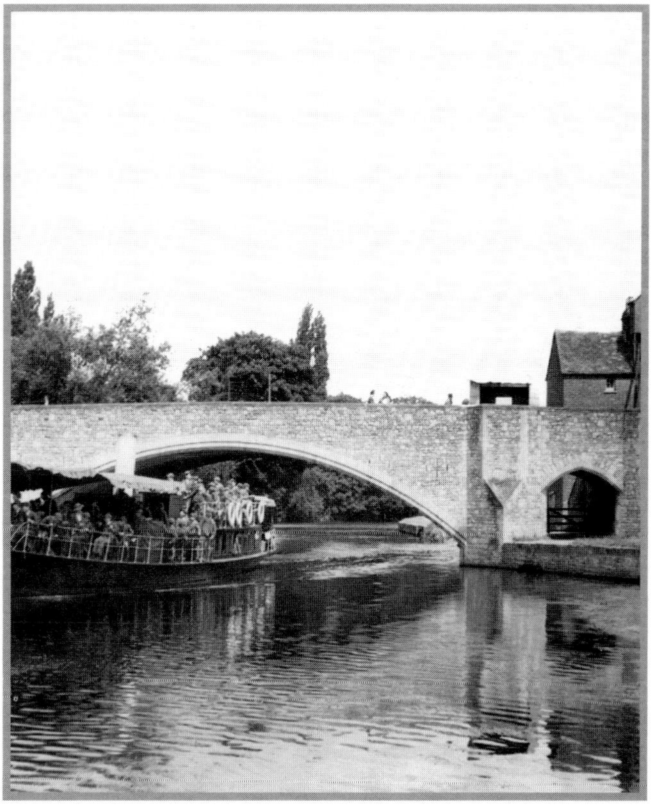

ABINGDON, THE BRIDGE AND A RIVER STEAMER c1955 A15501

STREATLEY
The Lock and the Weir c1955
Streatley is the village to the left of the river, and Goring is to the right. Every year, a regatta is held upstream, a colourful and vibrant event, where the villagers fight it out for 'top dog'. The large white building in the 1896 photograph has gone.

ABINGDON
The Bridge and a River Steamer c1955
Here we see the town bridge with a Salter Brothers steamer passing underneath. The 15th-century bridge was rebuilt during the 19th century. This town is best known as the original home of the MG sports car.

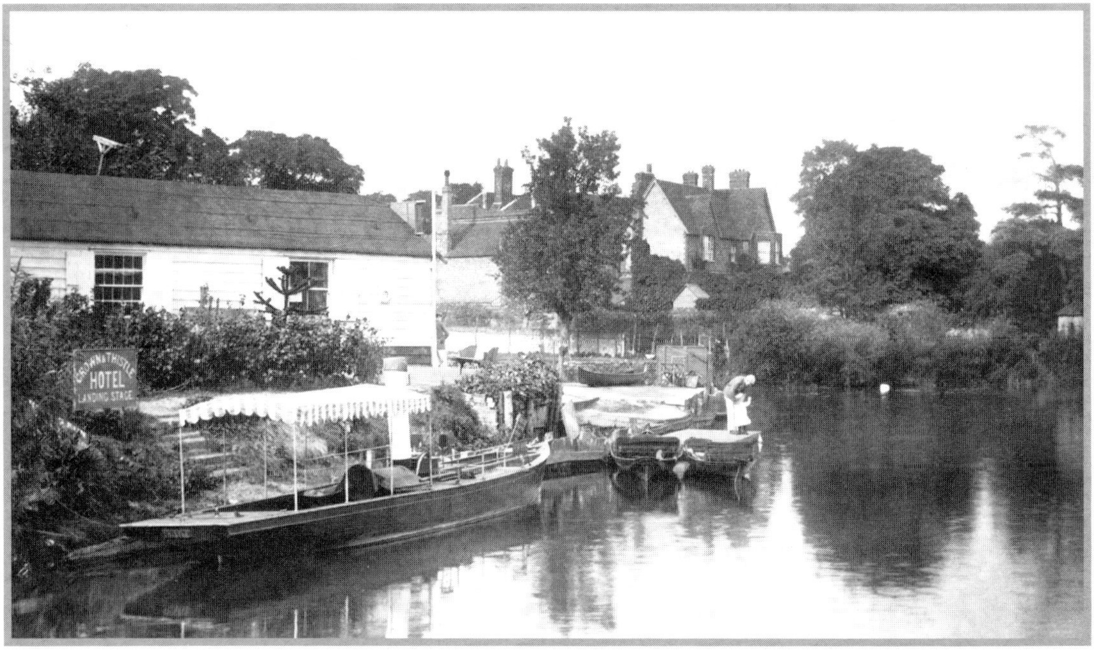

ABINGDON, THE BOAT HOUSE 1890 26987

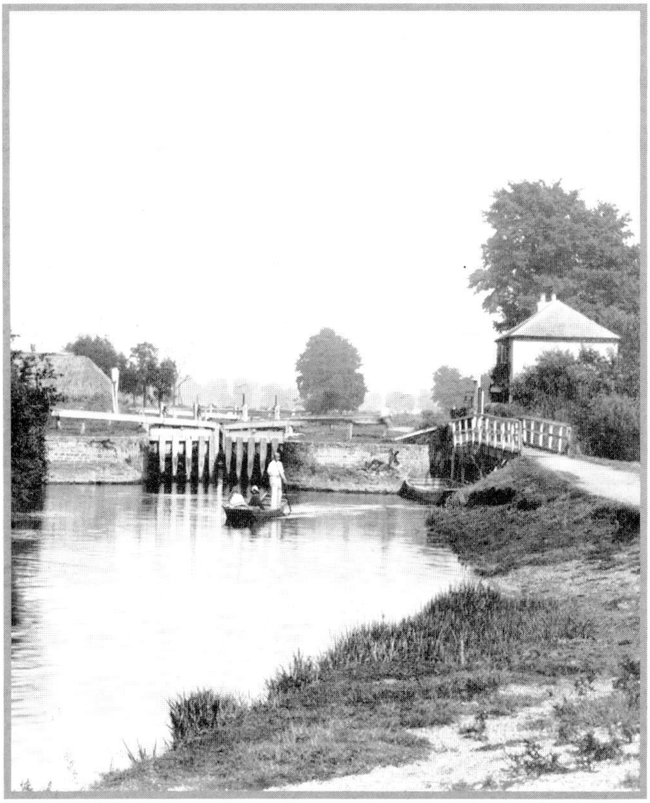

ABINGDON, THE LOCK FROM BELOW 1890 26990

ABINGDON
The Boat House 1890
A steam launch - the 'Thistle' - is moored outside the Crown and Thistle pub's landing stage just above Abingdon town bridge. This pub, a 19th-century coaching inn, is still open for business.

ABINGDON
The Lock from Below 1890
Two hundred yards upstream from photograph No 26987 is Abingdon Lock. The bushes to the left hide the site of the old abbey at Abingdon, founded in 676 and again in 955 after the original had been destroyed by marauding Danes. It was the mainstay of this area. After the Reformation, the town went into years of decline.

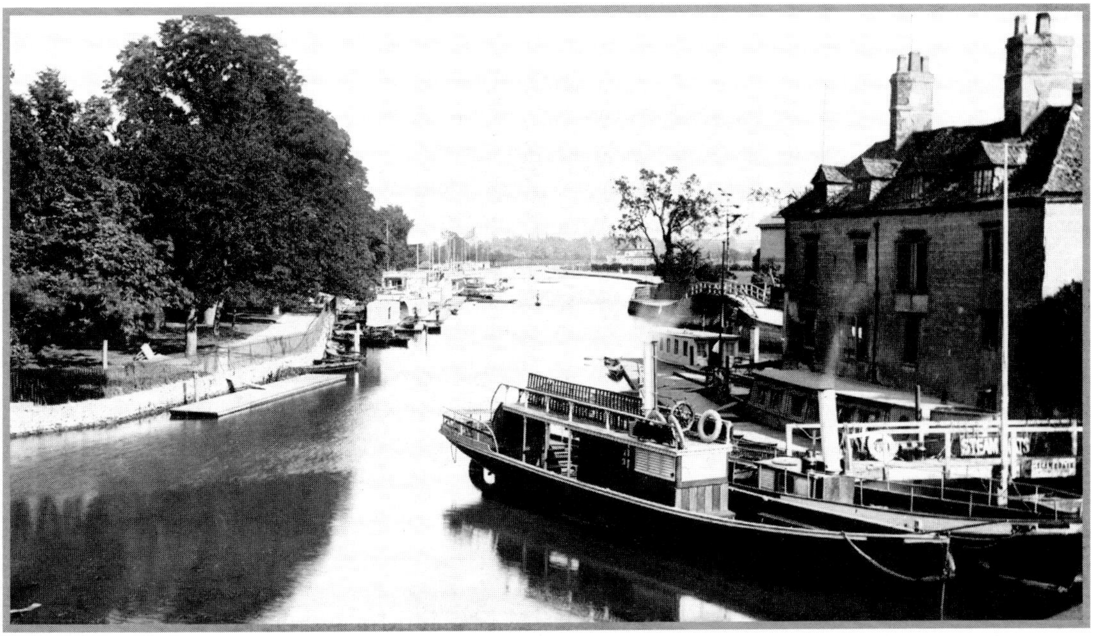

OXFORD, THE RIVER FROM FOLLY BRIDGE 1890 26948
By the time this picture was taken, Salter Brothers steamboats were well established on the river Thames, operating from their base at Folly Bridge. The company was formed as boatbuilders in 1858, and moved into passenger carrying in 1888.

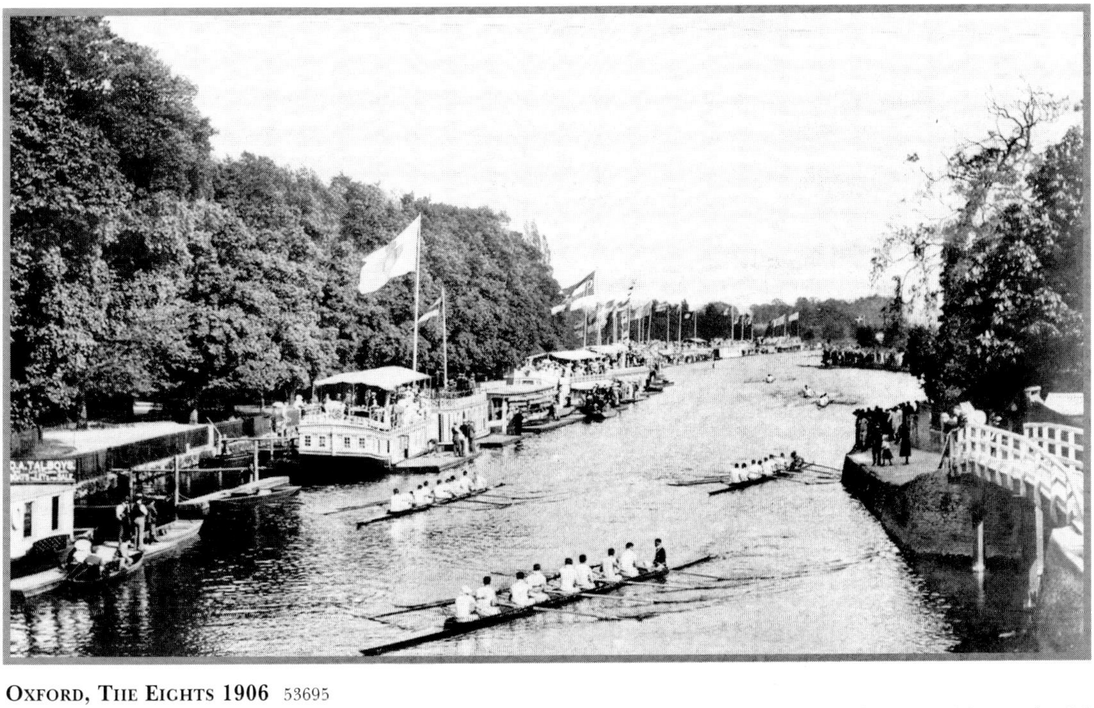

OXFORD, THE EIGHTS 1906 53695
This is the Medley section of the Thames - or Isis, as it is known hereabouts. Only a glance at this wonderful photograph gives an idea of the phenomenal popularity of rowing a hundred years ago.

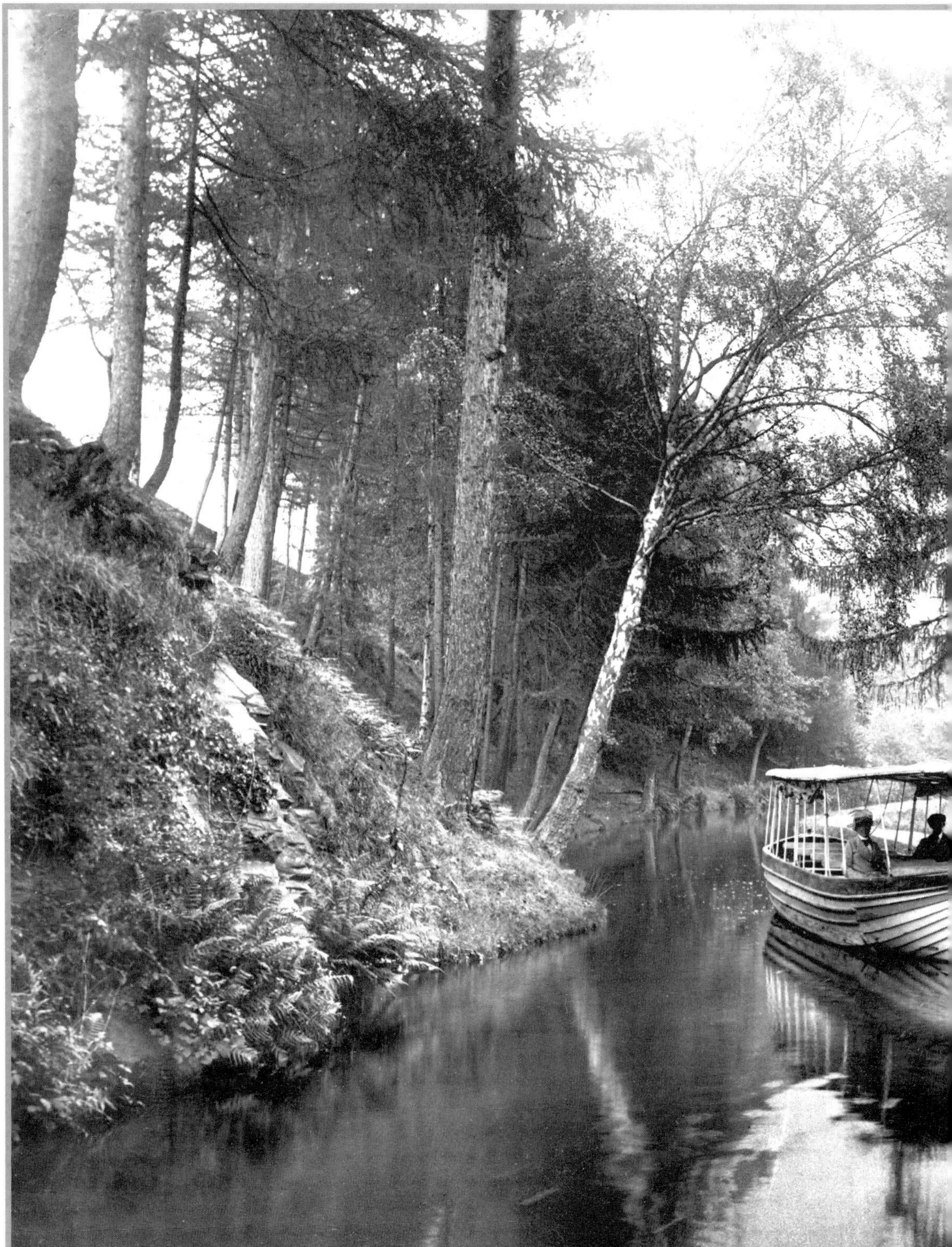

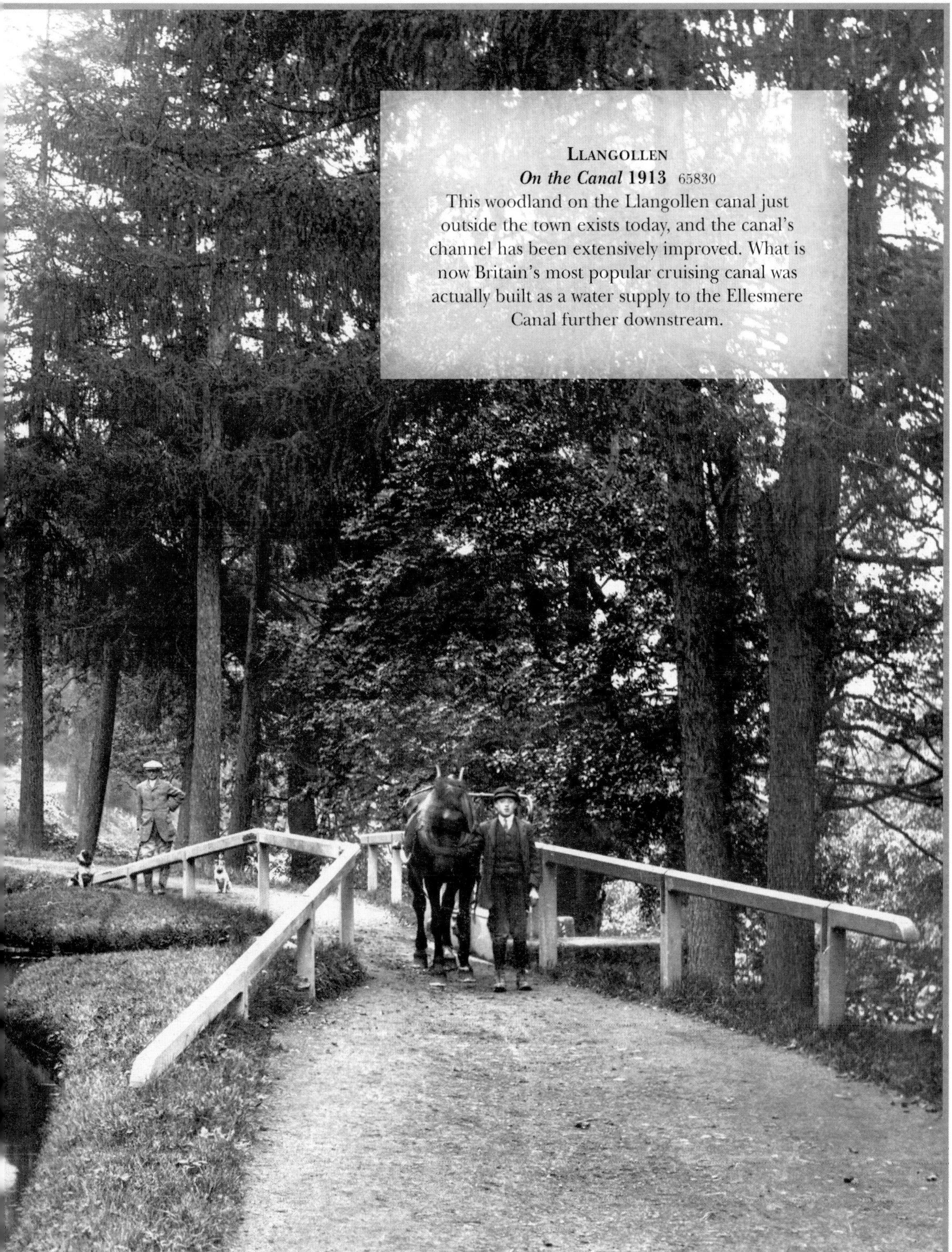

LLANGOLLEN
***On the Canal* 1913** 65830
This woodland on the Llangollen canal just outside the town exists today, and the canal's channel has been extensively improved. What is now Britain's most popular cruising canal was actually built as a water supply to the Ellesmere Canal further downstream.

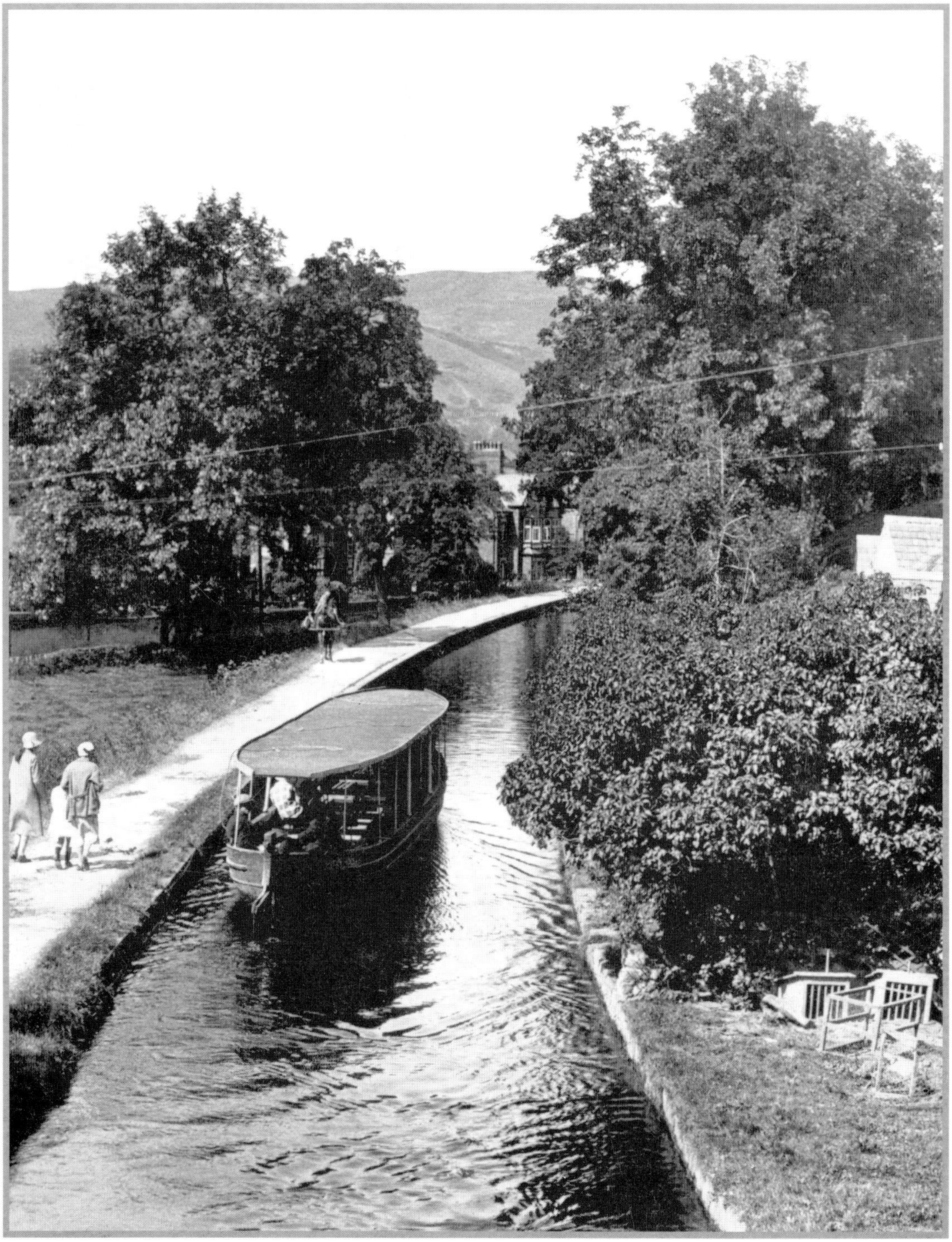

LLANGOLLEN, THE CANAL c1955 L76031
Long before the holiday boat industry took off, a trip behind a horse-drawn boat in Llangollen was a popular outing. The boats are towed to the end of the cruise and then both horse and rudder are moved to the opposite end for the return trip, thus solving the problem created by the lack of turning space.

Llangollen
The Canal c1955
A boat trip from Llangollen Wharf to the Horseshoe Falls is as popular today as it has ever been. This is probably the longest-lived operational horse-drawn trip boat on the canal system. The dog across the water is taking only a casual interest in the proceedings; he has seen it many times before.

Chirk
The Viaduct and the Aqueduct c1955
Here we see the Ceiriog river, which is also the border between England and Wales: the cameraman is on the Welsh side. 70ft above the river, the aqueduct was a most impressive stone structure built in 1801. Its majesty was attenuated somewhat when the Great Western Railway line from Wolverhampton to Chester came along and was built even higher.

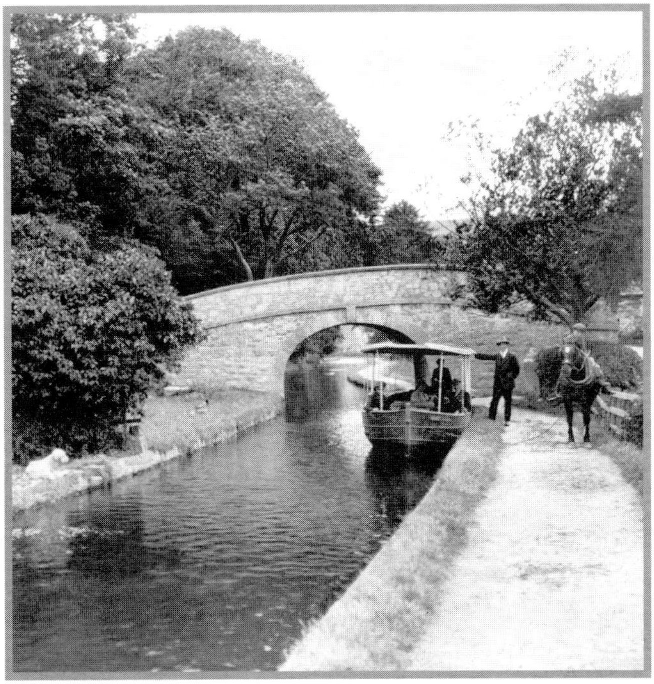

Llangollen, The Canal c1955 L76079

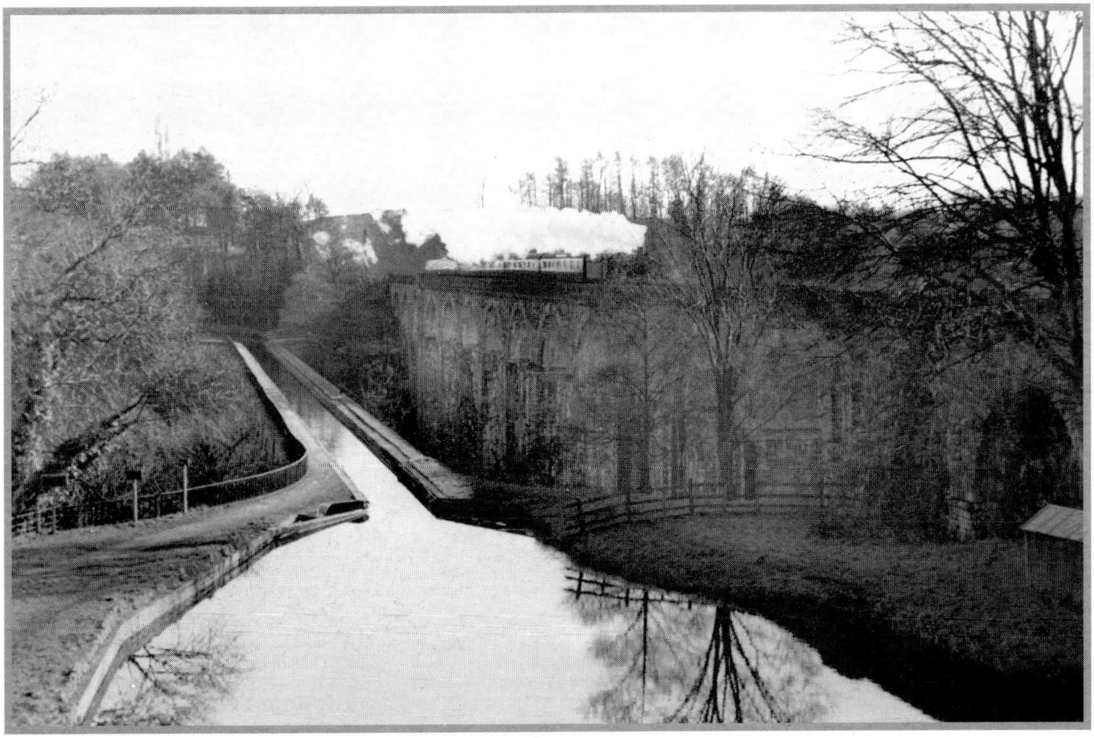

Chirk, The Viaduct and the Aqueduct c1955 C366039

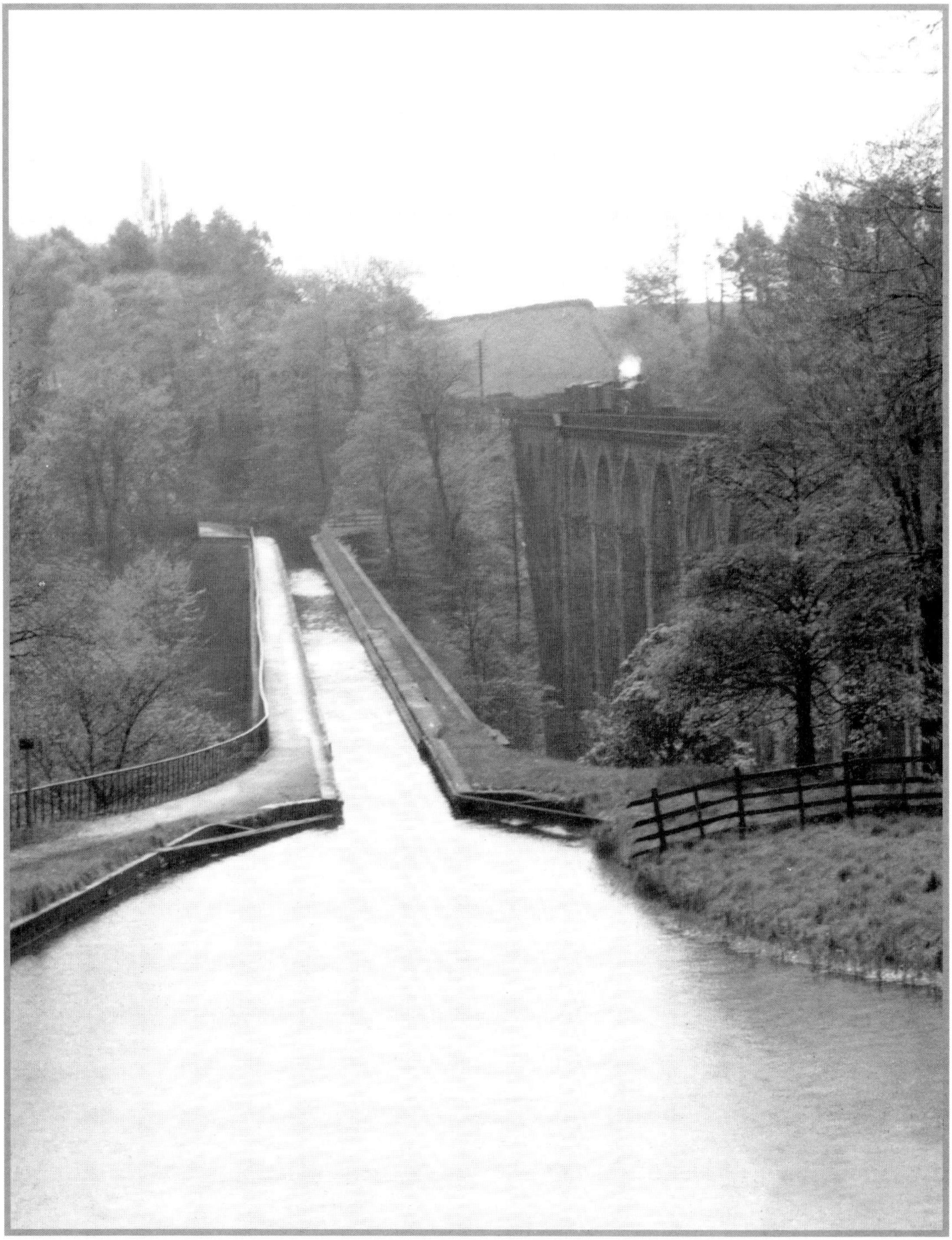

CHIRK, THE AQUEDUCT c1955 C366032

This view is similar to photograph No C366039, but with a different steam train on the viaduct. Of canal boats there is no sign. When this view was taken, the canal carrying age was over and the leisure boom had yet to explode. Directly under the cameraman's feet is the entrance to the 459-yard-long Chirk Tunnel.

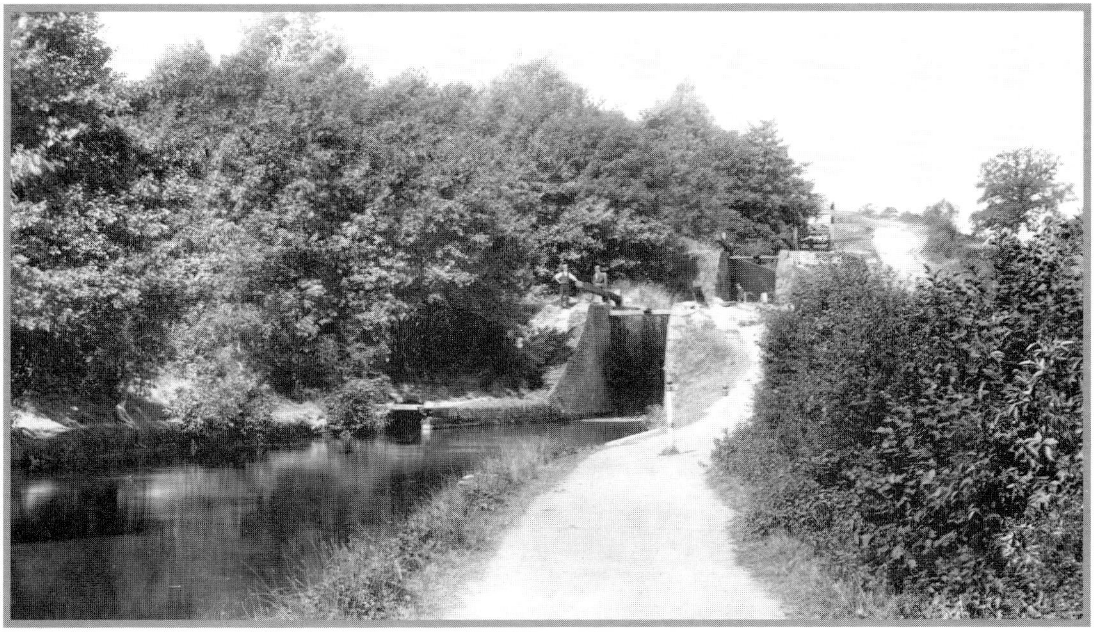

Newport, On the Canal, Fourteen Locks 1896 38707
The Monmouthshire Canal ran from Newport to Pontymoile with a branch to Crumlin, which is what we see illustrated. The fourteen locks at Rogerstone were still in use when this view was taken. They lift the canal 168ft by seven pairs of chambers; these are not staircase locks, which we have met before, but locks linked by a very short pound.

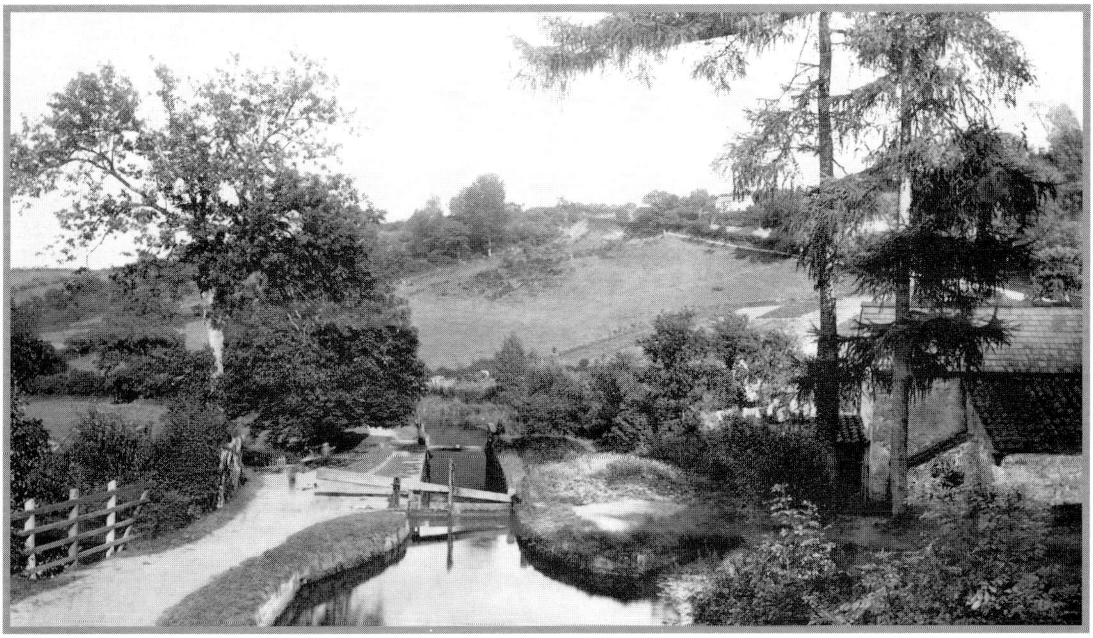

Newport, Allt-yr-yn, Above the Lock 1893 32637
Allt-yr-yn is the name of the hill in the distance. The lock chambers on this canal had their own individual size: 64ft 9in x 9ft 2ins - a most peculiar gauge. The canal became disused in 1930. At the top of the flight is a Visitor Centre with plenty of information, and it is possible to walk down the flight.

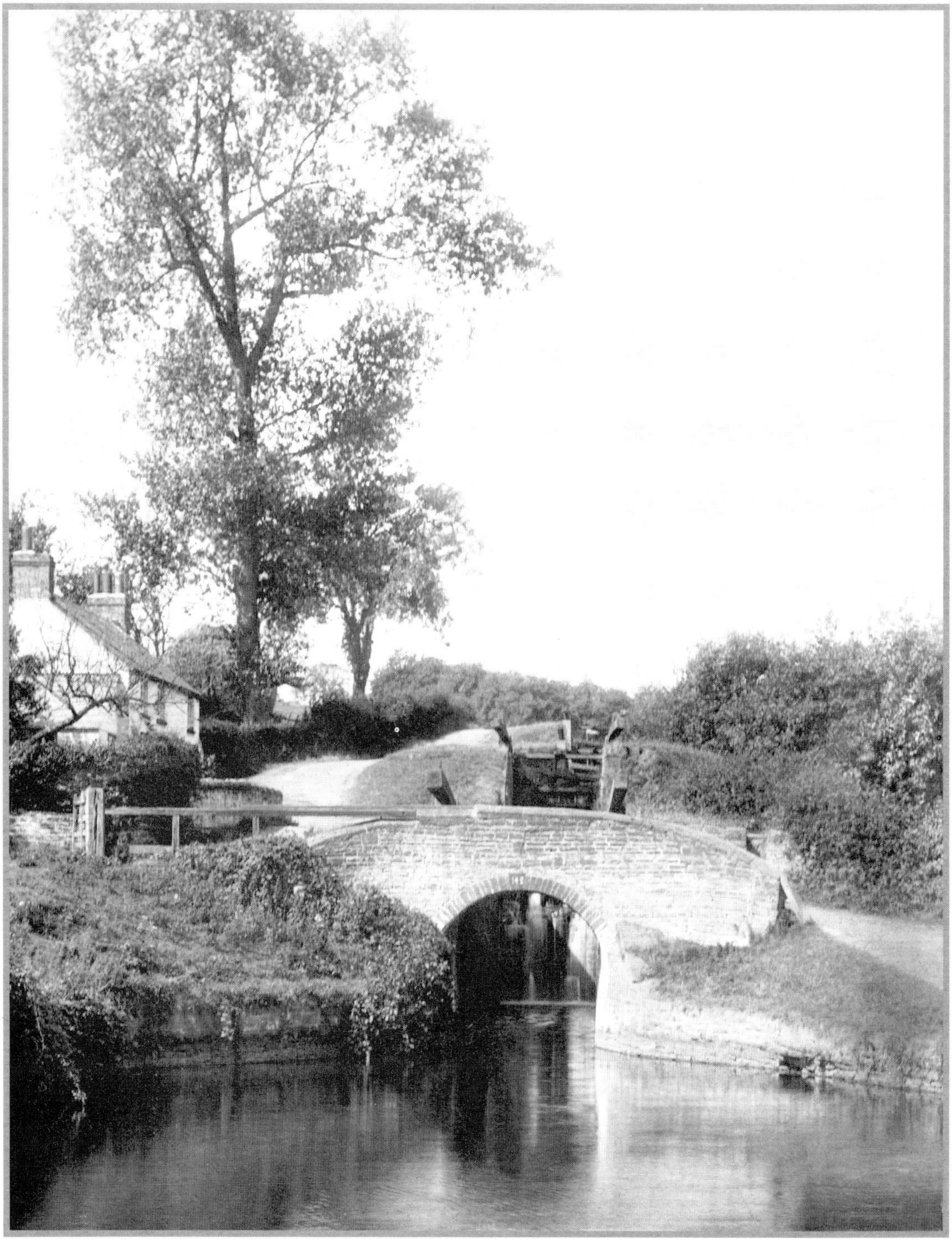

NEWPORT, ON THE CANAL 1896 38708
Although our long-dead photographer leaves us with no more information than that given, this is almost certainly another view of the Rogerstone Fourteen locks. The sobriquet 'Little Switzerland' is often added to the description of this area.

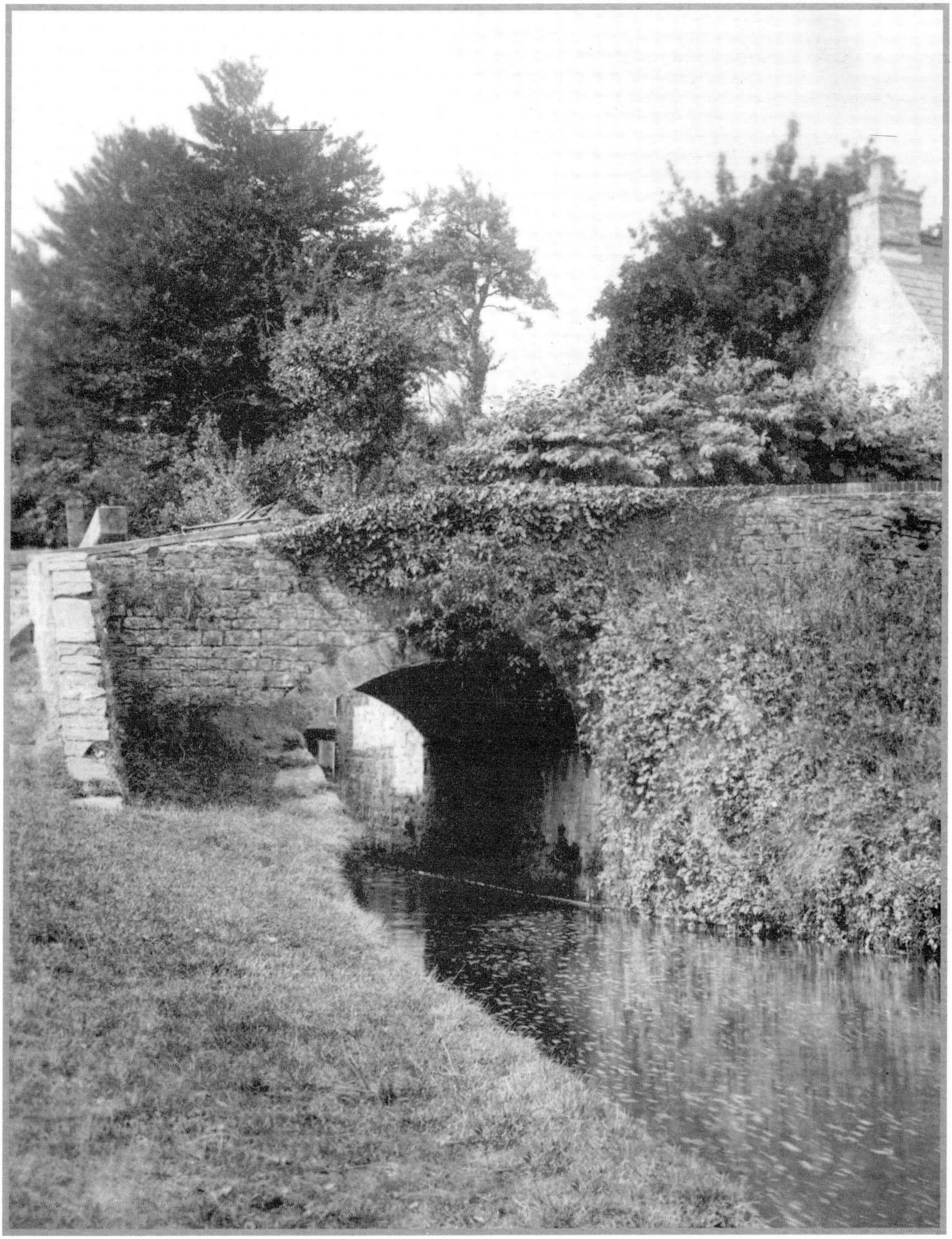

Brecon, On the Canal 1899 44733
The Brecknock and Abergavenny Canal ran south from Brecon to link with the Monmouthshire canal. When this picture was taken, the two had amalgamated and, in turn, had been taken over by the Great Western Railway. This is the entrance to Brynich Lock on the edge of Brecon.

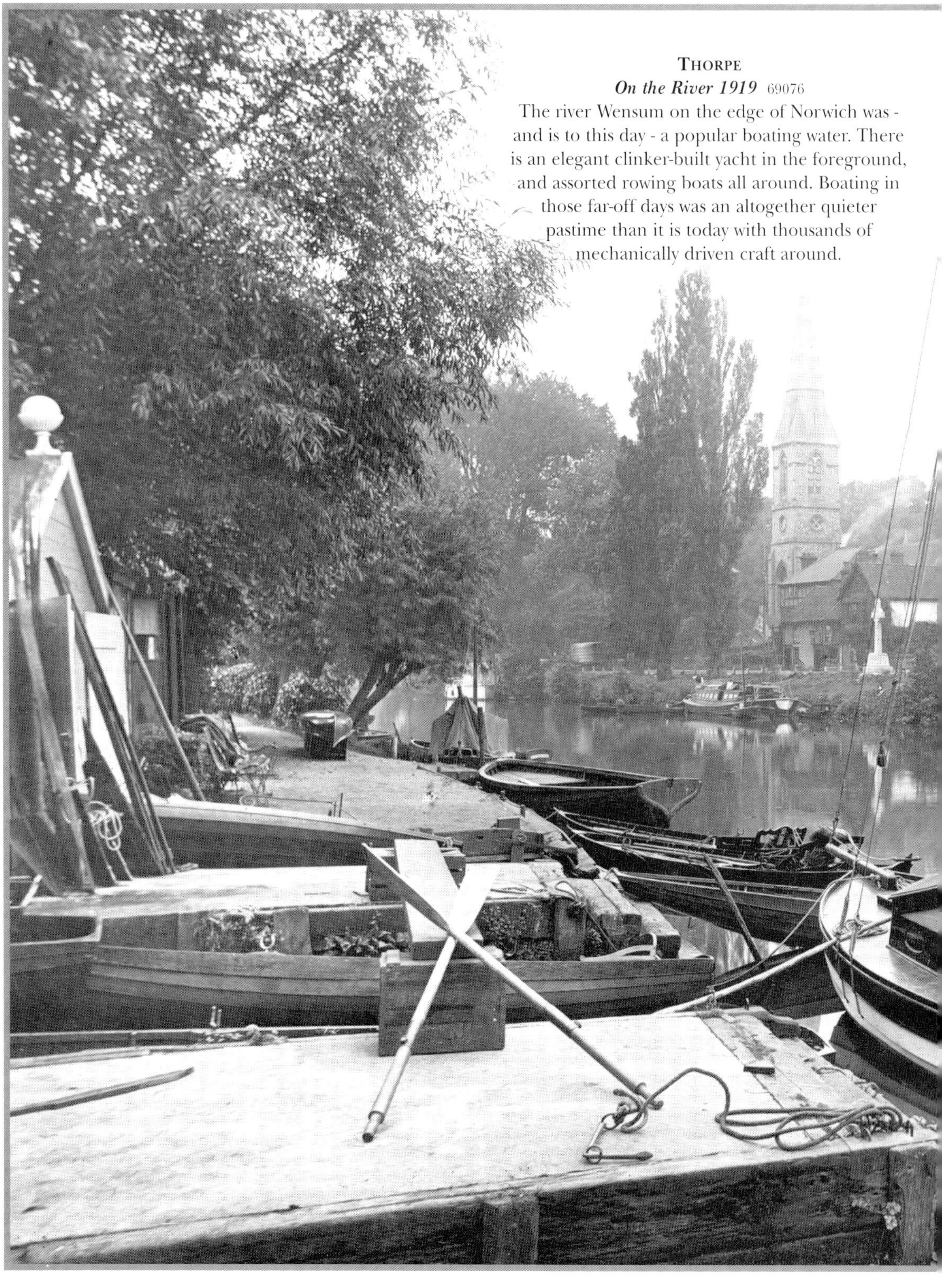

THORPE
On the River 1919 69076
The river Wensum on the edge of Norwich was - and is to this day - a popular boating water. There is an elegant clinker-built yacht in the foreground, and assorted rowing boats all around. Boating in those far-off days was an altogether quieter pastime than it is today with thousands of mechanically driven craft around.

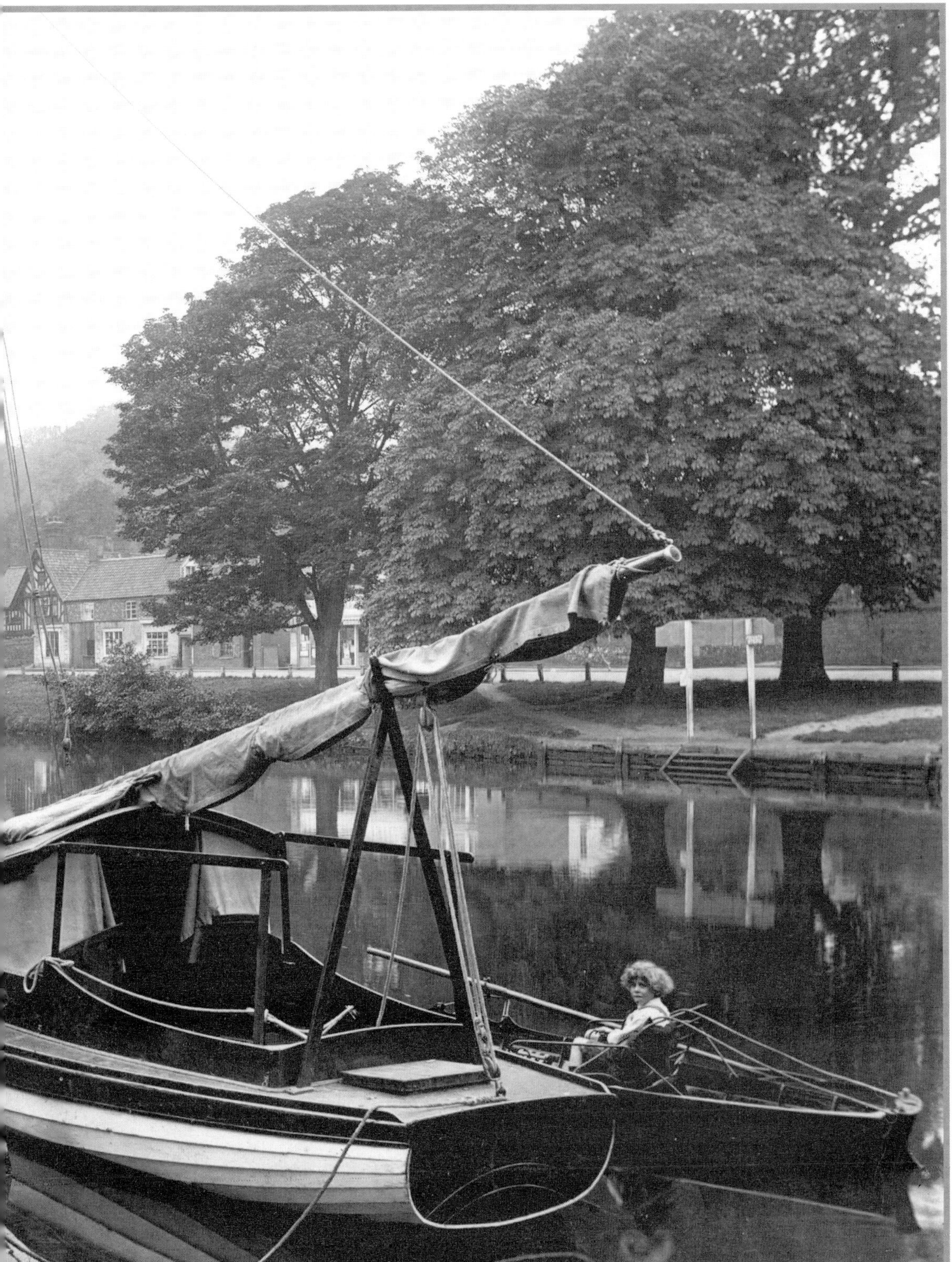

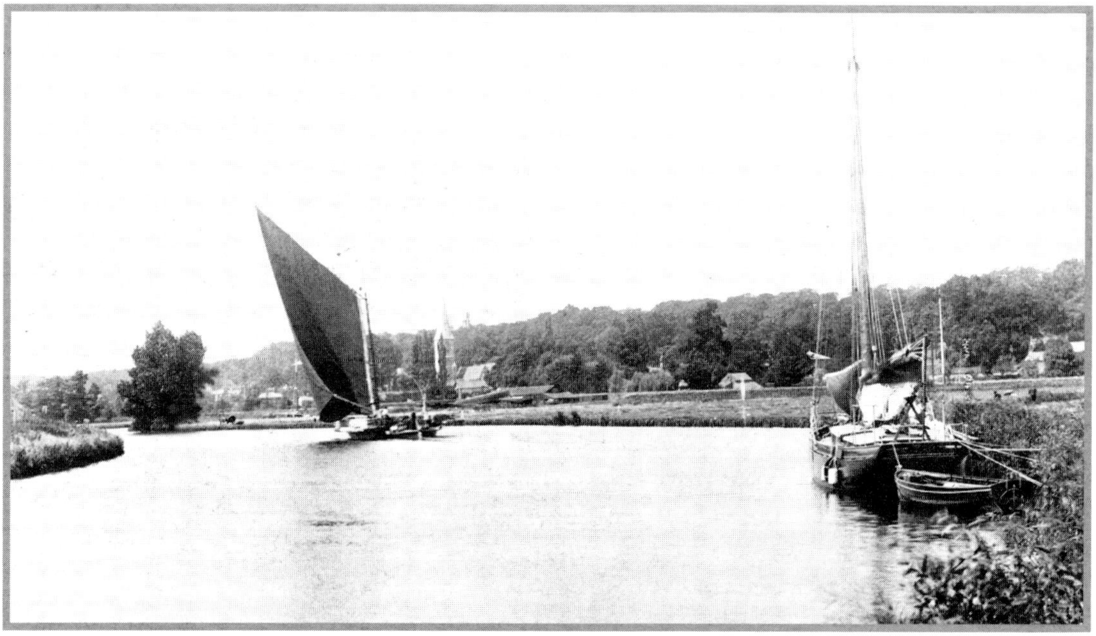

NORWICH, THORP REACH 1899 44478
Until the mid 20th century, the Norfolk sailing wherry was ubiquitous in these parts. Wherries carried both passengers and freight all around the rivers and broads of Norfolk. There are several preserved examples today, which seem like stately ladies in a world of modernity and rush.

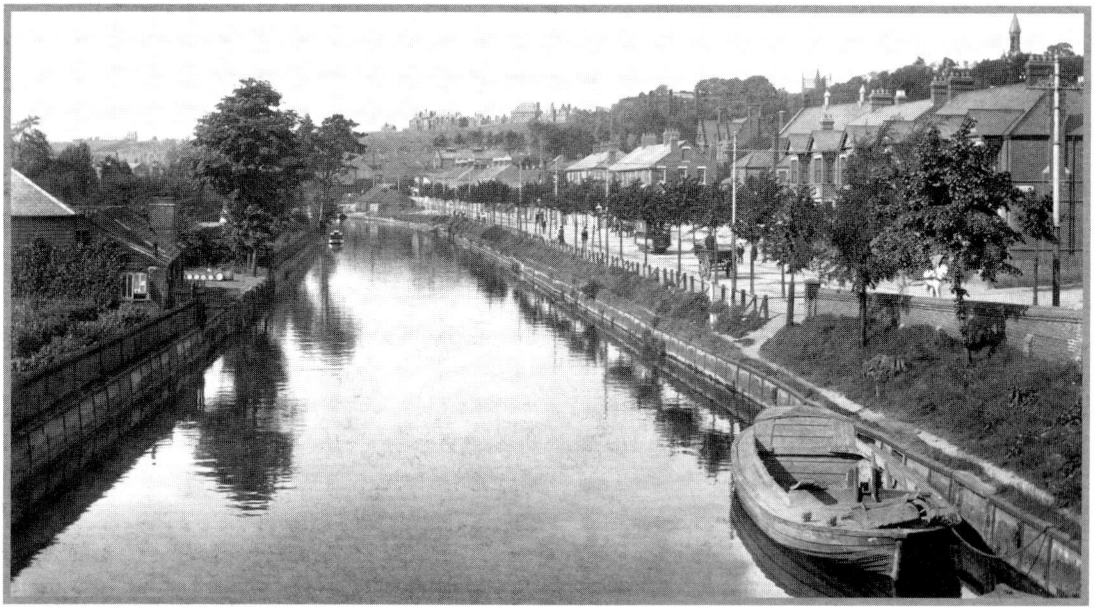

NORWICH, MOUSEHOLD HEATH AND THE RIVER WENSUM 1901 46678
The river runs along a neat channel here, but perhaps the greatest interest is alongside on the road. There are horses pulling carts and several pedestrians, but half hidden by the newly-planted trees is an electrically-powered single-decked tram car. The tall iron posts support the power wire. Amongst this modernity, there are still gas-fuelled street lights.

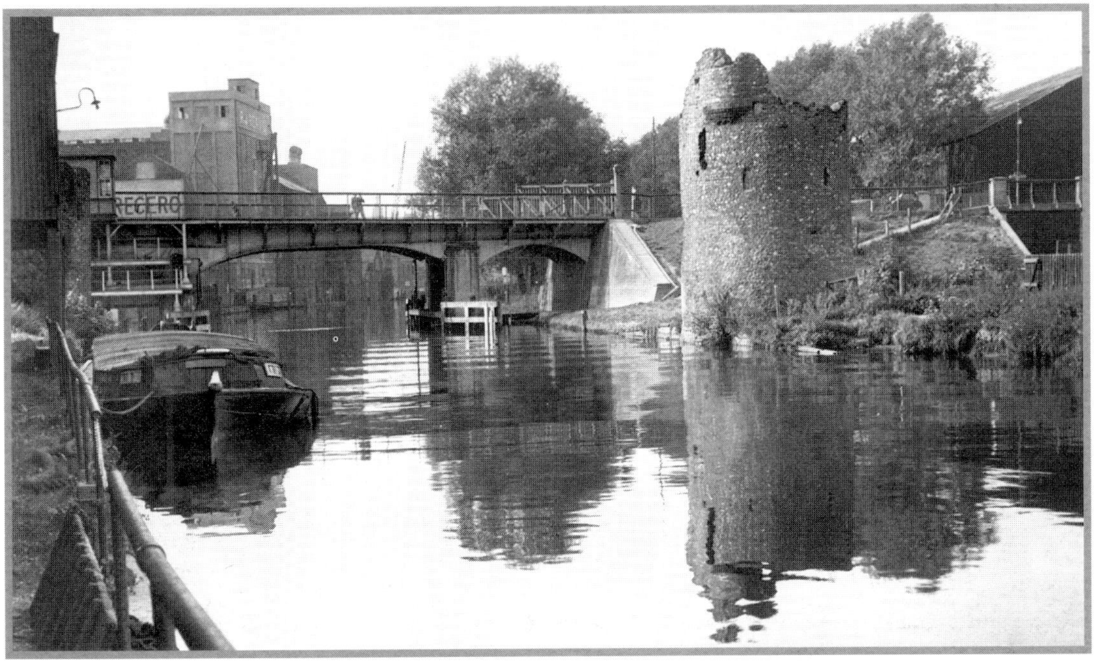

NORWICH, COW TOWER AND CARROW BRIDGE 1938 88664
Part of ancient Norwich, Cow Tower was once an integral part of the city wall. Much of this was dismantled in the 19th century, although it was reputedly in a poor state of repair. The area is now a pleasant waterside walk.

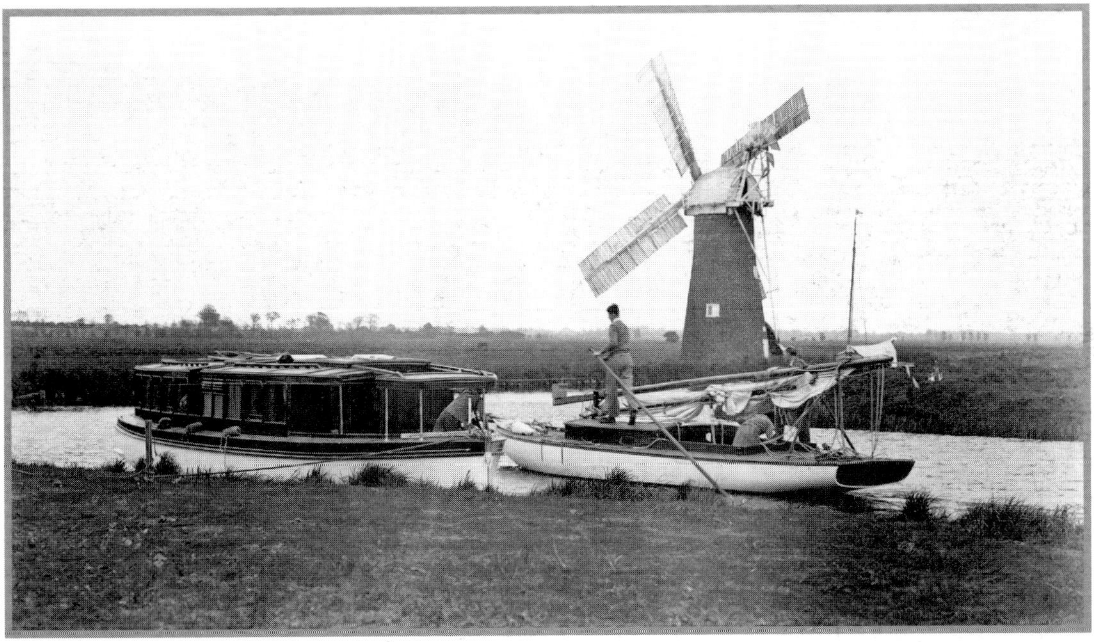

LUDHAM, THE WINDMILL c1955 L110083
There are windmills all over the Norfolk Broads. To give them their correct name, they are wind pumps, used to keep the water flowing from low-lying areas. A holiday cruiser is tied up as the yacht alongside poles out into the river before lifting his sail. This is known locally as 'quanting'.

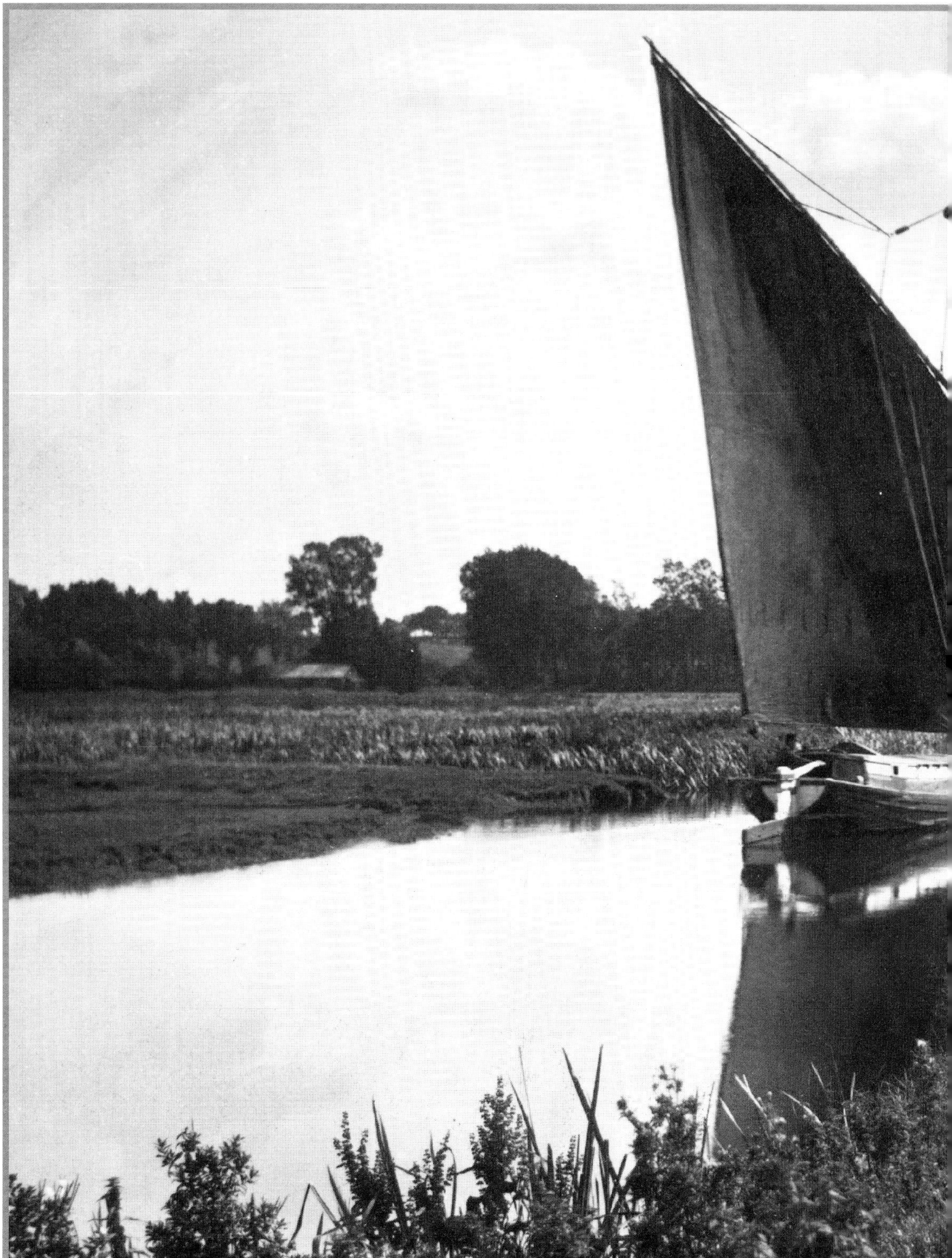

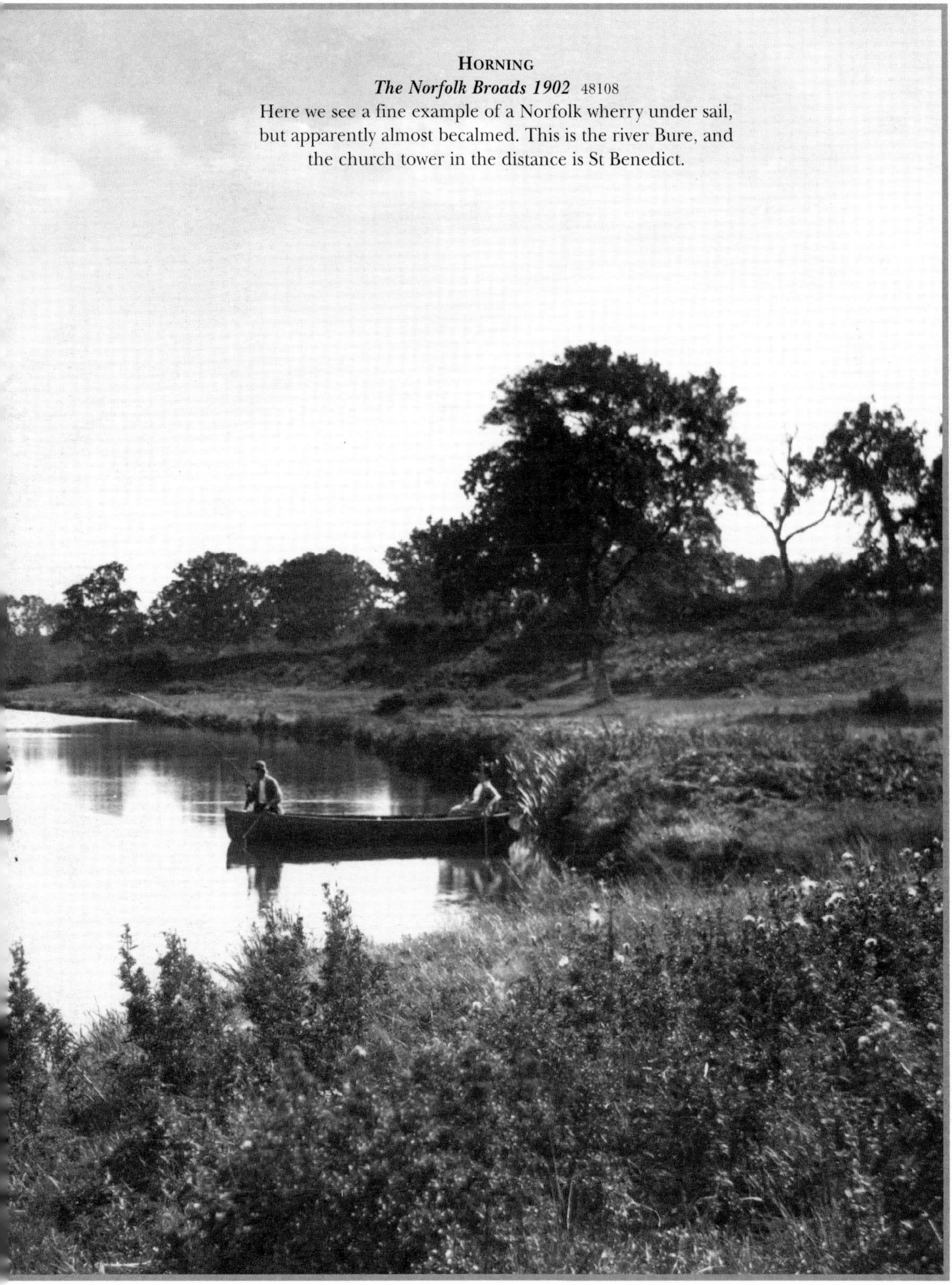

Horning

The Norfolk Broads 1902 48108

Here we see a fine example of a Norfolk wherry under sail, but apparently almost becalmed. This is the river Bure, and the church tower in the distance is St Benedict.

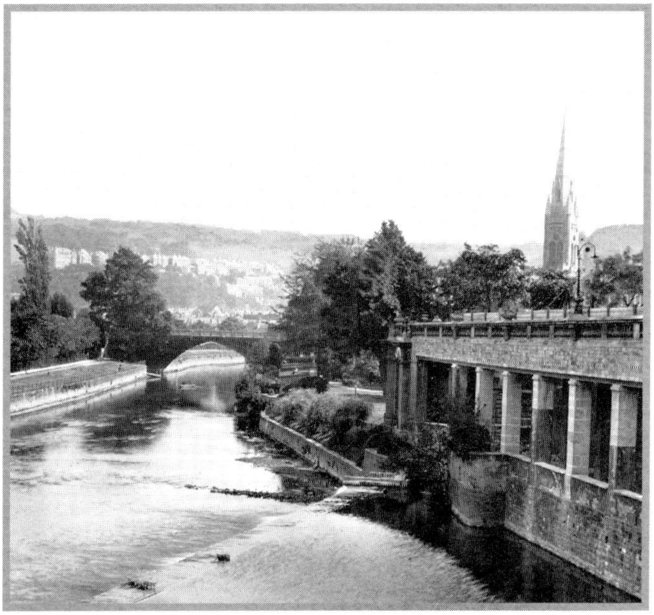

BATH, VIEW FROM PULTENEY BRIDGE 1914 67450

BATH

View from Pulteney Bridge 1914

Bath is, architecturally speaking, one of England's greatest cities. Established by the Romans on the banks of the river Avon, it was known to them as Aquae Sulis; the Roman bath-house is now open to visitors. The river here passes over a weir. Trip boats cruise above, pleasure boats below: and ne'er the twain shall meet.

BATH

The Old Bridge 1902

Attractive bridges over the Avon are part of Bath. This one is notable for its ironwork. Note how the street lights curve inwards in an attempt to get their feeble gas light towards the centre of the road.

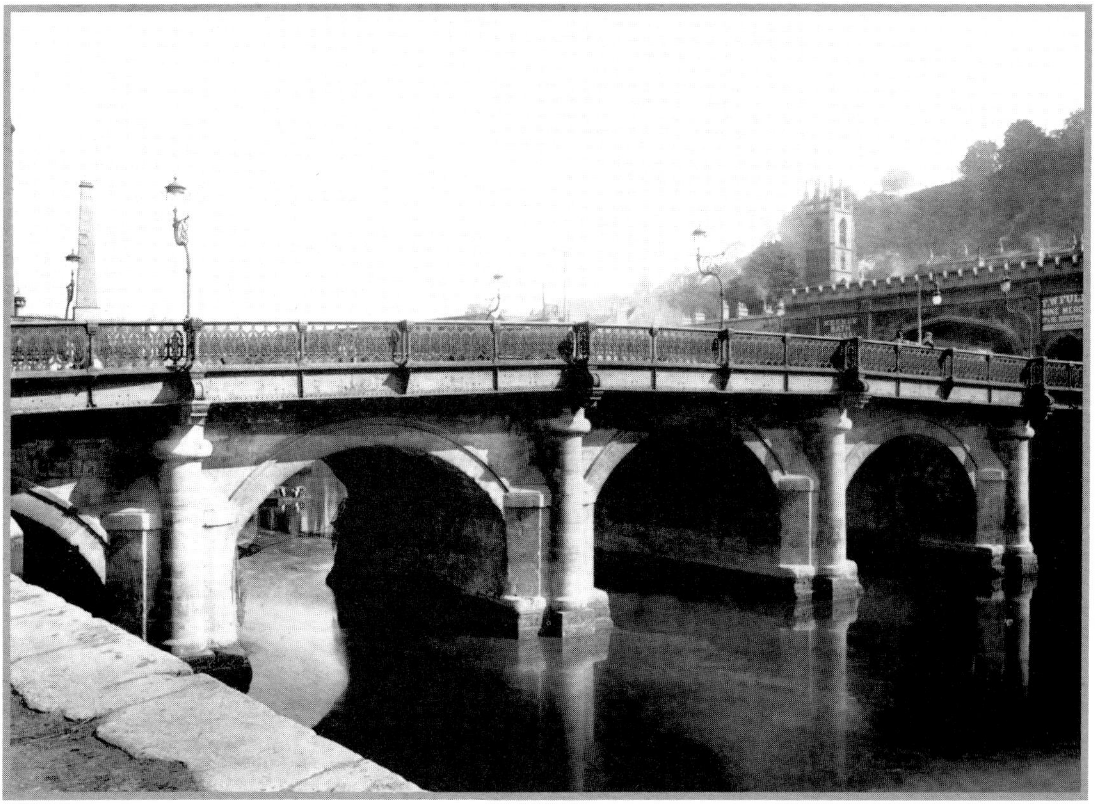

BATH, THE OLD BRIDGE 1902 48767

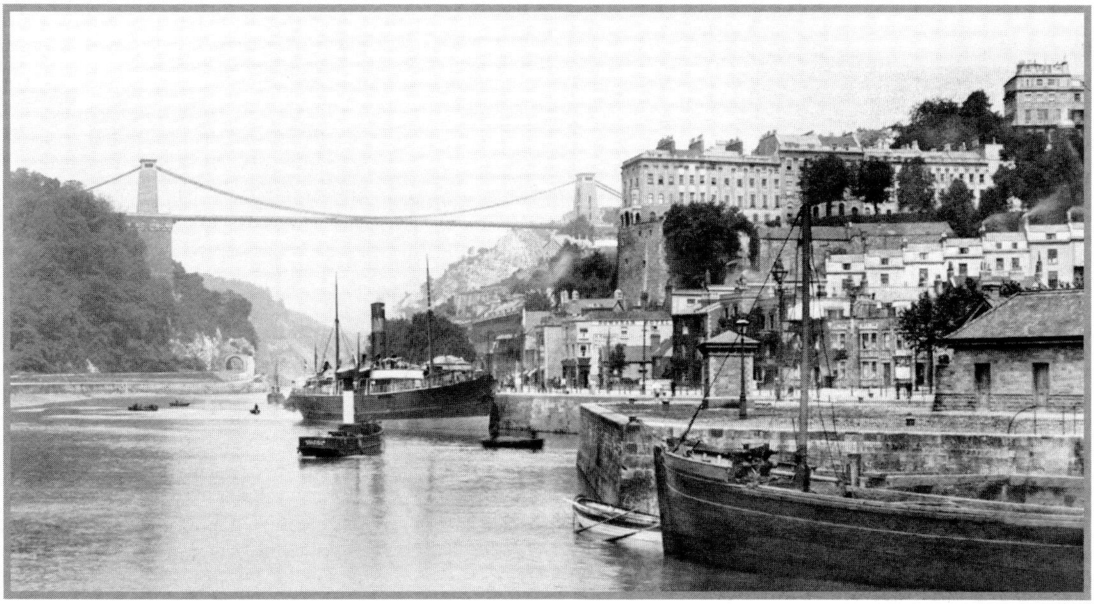

Clifton, The Suspension Bridge 1900 45555
Shipping still made its way up-river to Bristol when this photograph was taken. Today, the increase in size of vessels has led to a new port being created down-river at Avonmouth. Visiting ships now miss this magnificent suspension bridge. Designed by that great engineer Isambard Kingdom Brunel, it stands 245 feet above the river. Construction started in 1836, but owing to a shortage of funds, the bridge was not completed until 1864, six years after Brunel died.

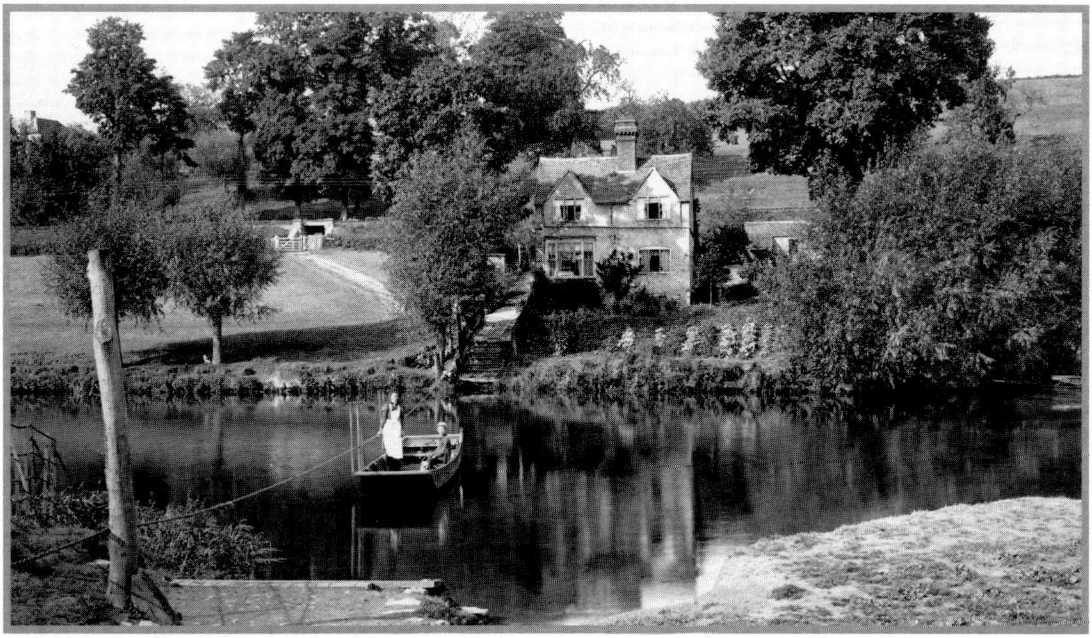

Evesham, Hampton Ferry 1895 36969
It is remarkable that more than a century after this photograph was taken, Hampton Ferry, to the west of Evesham, still exists, and it still operates in the same way: a cable is strung across the river and the ferryman pulls his boat across. Because of the volume of boating traffic, the cable now tends to be under water except when it is needed.

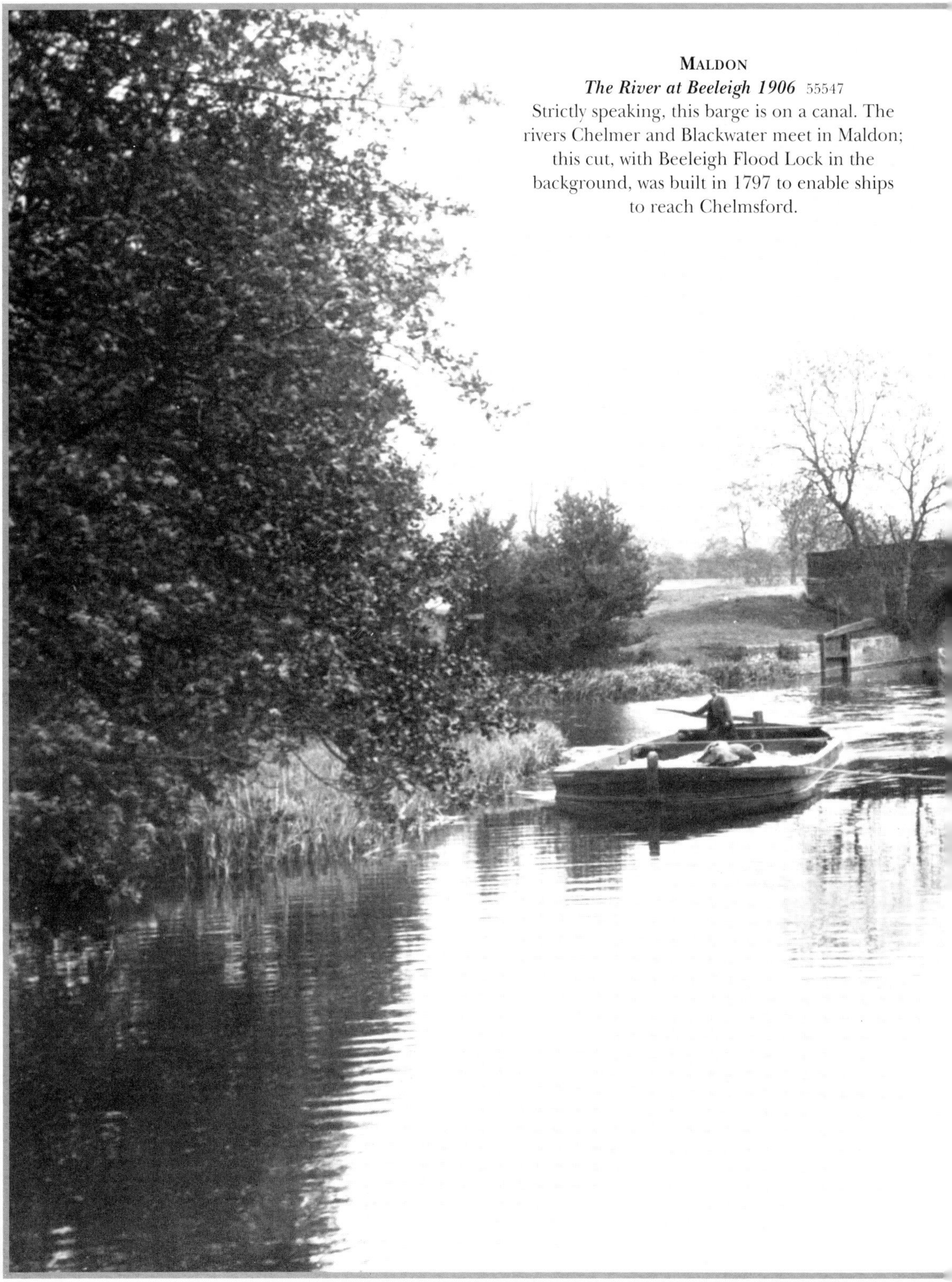

MALDON

The River at Beeleigh 1906 55547

Strictly speaking, this barge is on a canal. The rivers Chelmer and Blackwater meet in Maldon; this cut, with Beeleigh Flood Lock in the background, was built in 1797 to enable ships to reach Chelmsford.

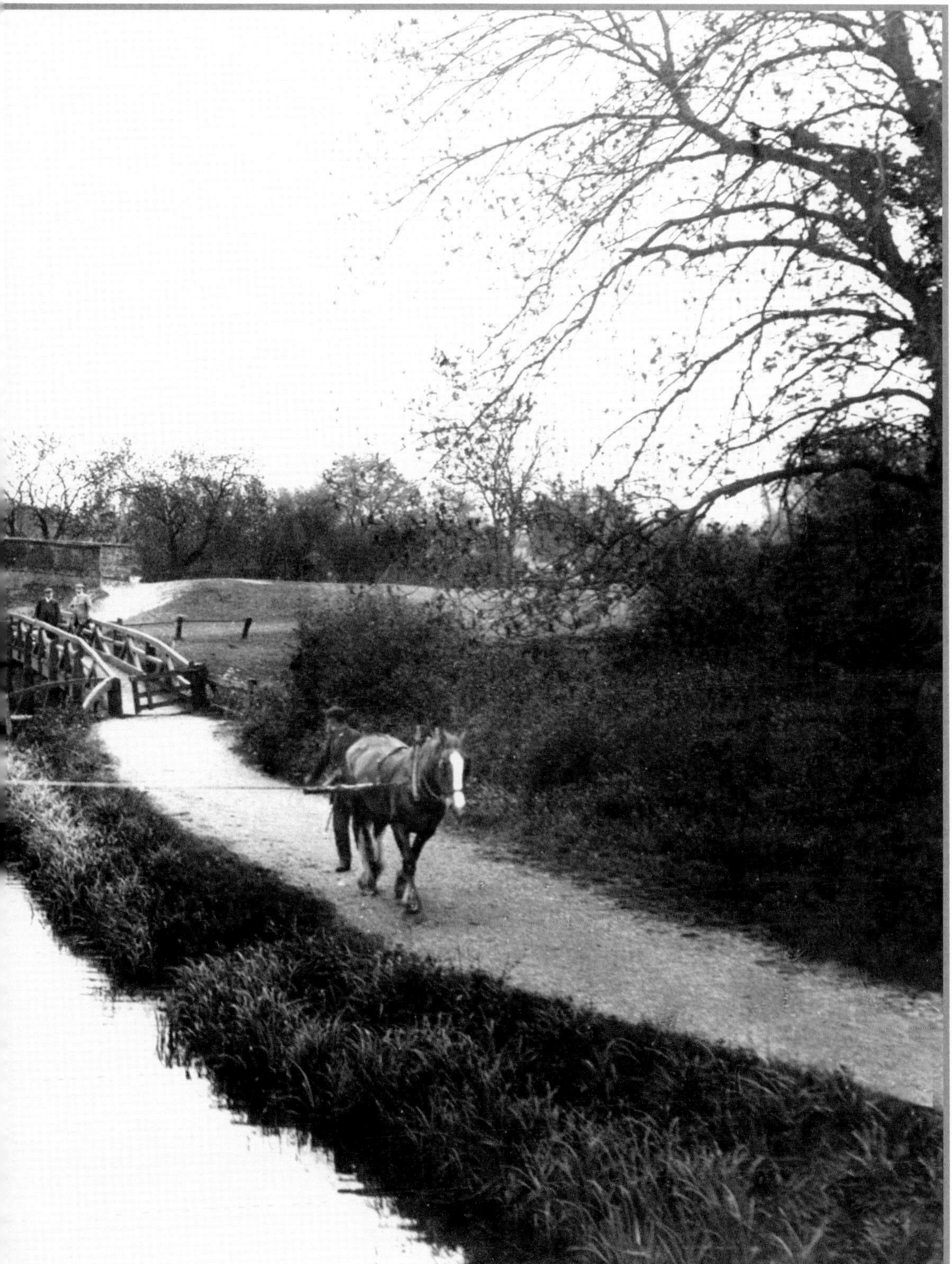

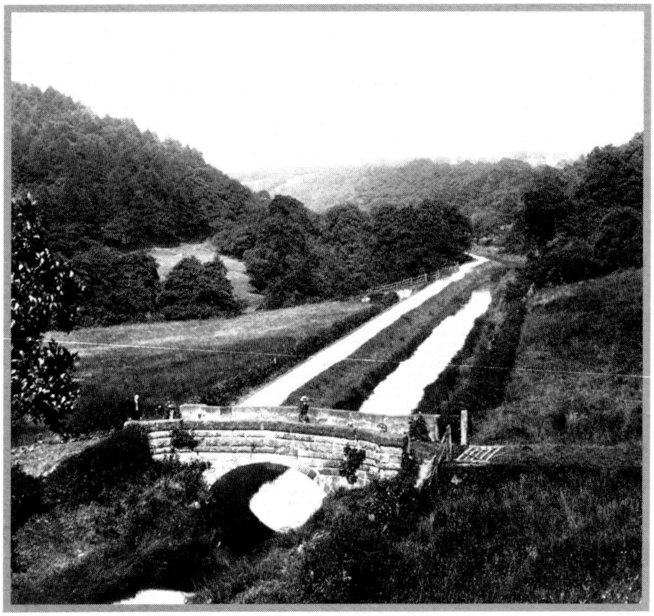

CONGLETON, DANE VALLEY BRIDGE 1898 42175

CONGLETON

Dane Valley Bridge 1898

Rising high in the Macclesfield Forest part of the Peak District, the river Dane heads west for some thirty miles before emptying into the river Weaver near Northwich. A most attractive stretch of water, especially in its upper reaches, it offers recreation both for walkers and fishermen.

WARE

The Canal c1965

The Lee and Stort Navigation north of London is a series of short canals linking the eponymous rivers. In this view, it is about to enter a canalised section in the industrial end of Ware.

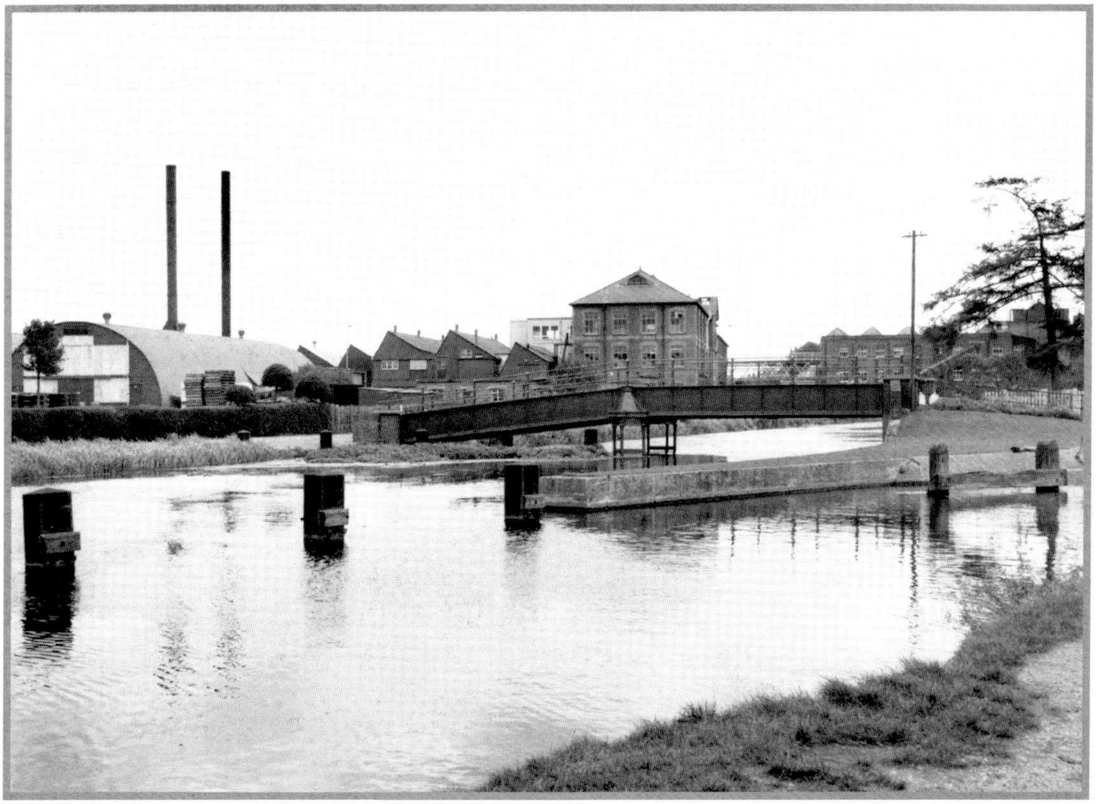

WARE, THE CANAL c1965 W24069

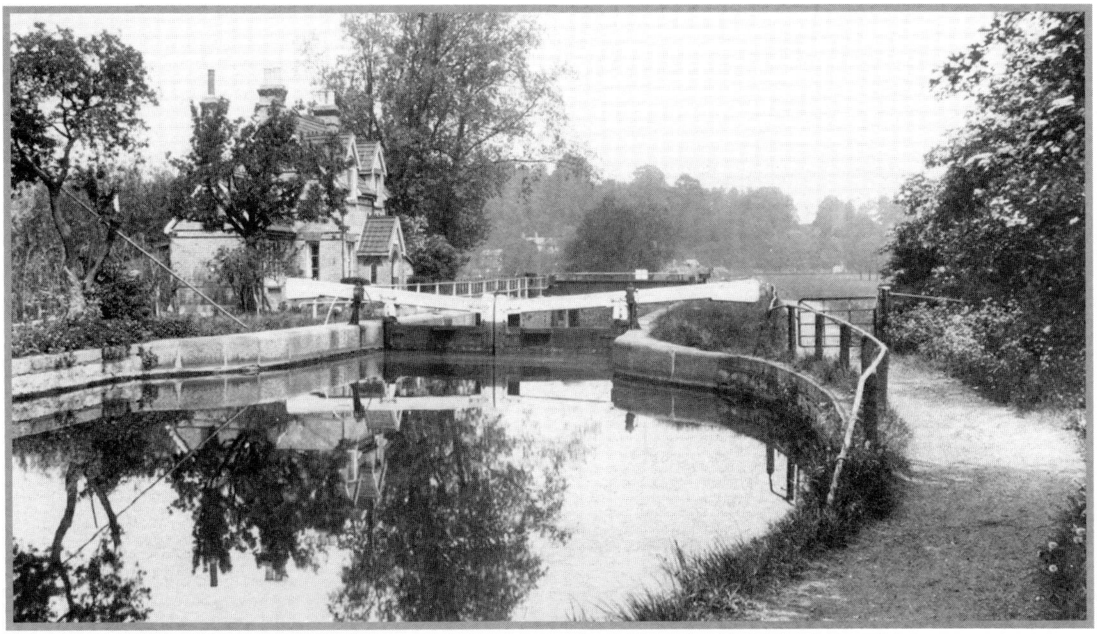

HERTFORD, THE LOCK 1920 81783

Hertford Lock is not in quite such a rural setting today. Some industry has now encroached to the right hand side, but the woodland has survived. Noise pollution is a problem now, with the buzz of the nearby M11 motorway omnipresent.

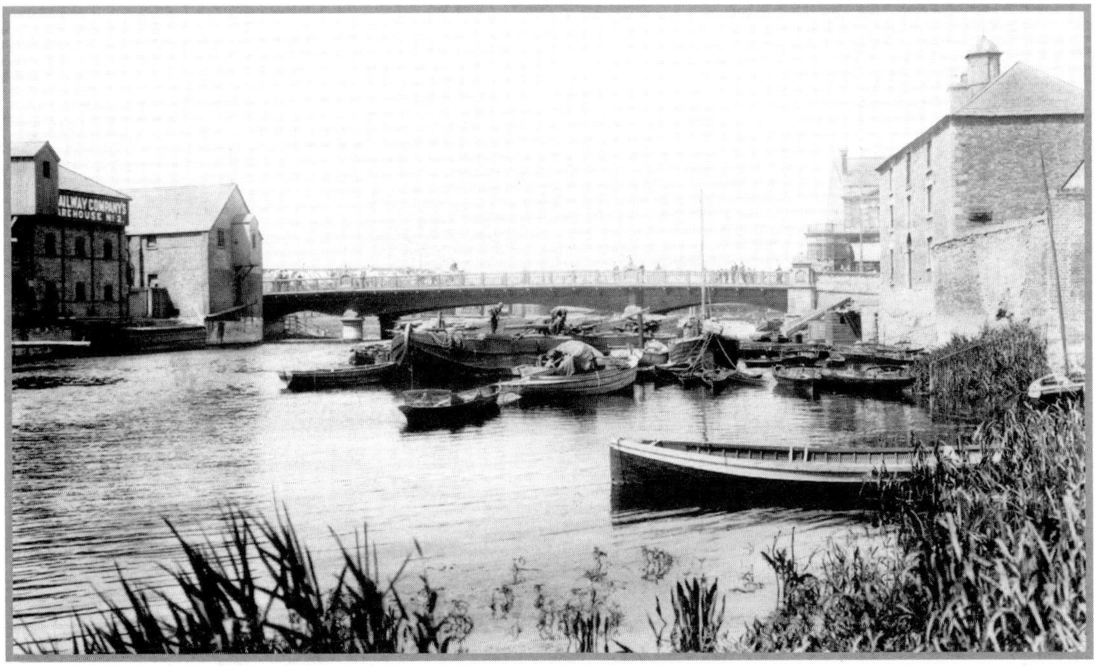

PETERBOROUGH, THE TOWN BRIDGE 1904 51560

This scene is now completely destroyed. The river still runs through the centre of Peterborough, but the old railway warehouses on the left are no more, and the rowing boats for hire on the extreme right have gone the same way.

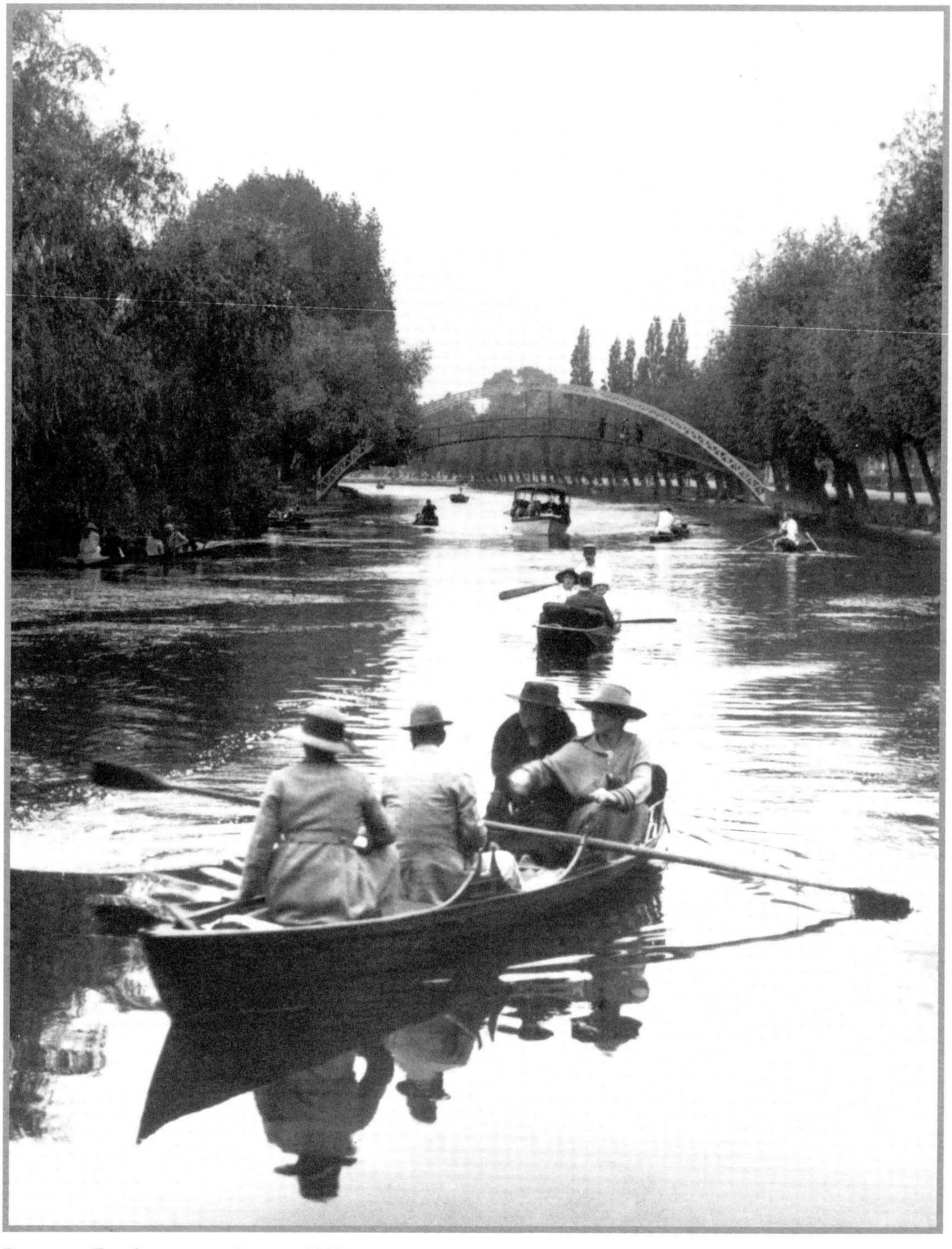

BEDFORD, THE SUSPENSION BRIDGE 1921 70446

The river Great Ouse in Bedford is as popular today with boaters, walkers and fishermen as it was eighty years ago when this picture was taken. The suspension bridge and park to the right are virtually unchanged, and you can usually see boaters out on the water.

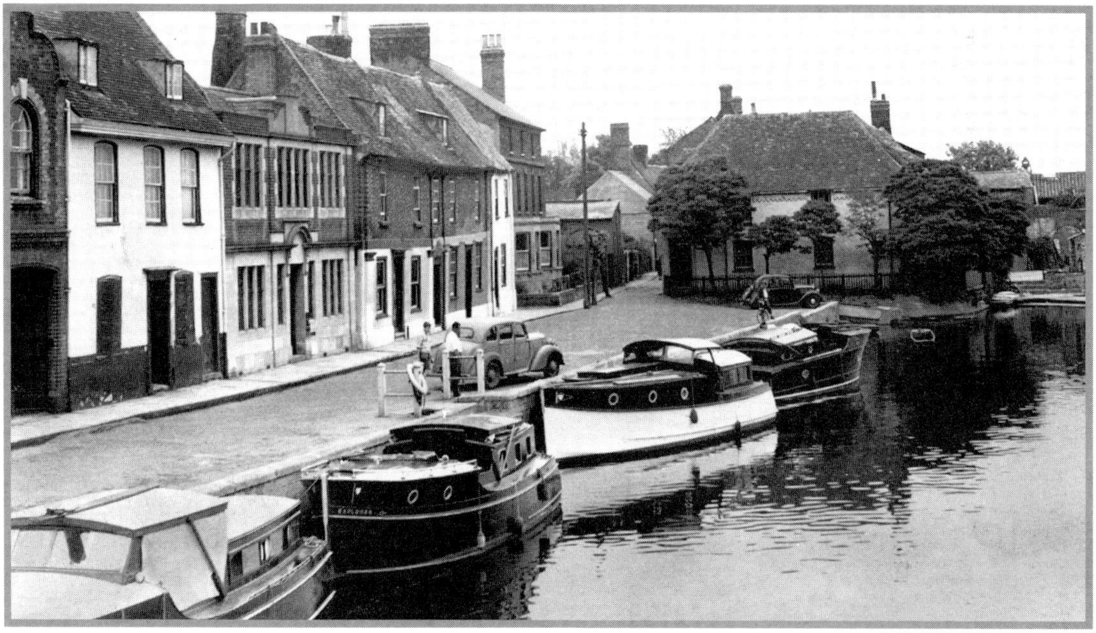

St Ives, The Quay c1955 S23005

Here we see an assortment of old holiday cruisers tied up at the quay in St Ives. Note the identical fold-back roofs fitted to each boat. This allowed everyone in the centre cockpit maximum exposure to the East Anglian weather. For centuries, the river was the lifeline of this attractive town.

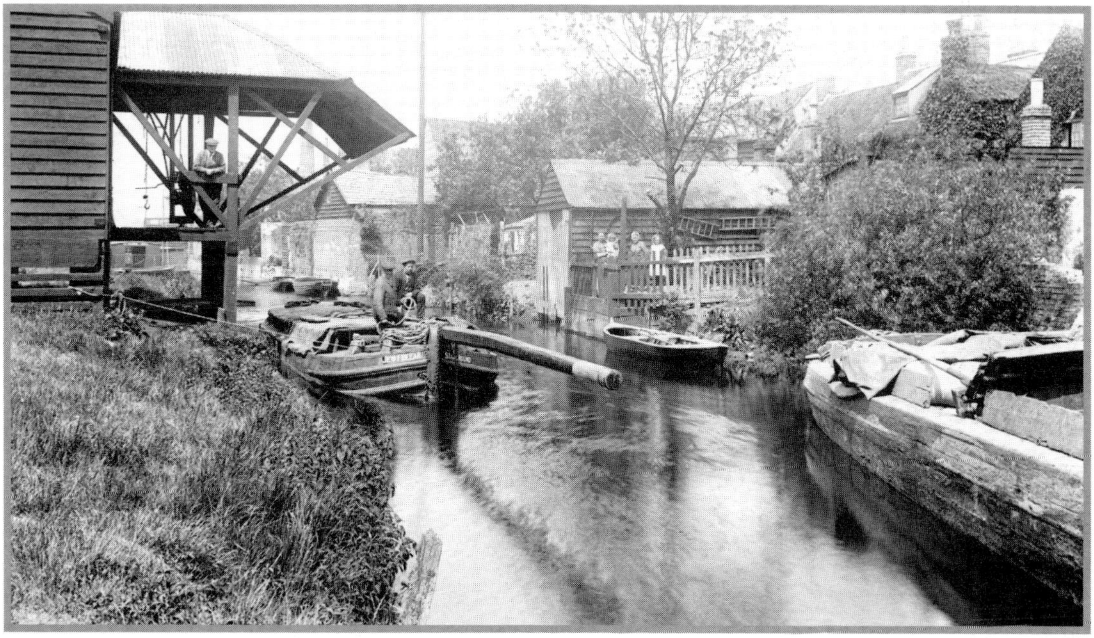

St Ives, The Old River 1914 66958

Even though the railway age was at its height, freight was still carried on the river Great Ouse, as can be seen from this view. The corrugated canopy on the left-hand building provided rudimentary shelter for both crew and cargo. Our cameraman seems to be attracting attention from the boat crew and the family across the water.

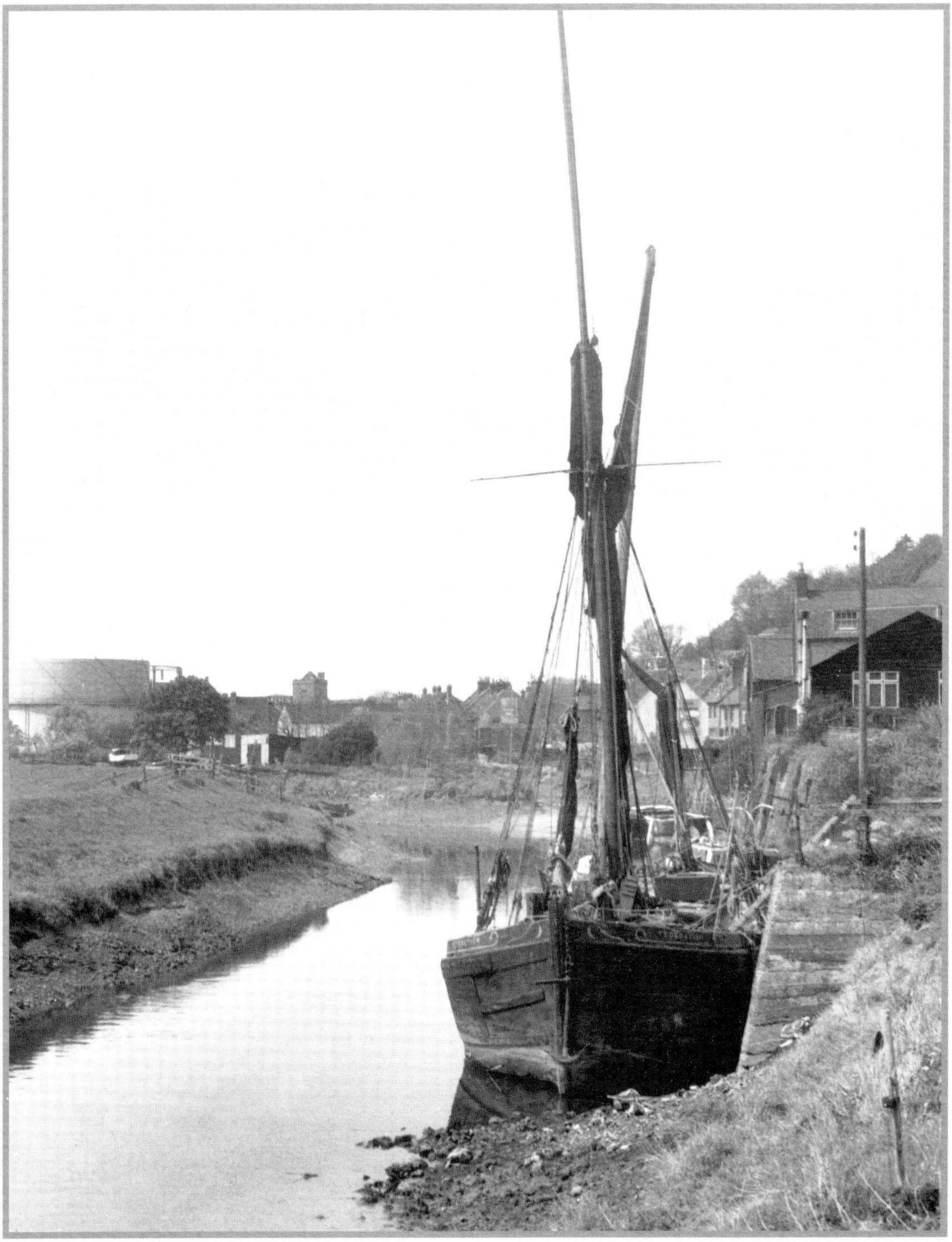

LEWES, THE RIVER c1960 L40080

The sailing vessel 'Federation' ties up close to the centre of Lewes, on the Ouse in East Sussex. As can be seen from the narrow water here, navigation is not what it was, although barges traded up to the cement works here right to the 1950s. There is scant boating activity on this tidal water today.

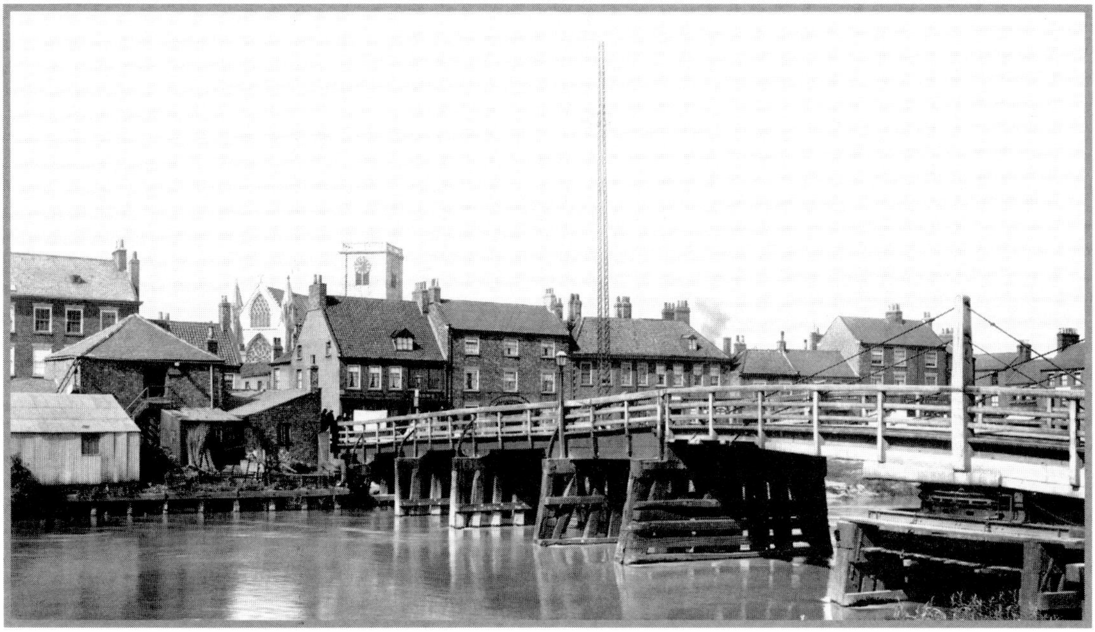

Selby, The Toll Bridge 1901 48027
This dilapidated structure still crosses the Yorkshire Ouse at Selby. The tide here is fierce, roaring up and down at several knots. Under the right-hand section of the bridge, the swivelling mechanism can be seen. This opens the bridge to river traffic, now but a shadow of what it was.

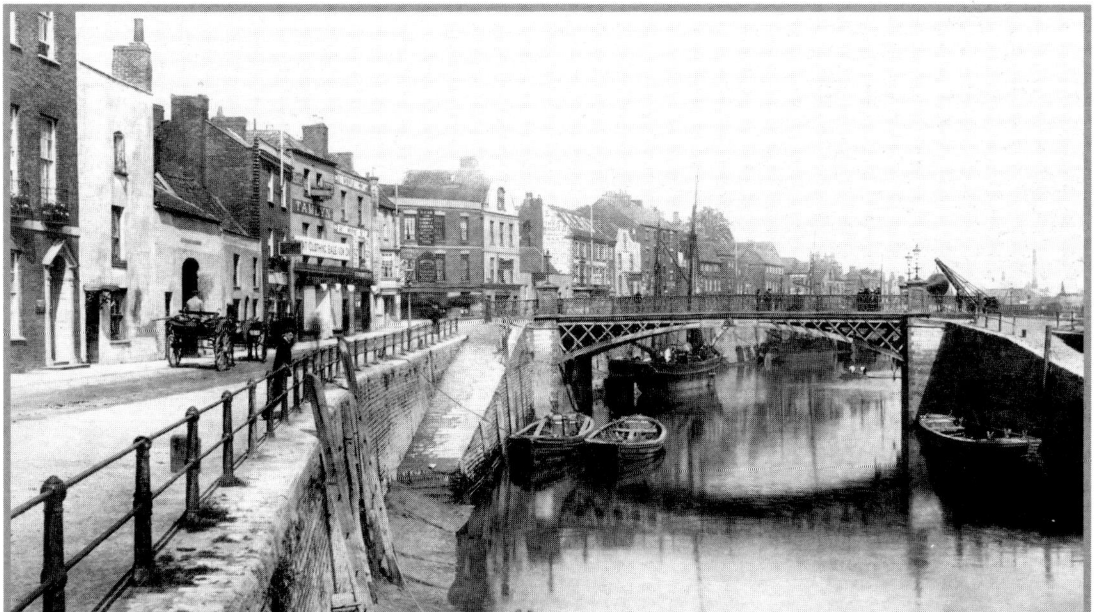

Bridgwater, The Bridge 1903 50451
In years gone by, the river Parrett carried a large volume of traffic. Although the Town Bridge was the limit for fixed-masted vessels, barges and similar vessels could - and did - trade up-river as far as Langport.

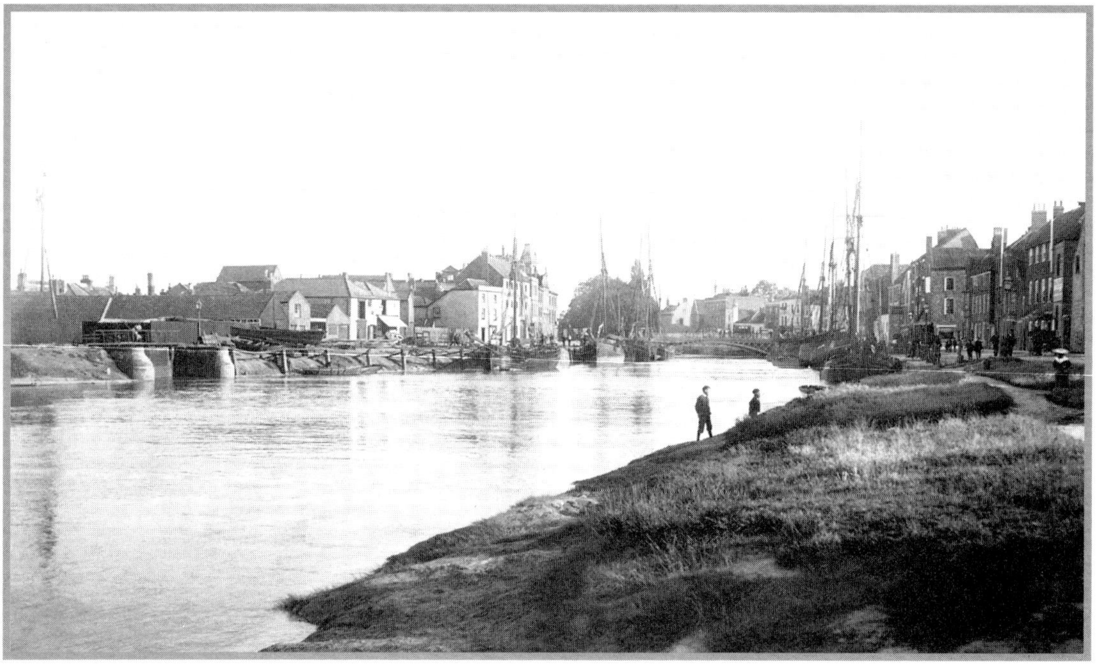

BRIDGWATER, THE RIVER PARRETT 1897 39998
This view shows the shipping staithes at Bridgwater, this time downstream from the Town Bridge. Inevitably, the town is much changed now, with made-up roads, much more building - and no ships.

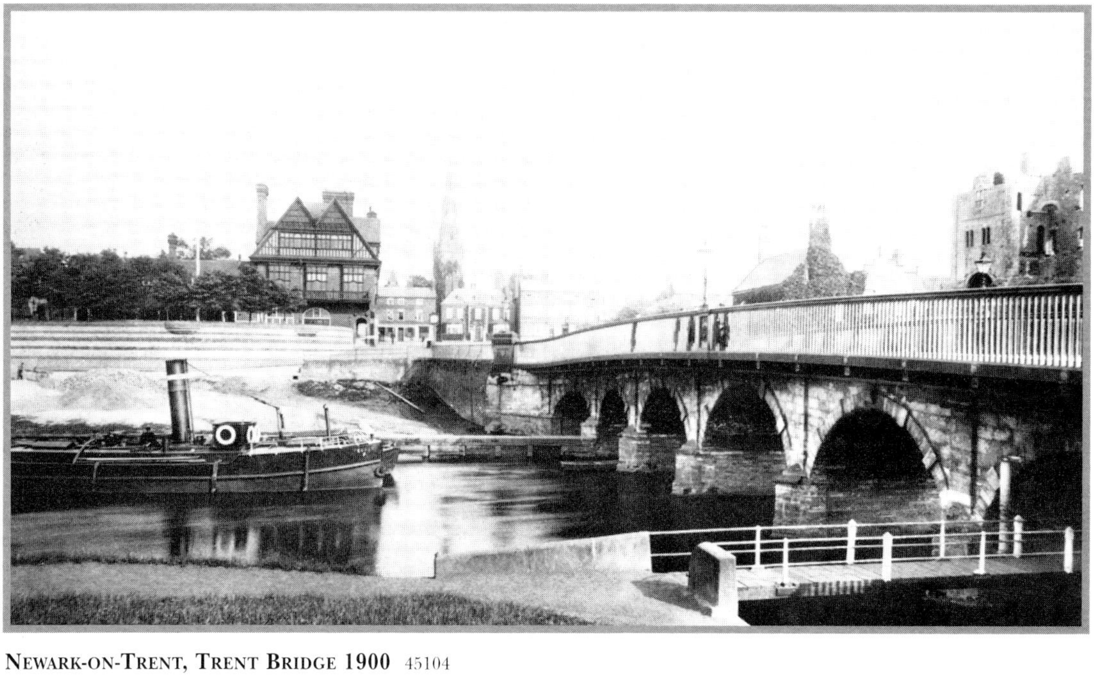

NEWARK-ON-TRENT, TRENT BRIDGE 1900 45104
For centuries, the Trent has been a water highway, carrying cargo up from the North Sea coastal ports. The bridge (right) is listed as an Ancient Monument. Beyond is the castle where King John died in 1216, the year after Magna Carta. The spire of S. Mary Magdalene (centre) is 240 ft tall.

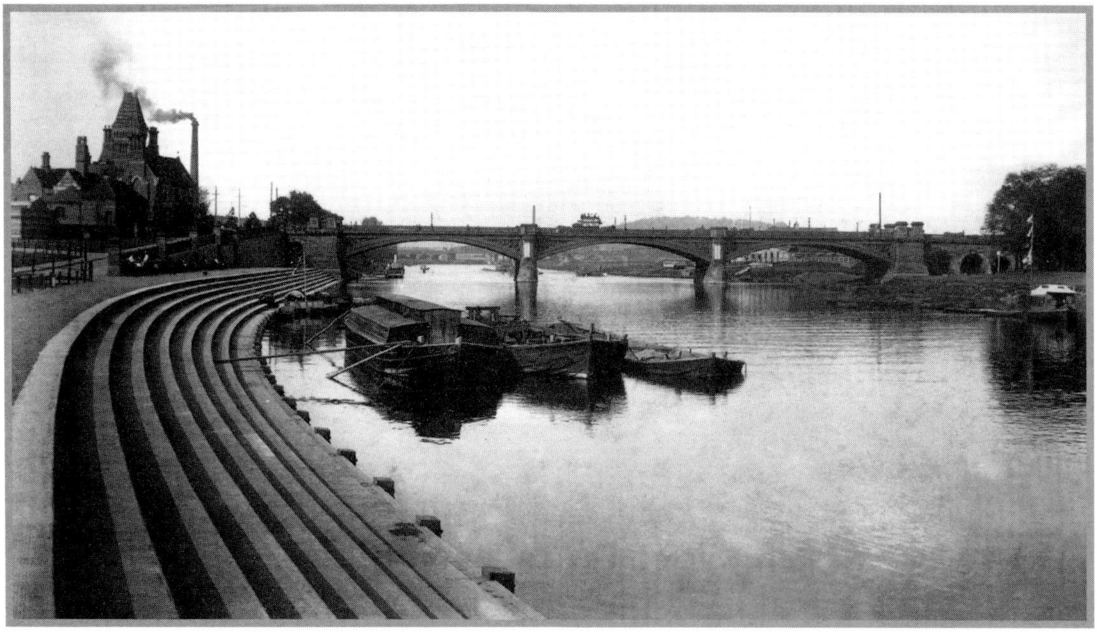

NOTTINGHAM, TRENT BRIDGE 1902 48329
This area of Nottingham around the river Trent is probably best known today for its sporting connections. Nottingham Forest and Notts County soccer teams are based here, as is the Nottinghamshire County Cricket Club. Forest and the Cricket Club are to the right beyond the bridge, Notts County to the left.

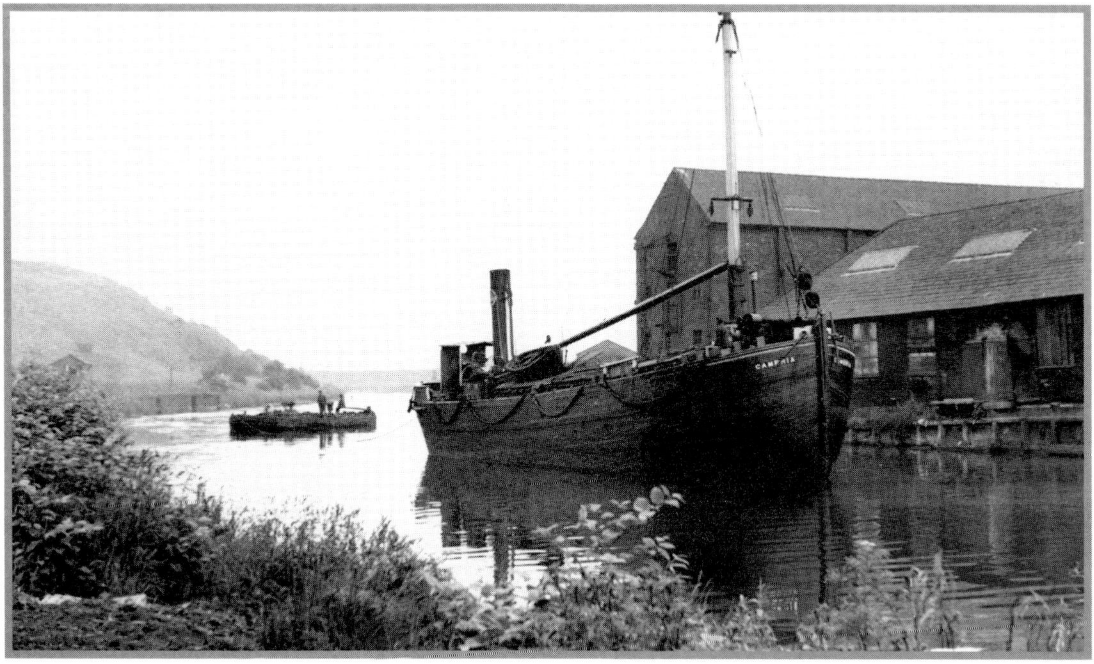

NORTHWICH, THE RIVER WEAVER c1955 N43011
Commercial traffic on the Weaver lasted for years. Northwich was noted for its chemical production - particularly salt. Now, most of its traffic travels by road, and this delightfully evocative scene is no more.

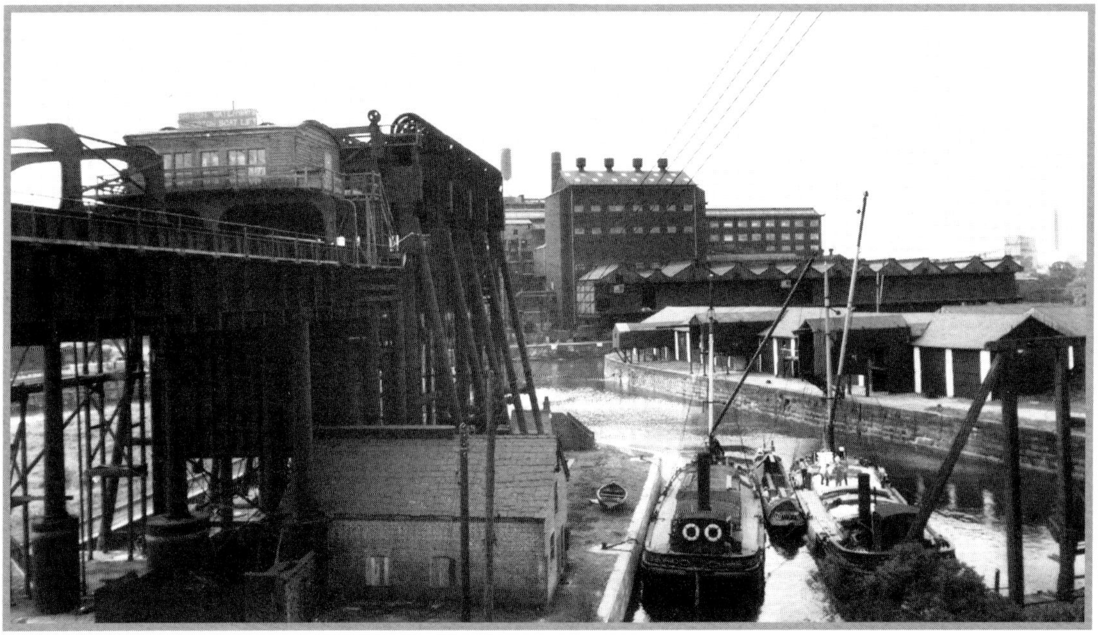

NORTHWICH, ANDERTON BOAT LIFT c1960 N43026
The Anderton Boat Lift linked the Trent & Mersey Canal (above) with the river Weaver below. Narrowboats entered a caisson along the trough to the left and were lowered down to the river. One such can be seen sandwiched between two barges.

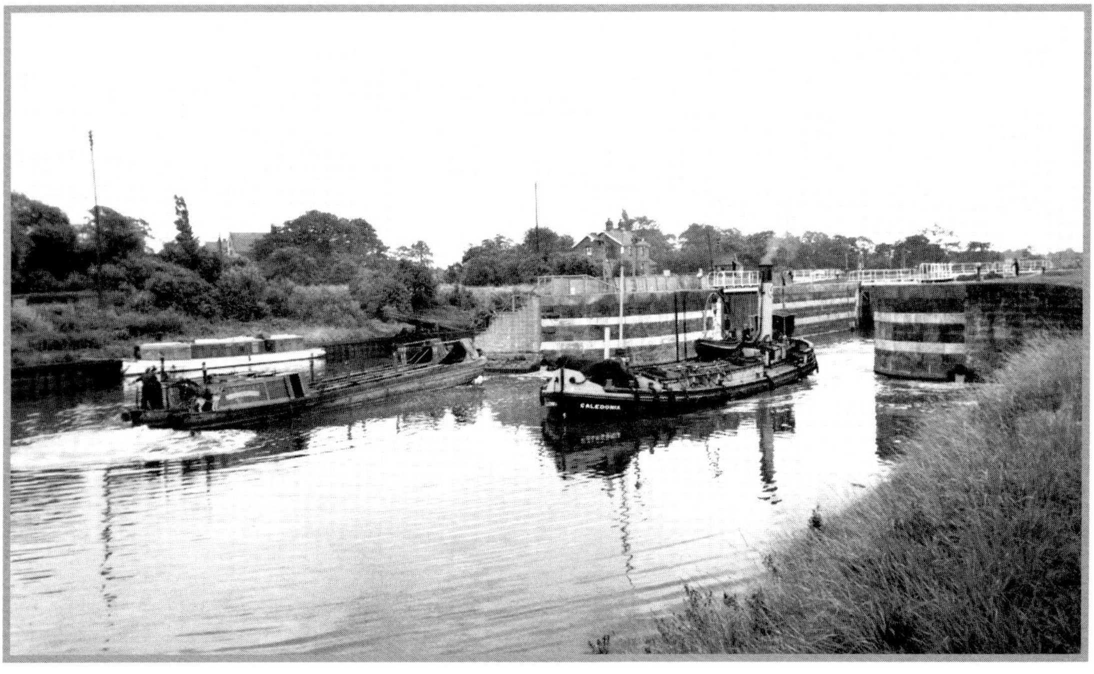

NORTHWICH, HUNTS LOCK c1960 N43024
As the steam-powered barge 'Caledonia' leaves Hunts Lock heading towards Northwich, a pair of narrowboats churn up the water as they line up to enter the lock.

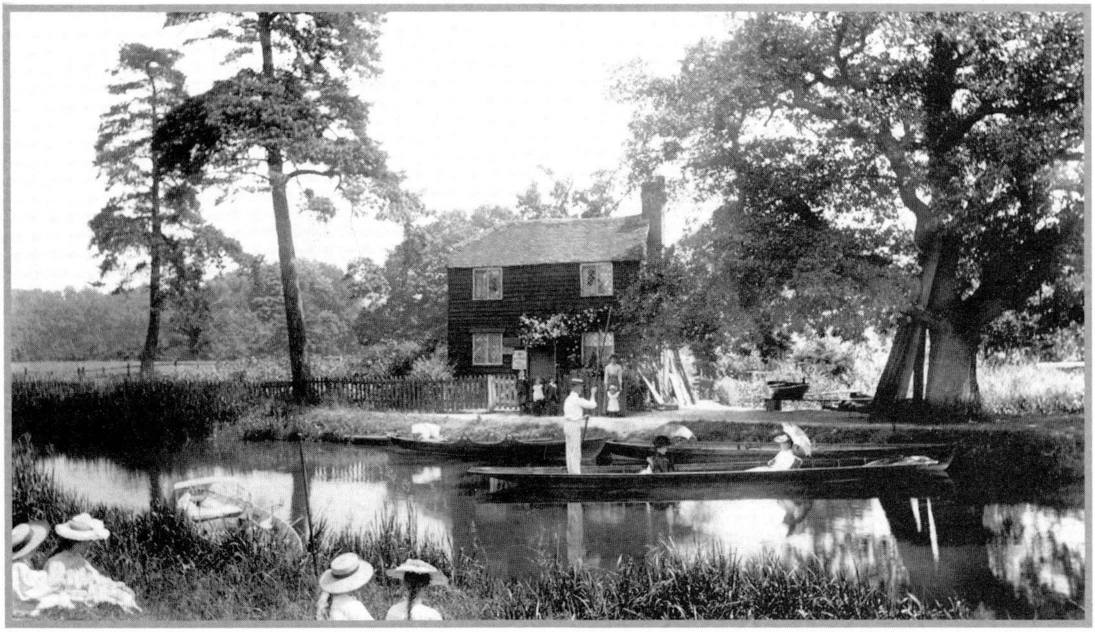

Shalford, River Wey, St Catherine's Lock 1904 51882
Two ladies - with parasols - take their ease whilst the gentleman punts them along the river Wey. The party in the bottom left-hand corner seem to have abandoned their boat for a rest on the bank. This view is upstream of St Catherine's Lock.

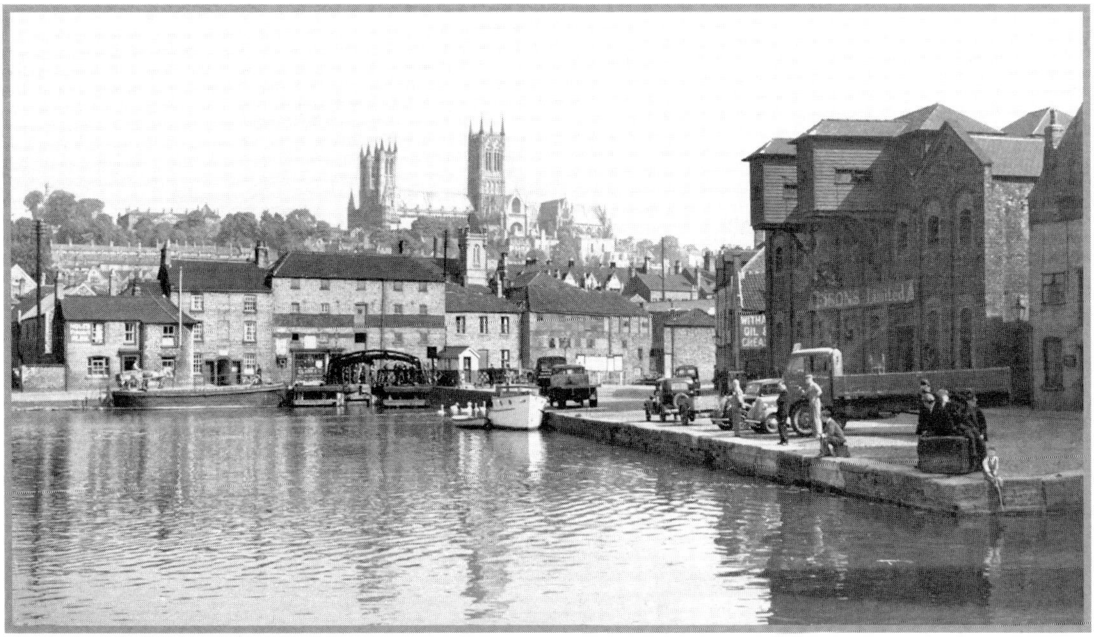

Lincoln, The Cathedral from Brayford c1950 L49051
The majesty of Lincoln Cathedral is seen from Brayford Pool. This is where the (un-navigable) river Witham and the Roman-built Fossdyke Canal joined. Fison's warehouse on the right is conveniently placed for deliveries by road or water, and the railway - just behind the cameraman - was also to hand.

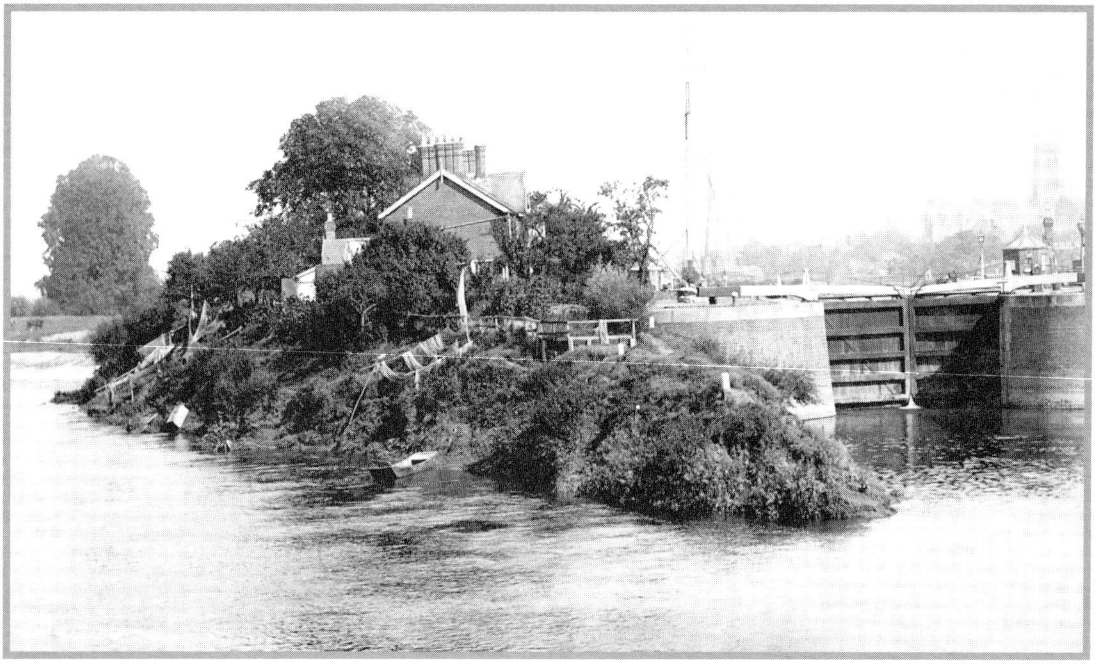

WORCESTER, DIGLIS LOCK AND THE WEIR 1891 29293A
Diglis Lock is to the south of Worcester on the river Severn. This lifts boats almost 8 ft, from whence they have the whole of Worcester to see. The cathedral on the right dates from 1074.

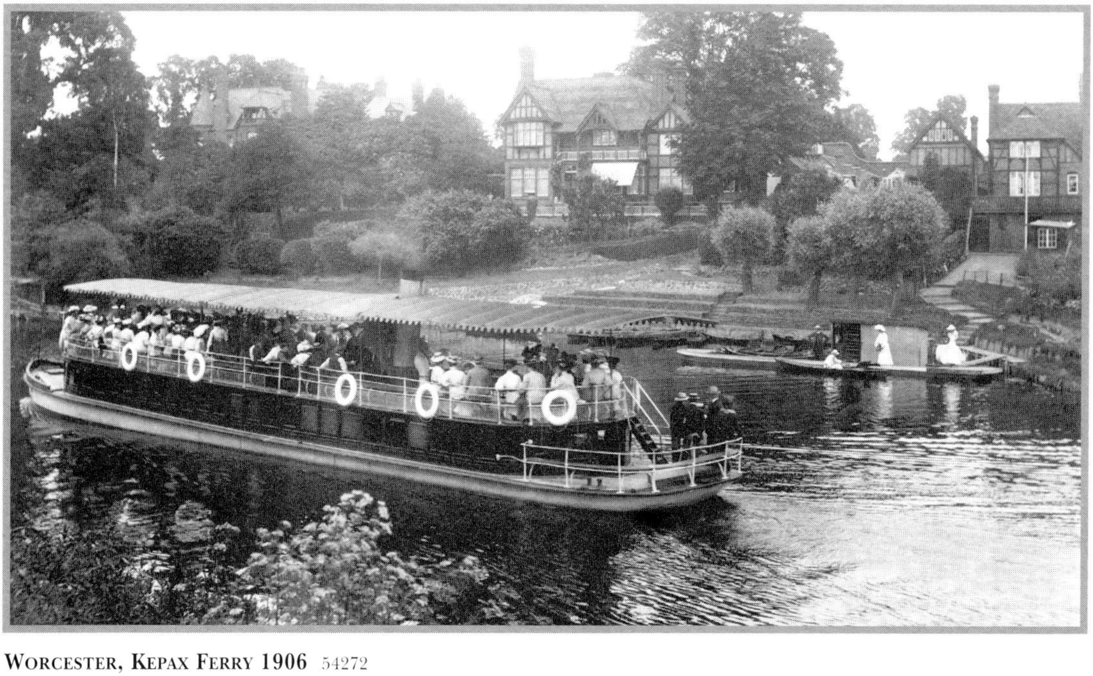

WORCESTER, KEPAX FERRY 1906 54272
Here we see one of the many pleasure steamers that used to ply on the river Severn in the Worcester area. The life-saving equipment - probably 10 buoyancy rings - would be considered just a little inadequate today, when one piece of equipment for every passenger carried is the law. Across the water, rowing boats are available for hire.

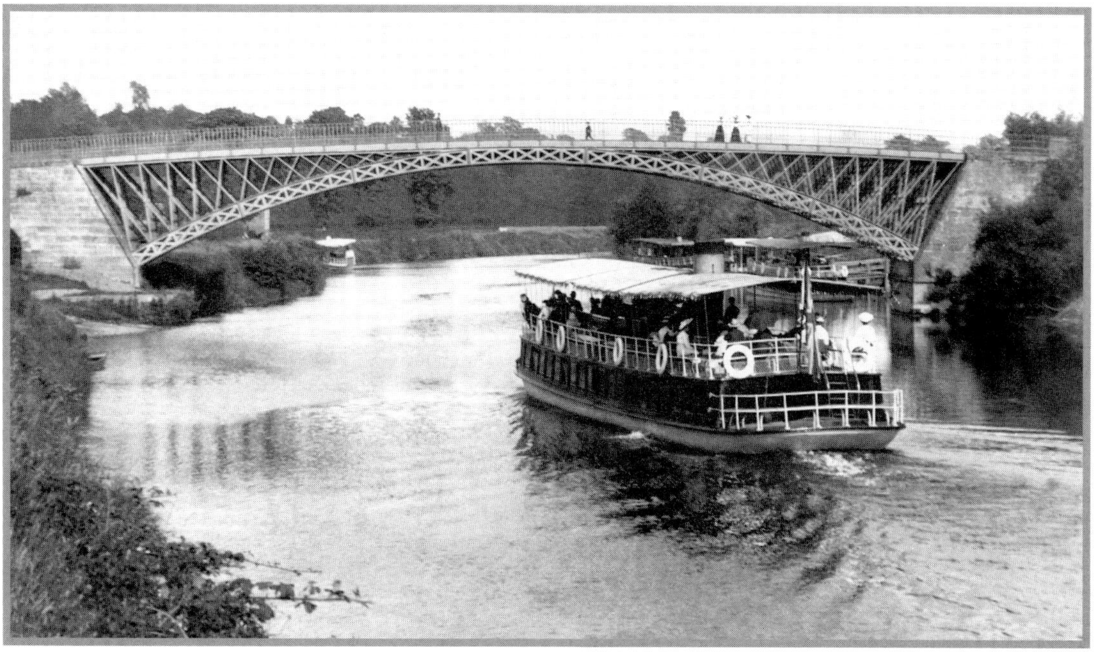

Holt Fleet, The Bridge 1906 54294

Holt Fleet
The Bridge 1906
This elegant single span over the river Severn takes the A4133 Droitwich to Tenbury Wells road. It was built in 1828 by that noted engineer Thomas Telford. Again, a plethora of trip boats can be seen.

Holt Fleet
The Hotel 1906
Patrons are enjoying the riverside milieu of the Holt Fleet Hotel. This building still exists today, rambling as much as ever. There is a good restaurant here, and Bass real ales are served.

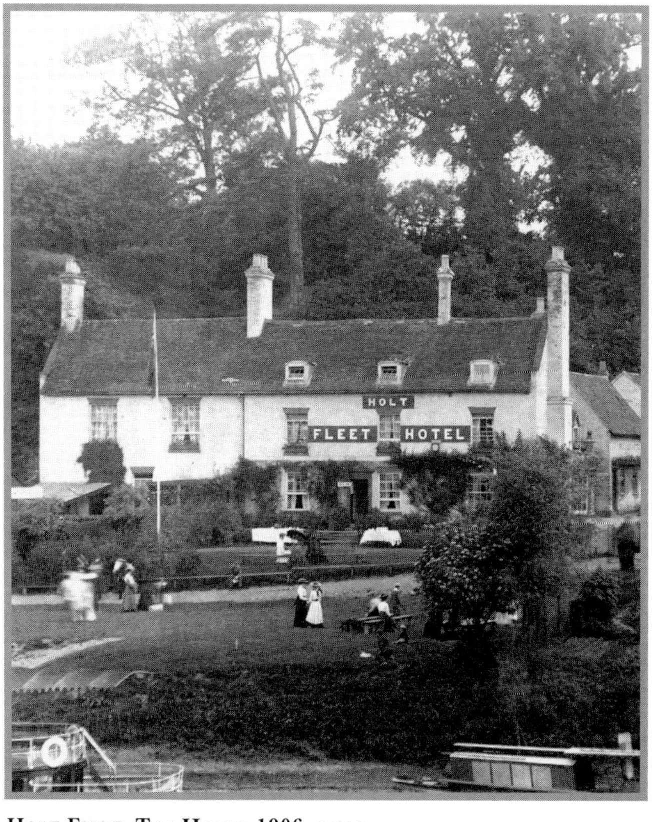

Holt Fleet, The Hotel 1906 54292

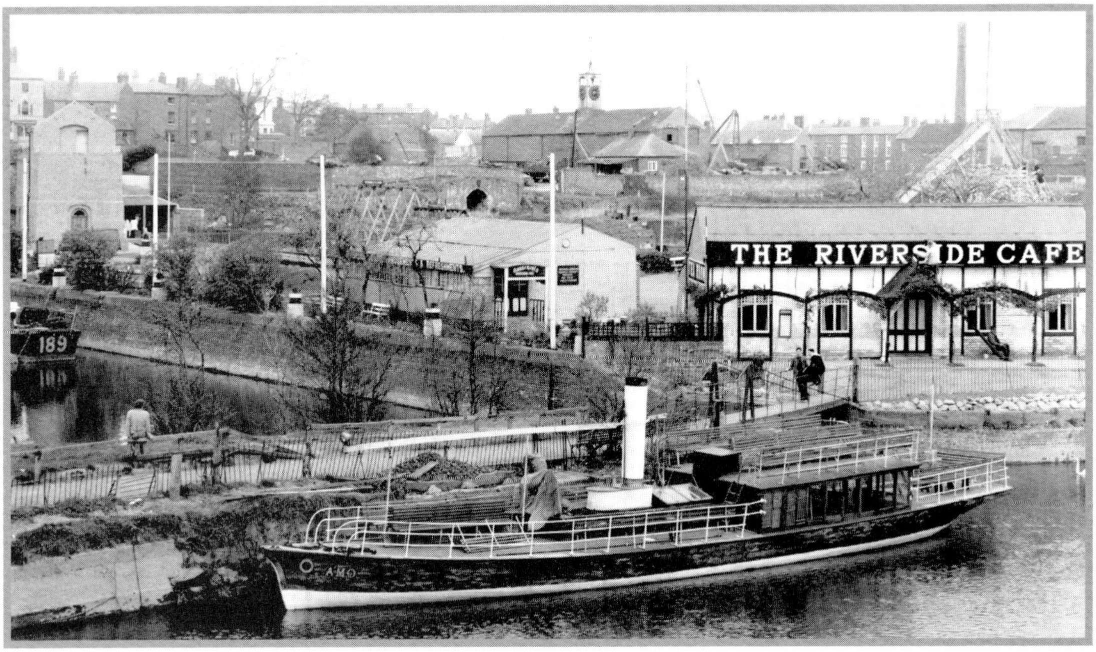

STOURPORT-ON-SEVERN, VIEW FROM THE BRIDGE c1955 S214022

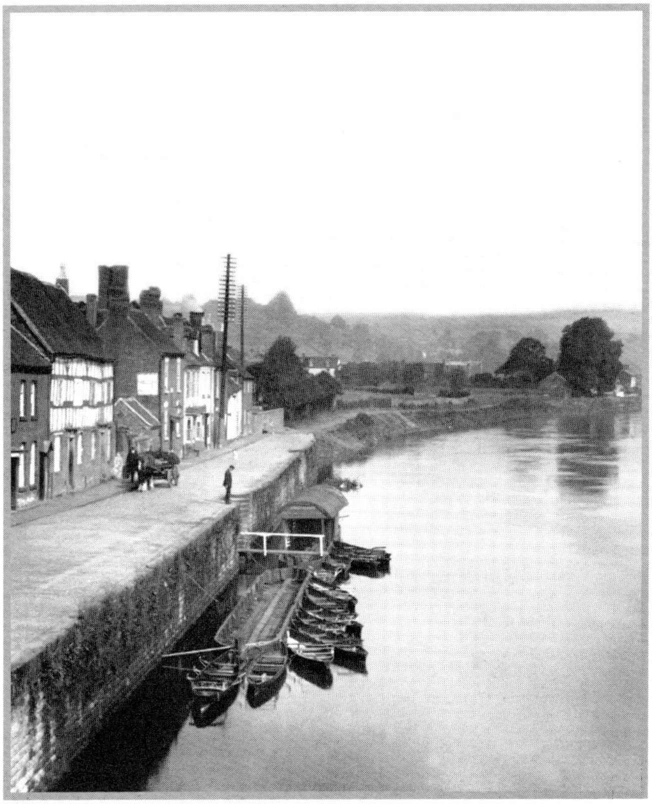

BEWDLEY, THE RIVER c1938 B82009

STOURPORT-ON-SEVERN
View from the Bridge c1955
This view is slightly upstream of the locks that give access to the Staffordshire and Worcester Canal. The area in the foreground is today a large amusement park. The bridge left of centre and above the amusement arcade is over the narrow canal lock which gives access to Stourport Basin and the excellent collection of buildings there.

BEWDLEY
The River c1938
Boats from further down the river generally do not reach Bewdley, although there is a statutory right of navigation. The rowing skiffs are as much activity as you are likely to see today. The houses here are very prone to flooding when rainwater from the Welsh mountains comes cascading down the river.

Index

Frith Book Co Titles

Frith Book Company publish over a 100 new titles each year. For latest catalogue please contact Frith Book Co.

Town Books 96pp, 100 photos. County and Themed Books 128pp, 150 photos (unless specified) All titles hardback laminated case and jacket except those indicated pb (paperback)

Around Barnstaple	1-85937-084-5	£12.99
Around Blackpool	1-85937-049-7	£12.99
Around Bognor Regis	1-85937-055-1	£12.99
Around Bristol	1-85937-050-0	£12.99
Around Cambridge	1-85937-092-6	£12.99
Cheshire	1-85937-045-4	£14.99
Around Chester	1-85937-090-X	£12.99
Around Chesterfield	1-85937-071-3	£12.99
Around Chichester	1-85937-089-6	£12.99
Cornwall	1-85937-054-3	£14.99
Cotswolds	1-85937-099-3	£14.99
Around Derby	1-85937-046-2	£12.99
Devon	1-85937-052-7	£14.99
Dorset	1-85937-075-6	£14.99
Dorset Coast	1-85937-062-4	£14.99
Around Dublin	1-85937-058-6	£12.99
East Anglia	1-85937-059-4	£14.99
Around Eastbourne	1-85937-061-6	£12.99
English Castles	1-85937-078-0	£14.99
Around Falmouth	1-85937-066-7	£12.99
Hampshire	1-85937-064-0	£14.99
Isle of Man	1-85937-065-9	£14.99
Around Maidstone	1-85937-056-X	£12.99
North Yorkshire	1-85937-048-9	£14.99
Around Nottingham	1-85937-060-8	£12.99
Around Penzance	1-85937-069-1	£12.99
Around Reading	1-85937-087-X	£12.99
Around St Ives	1-85937-068-3	£12.99
Around Salisbury	1-85937-091-8	£12.99
Around Scarborough	1-85937-104-3	£12.99
Scottish Castles	1-85937-077-2	£14.99
Around Sevenoaks and Tonbridge	1-85937-057-8	£12.99
Sheffield and S Yorkshire	1-85937-070-5	£14.99
Shropshire	1-85937-083-7	£14.99
Staffordshire	1-85937-047-0 (96pp)	£12.99
Suffolk	1-85937-074-8	£14.99
Surrey	1-85937-081-0	£14.99
Around Torbay	1-85937-063-2	£12.99
Wiltshire	1-85937-053-5	£14.99
Around Bakewell	1-85937-113-2	£12.99
Around Bournemouth	1-85937-067-5	£12.99
Cambridgeshire	1-85937-086-1	£14.99
Essex	1-85937-082-9	£14.99
Around Great Yarmouth	1-85937-085-3	£12.99
Hertfordshire	1-85937-079-9	£14.99
Isle of Wight	1-85937-114-0	£14.99
Around Lincoln	1-85937-111-6	£12.99
Oxfordshire	1-85937-076-4	£14.99
Around Shrewsbury	1-85937-110-8	£12.99
South Devon Coast	1-85937-107-8	£14.99
Around Stratford upon Avon	1-85937-098-5	£12.99
West Midlands	1-85937-109-4	£14.99

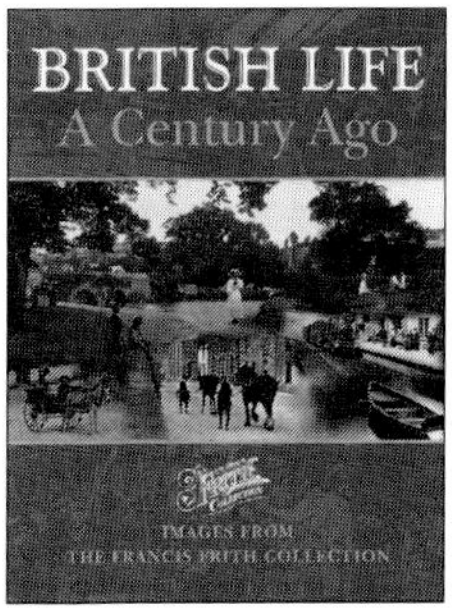

British Life A Century Ago
246 x 189mm
144pp, hardback.
Black and white
Lavishly illustrated with photos from the turn of the century, and with extensive commentary. It offers a unique insight into the social history and heritage of bygone Britain.

1-85937-103-5 £17.99

Available from your local bookshop or from the publisher

Frith Book Co Titles Available in 2000

Around Bath	1-85937-097-7	£12.99	Mar
County Durham	1-85937-123-x	£14.99	Mar
Cumbria	1-85937-101-9	£14.99	Mar
Down the Thames	1-85937-121-3	£14.99	Mar
Around Exeter	1-85937-126-4	£12.99	Mar
Greater Manchester	1-85937-108-6	£14.99	Mar
Around Guildford	1-85937-117-5	£12.99	Mar
Around Harrogate	1-85937-112-4	£12.99	Mar
Around Leicester	1-85937-073-x	£12.99	Mar
Around Liverpool	1-85937-051-9	£12.99	Mar
Around Newark	1-85937-105-1	£12.99	Mar
Northumberland and Tyne & Wear	1-85937-072-1	£14.99	Mar
Around Oxford	1-85937-096-9	£12.99	Mar
Around Plymouth	1-85937-119-1	£12.99	Mar
Around Southport	1-85937-106-x	£12.99	Mar
Welsh Castles	1-85937-120-5	£14.99	Mar
Around Belfast	1-85937-094-2	£12.99	Apr
Canals and Waterways	1-85937-129-9	£17.99	Apr
Down the Severn	1-85937-118-3	£14.99	Apr
East Sussex	1-85937-130-2	£14.99	Apr
Exmoor	1-85937-132-9	£14.99	Apr
Gloucestershire	1-85937-102-7	£14.99	Apr
Around Horsham	1-85937-127-2	£12.99	Apr
Around Ipswich	1-85937-133-7	£12.99	Apr
Ireland (pb)	1-85937-181-7	£9.99	Apr
Kent Living Memories	1-85937-125-6	£14.99	Apr
London (pb)	1-85937-183-3	£9.99	Apr
New Forest	1-85937-128-0	£14.99	Apr
Scotland (pb)	1-85937-182-5	£9.99	Apr
Around Southampton	1-85937-088-8	£12.99	Apr
Stone Circles & Ancient Monuments	1-85937-143-4	£17.99	Apr
Sussex (pb)	1-85937-184-1	£9.99	Apr
Colchester (pb)	1-85937-188-4	£8.99	May
County Maps of Britain	1-85937-156-6 (192pp)	£19.99	May
Leicestershire (pb)	1-85937-185-x	£9.99	May
Lincolnshire	1-85937-135-3	£14.99	May
Around Newquay	1-85937-140-x	£12.99	May
Nottinghamshire (pb)	1-85937-187-6	£9.99	May
Redhill to Reigate	1-85937-137-x	£12.99	May
Victorian & Edwardian Yorkshire	1-85937-154-x	£14.99	May
Around Winchester	1-85937-139-6	£12.99	May
Yorkshire (pb)	1-85937-186-8	£9.99	May
Berkshire (pb)	1-85937-191-4	£9.99	Jun
Brighton (pb)	1-85937-192-2	£8.99	Jun
Dartmoor	1-85937-145-0	£14.99	Jun
East London	1-85937-080-2	£14.99	Jun
Glasgow (pb)	1-85937-190-6	£8.99	Jun
Kent (pb)	1-85937-189-2	£9.99	Jun
Victorian & Edwardian Kent	1-85937-149-3	£14.99	Jun
North Devon Coast	1-85937-146-9	£14.99	Jun
Peak District	1-85937-100-0	£14.99	Jun
Around Truro	1-85937-147-7	£12.99	Jun
Victorian & Edwardian Maritime Album	1-85937-144-2	£17.99	Jun
West Sussex	1-85937-148-5	£14.99	Jun
Churches of Berkshire	1-85937-170-1	£17.99	Jul
Churches of Dorset	1-85937-172-8	£17.99	Jul
Churches of Hampshire	1-85937-207-4	£17.99	Jul
Churches of Wiltshire	1-85937-171-x	£17.99	Jul
Derbyshire (pb)	1-85937-196-5	£9.99	Jul
Edinburgh (pb)	1-85937-193-0	£8.99	Jul
Herefordshire	1-85937-174-4	£14.99	Jul
Norwich (pb)	1-85937-194-9	£8.99	Jul
Ports and Harbours	1-85937-208-2	£17.99	Jul
Somerset and Avon	1-85937-153-1	£14.99	Jul
South Devon Living Memories	1-85937-168-x	£14.99	Jul
Warwickshire (pb)	1-85937-203-1	£9.99	Jul
Worcestershire	1-85937-152-3	£14.99	Jul
Yorkshire Living Memories	1-85937-166-3	£14.99	Jul

Frith Products & Services

Francis Frith would doubtless be pleased to know that the pioneering publishing venture he started in 1860 still continues today. More than a hundred and thirty years later, The Francis Frith Collection continues in the same innovative tradition and is now one of the foremost publishers of vintage photographs in the world. Some of the current activities include:

Interior Decoration

Today Frith's photographs can be seen framed and as giant wall murals in thousands of pubs, restaurants, hotels, banks, retail stores and other public buildings throughout the country. In every case they enhance the unique local atmosphere of the places they depict and provide reminders of gentler days in an increasingly busy and frenetic world.

Product Promotions

Frith products have been used by many major companies to promote the sales of their own products or to reinforce their own history and heritage. Brands include Hovis bread, Courage beers, Scots Porage Oats, Colman's mustard, Cadbury's foods, Mellow Birds coffee, Dunhill pipe tobacco, Guinness, and Bulmer's Cider.

Genealogy and Family History

As the interest in family history and roots grows world-wide, more and more people are turning to Frith's photographs of Great Britain for images of the towns, villages and streets where their ancestors lived; and, of course, photographs of the churches and chapels where their ancestors were christened, married and buried are an essential part of every genealogy tree and family album.
A series of easy-to-use CD Roms is planned for publication, and an increasing number of Frith photographs will be able to be viewed on specialist genealogy sites. A growing range of Frith books will be available on CD.

The Internet

Already thousands of Frith photographs can be viewed and purchased on the internet. By the end of the year 2000 some 60,000 Frith photographs will be available on the internet. The number of sites is constantly expanding, each focussing on different products and services from the Collection.
Some of the sites are listed below.

www.townpages.co.uk
www.icollector.com
www.barclaysquare.co.uk
www.cornwall-online.co.uk

For background information on the Collection look at the three following sites:

www.francisfrith.com
www.francisfrith.co.uk
www.frithbook.co.uk

Frith Products

All Frith photographs are available Framed or just as Mounted Prints, and can be ordered from the address below. From time to time other products - Address Books, Calendars, Table Mats, etc - are available.

For further information:
if you would like further information on any of the above aspects of the Frith business please contact us at the address below:
The Francis Frith Collection,
Frith's Barn, Teffont, Salisbury, Wiltshire, England SP3 5QP.
Tel: +44 (0)1722 716 376 Fax: +44 (0)1722 716 881 Email: uksales@francisfrith.com

To receive your FREE Mounted Print

Cut out this Voucher and return it with your remittance for £1.50 to cover postage and handling. Choose any photograph included in this book. Your SEPIA print will be A4 in size, and mounted in a cream mount with burgundy rule lines, overall size 14 x 11 inches.

Order additional Mounted Prints at HALF PRICE (only £7.49 each*)
If there are further pictures you would like to order, possibly as gifts for friends and family, acquire them at half price (no additional postage and handling required).

Have your Mounted Prints framed*
For an additional £14.95 per print you can have your chosen Mounted Print framed in an elegant polished wood and gilt moulding, overall size 16 x 13 inches (no additional postage and handling required).

*** IMPORTANT!**
These special prices are only available if ordered using the original voucher on this page (no copies permitted) and at the same time as your free Mounted Print, for delivery to the same address

Voucher for FREE and Reduced Price Frith Prints

Picture no.	Page number	Qty	Mounted @ £7.49	Framed + £14.95	Total Cost
		1	**Free of charge***	£	£
			£7.49	£	£
			£7.49	£	£
			£7.49	£	£
			£7.49	£	£
			£7.49	£	£
				* Post & handling	£1.50
Book Title				**Total Order Cost**	**£**

Please do not photocopy this voucher. Only the original is valid, so please cut it out and return it to us.

I enclose a cheque / postal order for £ ....
made payable to 'The Francis Frith Collection'
OR please debit my Mastercard / Visa / Switch / Amex card

Number ....

Expires .... Signature ....

Name Mr/Mrs/Ms ....
Address ....
....
....
....
.... Postcode ....

Daytime Tel No .... Valid to 31/12/01

Frith Collectors' Guild

From time to time we publish a magazine of news and stories about Frith photographs and further special offers of Frith products. If you would like 12 months FREE membership, please return this form.

Send completed forms to:
The Francis Frith Collection, Frith's Barn, Teffont, Salisbury, Wiltshire SP3 5QP

The Francis Frith Collectors' Guild

Please enrol me as a member for 12 months free of charge.

Name Mr/Mrs/Ms ....
Address ....
....
....
.... Postcode ....